THE UNNOTICED
ENTREPRENEUR

THE UNNOTICED ENTREPRENEUR

GIVING ENTREPRENEURS THE TOOLS THEY NEED TO GET THE RECOGNITION THEY DESERVE

JIM JAMES

CAPSTONE
A Wiley Brand

Registered Offices
John Wiley & Sons, Inc., 111 River Street, Hoboken, NJ 07030, USA
John Wiley & Sons Ltd, The Atrium, Southern Gate, Chichester, West Sussex, PO19 8SQ, UK

Editorial Office
The Atrium, Southern Gate, Chichester, West Sussex, PO19 8SQ, UK

For details of our global editorial offices, customer services, and more information about Wiley products visit us at www.wiley.com.

Wiley also publishes its books in a variety of electronic formats and by print-on-demand. Some content that appears in standard print versions of this book may not be available in other formats.

Library of Congress Cataloging-in-Publication Data is Available:

ISBN 9781394195343 (Paperback)
ISBN 9780857089779 (ePDF)
ISBN 9780857089762 (ePub)

Cover Design: Wiley
Cover Images: Sunray pattern © NeMaria/Shutterstock, blue toolbox © Stephen Plaster/Shutterstock

Set in 11/15.2 pt Minion Pro by Straive, Chennai, India

SKY10069996_031924

15 MINUTES OF FAME IS NOT ENOUGH. A BUSINESS NEEDS TO GET NOTICED ALL THE TIME.

Entrepreneurs know that their key role is to share the vision of the company. If you can sell the why, customers will buy the service.

Most business owners don't trust their own creative instincts, think an agency will cost a bomb and let them down, and believe that fame is the preserve of the big company.

This book delivers ideas and examples so that you don't have to be frustrated at being unnoticed.

Recognition is not a function of scale nor budget, but of simple and authentic ways to help people to understand you and your business.

Let my guests and I share with you how to #getnoticed for free.

You can do this. SPEAK|pr™

FRUSTRATED AT BEING THE UNNOTICED?

Fifty experts share how you can get noticed for what you do.

Who this book is for.

I dedicate this book to entrepreneurs who are passionate about creating value from nothing; the people who take risks themselves so that they can make a difference for the benefit of others.

My hope is that the ideas in this collection of essays will give you the ideas, connections, and motivation to get noticed for all the good that you do.

Contents

Prologue: The Need for Thymōs

I drove the Morgan Roadster into the Forbidden City in Beijing without a permit and felt the excitement of creating a spectacle which was at once both foolhardy and audacious. The dark blue uniformed police were making their way towards my film crew, and I held back the clamouring crowds craning their necks to see this British sports car that looked as though it had arrived by time machine. I shouted instructions to the photographers from a Chinese magazine to keep filming; I would not lose this perfect PR moment. This British racing green sports car with top down, chrome spoke wheels gleaming in the sunshine within sight of the portrait of Chairman Mao was going to be the cheapest, cheekiest, and most impactful public relations launch in the Middle Kingdom. And so it was. The Autocar publishers laid out the photos of my tan interior 4-seater Roadster across the pages of their magazine, and I had launched my business in China for free.

I have spent my life building brands by using public relations, with conventional campaigns augmented with moments like the Forbidden City photoshoot in 2011. I first got a taste for public relations when I needed to raise money at 18 by jumping out of an aeroplane, and convincing a store in my hometown of Canterbury to give me expedition equipment in return for media coverage. In Manchester, at postgraduate University, my friends and I organised the Manchester Marketing Mix and raised money for charity. After 5 years working variously in an advertising agency, a food import business, and a music technology company, in 1995 I left for Singapore to start my agency, EASTWEST Public Relations. I was 28 and so full of ambition and belief. When China entered the WTO in 2001, I was drawn to this magnet of entrepreneurial opportunity. I moved to Beijing in 2006 to start a communications business in a country where I couldn't speak the language.

For a person who has always enjoyed talking, as my family will tell you, being in a place where I could neither understand nor be understood created a massive learning experience, especially when I was in the business of helping others to communicate. Over a period of 13 years, I built several businesses, including the official importer of the Morgan Motor Company, my own EASTWEST Public Relations, and Wake Drinks. I also created the British Business Awards, the British Motorsport Festival and was hired as the interim CEO of Lotus Cars in China. I built all of these without spending money on advertising or expensive events. Just as I had done when I made my expeditions to Australia and Central America self-funded through sponsorship. What I have wanted to do with this book is have industry experts and technologists explain how you too can #getnoticed, with my experience being used to curate their insights for you.

For over 25 years, I have enjoyed both success and failure in business, and I think I can save you some of my mistakes, as I've asked experts on your behalf what will improve your chances of success. I've been a founder, an employee, and a consultant, and so I know the pain of wasting money and not being allowed to spend money, and watching others spend it unwisely. In all these situations, though, I came to appreciate that effective communication is an essential element of personal and professional success. Building businesses in China without a budget and not able to read or write Mandarin, and in a market of immense scale, taught me the valuable lessons of focus, visualisation of messaging, and the essential need to use technology for the entire process.

Back now in the UK, with time to reflect and COVID enforcing long periods of concentration, I wanted to help other business owners communicate, not by asking them to become PR professionals but by sharing free and effective means to #getnoticed. When I returned to England in 2019, I saw my brilliant sister struggling to share her much needed message about the impact of light on children simply because she didn't know how to build a story and to share it. I saw so many people struggling under COVID, who needed new marketing skills just in order to survive. I wanted to help in a way that used my skills to the best effect. So in June 2020, I started "The UnNoticed Show" podcast, to help all those amazing entrepreneurs like my sister who can't afford an agency, and frankly don't really need one either, but can do such good if they can find ways to share their message.

I have sought experts, entrepreneurs, and technologists who are solving the problems founders face every day, and put them into a framework so that this is public relations for people who don't want to become PR professionals, just to use PR for their purposes. First though, let's address the poor reputation of public relations itself, that it is just "spin" or "gin-slings." Getting noticed goes much deeper than that.

Getting noticed is more than just a business issue, it's personal. Thymōs is the Greek term for the need for recognition, and in Platonic philosophy is that area of the soul where feelings of pride, indignation, shame, etc. are located. In his book *The End of History and the Last Man*, Francis Fukuyama coined the terms: "Megalothymia" which refers to the need to be recognised as superior to others, and "Isothymia" is the need to be recognised as merely equal to others. In Homeric poems, thymōs is one of a family of terms associated with the internal psychological processes of thought, emotion, volition, and motivation.

Today, we know that feelings of pride and self-esteem impact levels of the neurotransmitter serotonin in the brain, releasing the "happy chemical" at a biological and sociological level, meaning that we need to get noticed as people. As entrepreneurs we are the business, we put our heart, souls and bodies into these ventures with all kinds of dreams, and anonymity does nothing to validate our aspirations, nor deliver sales. Anyone who has undertaken investor relations will know that the third-party validation of media or analyst coverage can affect valuations, recruitment is easier when candidates have heard of your company, supplier credit terms are better and of course sales pipelines fill up much more quickly.

I've compiled this second volume of The UnNoticed Show© to give you ways to release more serotonin into the collective bloodstream of your company. This book is a curation of just 50 articles drawn from the >200 interviews, which I've held since June 2020 with entrepreneurs, experts, and technology providers on the 20-minute format podcast. The style that you are going to read is conversational because these are curated versions of the transcripts, not elements drafted into a new article. I've taken this approach intentionally because I want to share the energy, tone, and personality of my guests as if you were to meet them.

I kept each episode intentionally short for two reasons: (i) You won't have a lot of time, and will want to get to the details; and (ii) You don't want to become PR experts, just to learn enough to give directions to others to take the right strategy. It was hard to decide on just 50, but I want to keep to the philosophy of being economical with your time.

Besides the guest essays, I introduce the SPEAK|pr™ programme as a framework for approaching public relations. This is a five-stage method I have developed to help structure the approach. There is a wealth of tactical information available on the internet, but it seems to me there is a dearth of strategy, and yet as business owners, we need to create a consistency and automated flow of information that, once set up, we can give to others to implement. I want to provide a broader overview of what thinking needs to go into developing a consistent communications campaign. I'll introduce a framework which I have been working under the name "SPEAK|pr™" which stands for: Storify, Personalise, Engage, Amplify, Know. I have curated the interviews nominally by each stage of the framework, although there is overlap of course and ask for you to forgive the omissions or repetitions for which I am entirely to blame. I invited my guests to answer one of two questions:

Entrepreneurs to answer — "How do you get noticed?"

Technologists and experts to answer — "How do you help entrepreneurs get noticed?"

In doing so I have hoped to create both an inside-out and outside-in approach, which serves you in whatever role you play. This isn't of course a textbook, it is a series of conversations and formatted that way, with practical, easy to implement ideas which you can use to improve the recognition that you and your organisation receive from the people that matter. I have an online programme and mastermind for the SPEAK|pr™ programme for anyone who would like to go into more depth, but the goal of this book is to include you in the conversations I have had with 50 people around the world who are solving the same problems that you are facing every day.

I am most grateful to all of my guests for sharing their time and insights with me and allowing me to share these in the podcast, articles, and now this book. I am also grateful to everyone who has listened to The UnNoticed Show and been patient with me as I have rambled, stumbled, and stuttered whilst learning this new medium. I couldn't believe it when I learned that the show has reached the top 3% ranking of worldwide podcasts, with listeners from 121 countries and 2151 cities. It just goes to show that there are people like us all over the world who experience frustration daily at being unnoticed and having a business which has potential that is unfulfilled. We are all searching for Thymōs for all the right reasons – as the Champion of the UnNoticed, I want to help you find yours.

Keep on communicating!

JIM JAMES

PART ONE
Storify

Chapter One
Introduction.

"Marketing is no longer about what you sell, but about the stories you tell."
— Seth Godin, Author

When I started the Morgan business in China, I knew I had to tell the story of this 100-year-old brand from the UK with a locally relevant context. If I were to simply promote a hand-built car being sold to retirees in the UK as being available to the newly rich in China, I would fail. Instead, I had to make the ownership of a Morgan be seen as a part of the life story of those Chinese who aspired to be seen as international, as cultured, and as this was China, a healthy dose of Megalothymia. This had to be their story being told through the ownership of my cars.

People love stories, and yet in business, we often cannot remember that this simple narrative device is how we all learn and engage with concepts and with other people. Storify stands for the process by which you can think about your business as if it were a story in a novel or a film, with a cast, a plot, and set of circumstances and challenges to be overcome. The traditional approach to public relations is that the hero for the story of the company is the founder or CEO, but actually, the most successful campaigns are when the hero is the customer and the company is the facilitator, the mentor that enables that hero, who is the centre of your story, to accomplish their objectives.

Underpinning the idea of storification is that you are placing yourself and your business in a position of service to your clients. When we talk about storification, it's really liberating because your communication is about the story of your customer, staff or partner, and how you help them fulfil their journey with you in a supportive role. In practical terms, this meant that I was constantly looking at my 3D strategy of "Drive, Display, and Digital" to create stories around the Morgan brand with Chinese as the central characters in my cast.

In this section, I've covered interviews which will help you define what your story is, how to tell it, to brand yourself and your company, and a case study of how a focus on one story helped an Agency in America to grow. John Lee Dumas shared with me three central chapters from his best-selling book, *The Common Path to UnCommon Success* culminating from his podcast EO on Fire which has interviewed over 3000 entrepreneurs. Park Howell, "The World's Most Industrious Story Teller" gives a three-part series which is a synopsis of his book and course, which shows you how to construct the narrative for your business. Branding guru Gerry Foster has coached over 100 000 business owners and shared his approach "To be distinct or extinct," and Michelle Griffen delivered the "5Cs" of personal branding to complement Gerry's masterclass. Eight seconds is all we have when pitching, or the audience will lose concentration, and you'll lose the sale, and Martin Barnes explains the core concepts of great presentations so that the story doesn't get lost in the PowerPoint animation. Finally, just to prove that story really works, Chris Martin of Atlas Marketing is focused on the construction industry, and shares a case study of how they solved a clients' PR problem with a story about the willingness of their client to work to the peculiar time table of their clients.

The power of story is that when done well, it becomes retold by those who are part of it. Ultimately, in order for the story of your company to be told beyond your own network, it's necessary for others to share it with their networks. By understanding the power of story, and placing your customers, team, and partners at the centre of that story you will have amplification; but we will talk about that later on.

Chapter Two
The Common Path to Uncommon Success.

Interview with Puerto Rico based John Lee Dumas; the best-selling author and host of the EO on Fire podcast.

If you don't know John Lee Dumas, he is the founder and host of the award-winning podcast "Entrepreneurs on Fire." He has over a million monthly listeners and seven figures of annual revenue, which he very generously and transparently shares. He also has a new book entitled *The Common Path to Uncommon Success.*

In the past eight years, John has done 3000 interviews with successful entrepreneurs. He has spent thousands of hours talking with people who have achieved massive levels of success. From those conversations, he has discovered that there is a very common path to uncommon success.

Step 1: Identify Your Big Idea

One misconception John first wants to address is how people are made to believe that the path to success is complicated or hidden, but that's not true. The path to uncommon success is simple and clear, which is why he has created a 17-step roadmap, and this begins with your big idea. So many people never think about what their big idea is, what that looks like, or what that means, which is why they don't achieve success. John's big idea, back in 2012, was to do the first ever daily podcast interviewing entrepreneurs. Because he was the first and only daily podcast interviewing entrepreneurs, that meant he was the best, but he was also the worst.

Back to his book, John has interviewed 17 amazing entrepreneurs that contributed to his 17 chronological steps, each one specifically because they are experts in that one specific step. Hal Elrod is the entrepreneur John interviewed for his big idea and his basis for writing Chapter One of his big book, and he shares that Hal's big idea was creating a Miracle Morning, which everybody needs to start, and he hopes people realise that that is where the power lies.

The Three Common Traits All Successful Entrepreneurs Have

One important lesson John has uncovered is that no one is born an entrepreneur. John gave entrepreneurship a try at 32 years old, and here he is now, so it is never too late. The successful entrepreneurs he's interviewed have specific characteristics in common, the first of which is that they are all productive, meaning they are producing the right content. The second common trait these entrepreneurs have is discipline, because without the daily plan of action, you're not going to achieve the level of uncommon success you want. The third shared trait is being focused, which is where you follow one course until success. If you have one big idea and you focus laser-like on that one big idea, you stand a chance of achieving success.

If you fail, John says it's because of one reason: you haven't created the best solution to a real problem, which is a simple concept that most people don't seem to grasp. Entrepreneurs on Fire did so great even back in 2012 when it was first launched, because it was the best solution to a real problem, the problem being that people wanted more interviews and entrepreneurs to listen to. Nobody was doing it, so John created the only, therefore the best, solution to a real problem.

Step 2: Niche Down

Most people create a watered down solution to a hypothetical problem and nobody cares, but what his book does is it takes you on that journey to help you identify your big idea and then move into Chapter Two, which is about discovering your niche within that big idea. For John, there's no niche too small, because even a niche of one is big enough. Niche down until you can be the best solution to a real problem, he says. Whether it might be six or seven levels down, or only two or three, you need to go through that process.

Step 3: Create Your Avatar

Step three is creating your avatar. That's the perfect customer, client, listener, follower, or consumer of your content, products, or services. Having multiple avatars will cause you to fall back onto having generic marketing, and you will blend in and not be heard or discovered. John's avatar back when he launched Entrepreneurs on Fire was a 32-year-old father of two young children in a 25-minute commute to work whose name is Jimmy. This didn't mean that other people weren't listening to his podcast, but he served his avatar better than anybody else, and he achieved success as a result.

John has really managed to communicate his value around the world, and he says that he's been able to do so by keeping things simple and clear. He goes back to his beginning steps about identifying a big idea and discovering the niche within that big idea that you can be the best solution to a real problem. And then, once you create your avatar as a next step, you go out and find them. That avatar could be listening to podcasts, on YouTube, watching shows, on social media, reading blogs, or more. Though his book outlines this simple concept, John cautions that it is not a simple process, because if it was, everybody would be doing it.

Now, in terms of the timeline, John says an entrepreneur should be able to implement these 17 steps realistically in 3–6 months and build a foundation for a successful business. In the end, John's goal is to release people from that inability to get behind things that they believe in. John and his partner, Kate, have been able to donate multiple six figures to causes they believe in. Over the years, they have built five schools in developing countries such as Guatemala, Laos, and Cambodia. They are giving the gift of education, because they're financially in a situation to be able to do that, which is admirable. Apart from that, he wants to give the common path to uncommon success to his audience, so that they can achieve the type of uncommon success that they want to and the type of financial freedom that they can so they can ultimately support and give back to something that they believe in.

Why You Need to Find or Create the Right Mastermind

On his podcast, John ends every single one with, "Hey, Fire Nation. You're the average of the five people you spend the most time with. You've been hanging out with myself and Jim today, so keep up the heat," and one of the steps in his book is teaching people how to create or join a mastermind. If you're not in a mastermind, John says you're missing out. The accountability, the companionship, the lessons, and the collaboration are all critical, which is why he teaches you how to find the right mastermind or how to create the right mastermind, and then how to make sure your mastermind is being run correctly, which is also key. If that's not part of what you're doing on a weekly basis, you're never going to achieve the levels of uncommon success that you're capable of.

To learn more about John, you can visit his website.*†

---

* There, he explains in a video more details about his book, of which there are five bonuses that come with the pre-order. They are going to slowly start to take those bonuses away, so it is a timely thing to jump on it now and lock in all five of those bonuses. If you live in the US, one bonus is free delivery of all three of his journals, the Freedom, Mastery, and Podcast Journals. If you're outside the US, you still get immediate access to all three of those journals, which are all bestsellers and are on sale on Amazon for $45.

† There are so many lessons to be learned from John Lee Dumas. Again, his book, *The Common Path to Uncommon Success*, is available for pre-order. So, don't forget to identify your big idea, find your niche, and create your avatar. With the SPEAK|pr programme, this will help you Storify your business, personalise the avatar, create compelling content, amplify that through technologies, and then use the Active Communications Index to track how much you're doing against your goals so you can achieve the success you envision.

Chapter Three
The Business of Story.

Interview with Phoenix, Arizona, based Park Howell; "The world's most industrious storyteller," author of Brand Bewitchery, The Narrative Gym for Business, *and top rated podcast "The Business of Story."*

Fresh from launching his book, *Brand Bewitchery* Park was so full of great information and energy that I asked him to come onto three separate 20-minute episodes. The result is three articles which summarise how you can create a story for the heroes of your business.

Albert Einstein once said that if you want your children to be smart, tell them stories. But if you want them to be brilliant, tell them more stories. Park Howell is known as, by all accounts, "The world's most industrious storyteller," and he's launched a book called *Brand Bewitchery: How to Wield the Story Cycle System™ to Craft Spellbinding Stories for Your Brand.* Aside from that, he has his Business of Story podcast where he shares how he can help you and your business grow.

The Story of the World's Most Industrious Storyteller

Park has been in the advertising branding-marketing world for 35 years. Before that, he studied and got his degree in Public Relations from Washington State University. He was in the PR world and worked for a couple of agencies where he found himself in a cubicle writing, which he got bored of. He was lucky, though, because the PR firm he was working for, which was also his very first employer, had a very small, struggling ad department, and they were getting overwhelmed with work, so they asked him to write a few ads. This was something that he discovered he enjoyed doing. So, he then worked in agencies that had both advertising and PR, and eventually started his own firm in 1995 called Park & Co. 2006 is when Park started looking for an answer, and that's where he found story. That was the genesis of him finally writing and producing *Brand Bewitchery*, his new book.

He said it was really easy back then, when the brands owned the influence of mass media. They had radio, TV, billboards, outdoor direct mail events, public relations, and no Yelp. In 2006, all of that started to change with the advent of the internet, e-commerce, and blogs. Today, 14 years later, it has extremely shifted. When before, brands used to own the influence of mass media, now, the masses are the media, and they own your story. People are so bombarded with content that the brain cannot remotely digest at all.

When it comes to what made him believe that a story should emerge out of this sea of digital and social media, he says it was around the time that his middle child, his son Parker, had just started film school at Chapman University in Orange, California, which is a prominent film school. His son graduated in 2010, has been in Hollywood ever since, and is a director who does a lot of work in virtual reality and mixed reality motion graphics. With his son being in school, this pushed Park to evolve as a communicator. He said to himself, "My son is going to school to become a competitive storyteller in the storytelling capital of the world, LA. What do they teach him? What does Hollywood know that I should know that could give me an advantage over my competition and help me understand how to communicate with my clients and help them hack through the noise and hook the hearts of their audiences?" That's where he found storytelling.

How Can You Be Your Customers' Hero with Brand Bewitchery?

In *Brand Bewitchery*, Park writes about the need for the business owner to be a mentor to their customer's hero. It's not like telling stories at bedtime. This is really about how you convert your story into a promise, a client, or a customer, and it begins by thinking as a storyteller and thinking through the narrative mind. As Park's son was going to Chapman, he told his son to send him his books once he's through with them, since he's paying for them anyway. He wanted to know what they were teaching him, and there, he came across the hero's journey and saw it as an amazing strategy that he could use in business storytelling, and that was the inspiration for his 10-step Story Cycle System.

The key to the hero's journey and the key to every great story, Park says, is always about a single character or protagonist. It's not about a family or group. It's always about a single individual and the journey they're on. That got Park to thinking back in the olden days, before 2006, when brands owned the influence of mass media and were very brand-centric. They were just cramming content down people's faces and saying, "You have to do it our way. If you want to be cool, you have to buy our product." That changed when people started telling their own stories online, calling brands out, and asking for authenticity and honesty. Now, brands have to make a significant paradigm shift and realise they are not the centre of their brand story; their customers are. Once you put your customer at the centre of your story, it requires you to understand them, what they want in life, where they are on their journey to get what they want, and how you can be there as their mentor to guide them through that. It's a total paradigm shift of taking yourself out of being the centre of the story and placing your audience there. Doing that will give you a whole new view on how to communicate your brand.

Park also talks about nine different descriptors in his book, which came about through helping people pull together their brand story strategy using the Story Cycle System. It was what people started naturally doing, and he calls it the "OOOH" exercise. The three Os, your power threes, stand for Organisation, Offering, and Outcomes. Then he asks you to think of three one-word descriptors that describe your organisation in general, and then finally, to give three one-word descriptors that describe your outcome. What do people actually achieve by using your product or service? Once you have those nine, which is divisible by three, the power of three, tell a story. Grab each one of those words, and you're going to end up with nine different stories. Tell a story about each particular word, about your real world impact, and how your brand expresses itself and shows up in the world.

It's a beautiful way to prove what you're trying to do when you're creating your brand story, because people are so often very aspirational, as they should be, but sometimes, it's hard to get your employees on board, but then you overlay these stories and realise that it actually is very much like that. Not only does it prove that what you really stand for is true and authentic, but it also gives you amazing content that you can use in public relations, in inbound and outbound marketing, and on your website. It also changes your focus from telling case studies, which are typically brand-focused, to what Park calls case stories, which are, again, placing your audience or your customer at the centre of the story, and where you show up at the very end to help them achieve something. But again, the story is about them, not about you.

The Business of Your Story

For the Business of Story, Park's podcast or organisation, he has three words. The first is *mage,* which is a sorcerer that describes himself to be. His next word is *industrious,* as the world's most industrious storyteller as coined by one of his clients, which he liked so much and just ran with it. He also says industrious, because he uses story to build careers, to build businesses, and to build brands. The last word is *optimistic,* because Park considers himself very optimistic. The Business of Story is about optimism, and a true, well-told story typically has an optimistic view to it. He says it's a word about his offering. The Business of Story is primal. It is a very primal way that *Homo sapiens* communicate, as *Homo sapiens* are the only known being that actually use story, story structure, and problem-solution dynamic. In his offering, what he demonstrates is how primal this is and how people can move from being intuitive storytellers to intentional ones.

Park then mentions this excerpt from his book: "The various narrative frameworks you can use to tell a story have a rich, proven history of effectively connecting with people and moving them to action. In fact, they are primal to us storytelling monkeys. In the fall of 2018, I was working with 60 engineers and executives at the Palo Verde Nuclear Generating Station in Phoenix. They were a smart and very logic-driven crowd, so I shared with them how our minds are hardwired for story by telling them a tale of Fog, the caveman, which is one of my favourite tales to tell. One evening, Fog returned to his cave looking a little worse for wear. His plump cavern roommate, Larry, grunted, "Fog, you don't looks so good. What happened?" He explained, "Fog go to stream to catch sabre tooth salmon for dinner." "Uh huh," grunted Larry, "but sabre-toothed tiger show up. Fog give tiger salmon. Tiger like salmon better than Fog, so here I am safe in cave with you." "Aha," grunted Larry, nodding at the end sight.

And there you have it. Park says it's a perfect three-act story structure delineated by Larry's "Uh huh" setup, "Uh oh" conflict, and "Aha" resolution. Its story structure is so basic, even a caveman can do it.

It's setup, problem, and resolution, and then he goes on to teach people how to use the "And, But, Therefore" (ABT) framework which is the exact same story dynamic, but this can be used in public relations, marketing, and branding, and it is extremely powerful. He's also got different stages: heroes, stakes, disruption, antagonist, mentor, the journey, the victory, the moral, and the ritual part. To make sense of that, Park brings back to the 10-step Story Cycle System that was inspired by Campbell's hero's journey, which is anywhere from 12 to 17 steps, depending on where you read it. This is mapped to business, and you can think of it in the three-act structure.

Act One of Brand Bewitchery

Act one is simply setup, and those are the first three steps of the Story Cycle System. As you're thinking about your brand and the narrative framework, the setup is your back story. What he means by that is, what is your number one position in the marketplace? What do you functionally do differently and more distinctively than your competition? This, by the way, in the 10 steps, is the only time one thinks about function. Everything else is humanised.

Step two is heroes, and people say, "Well, people aren't really heroes," which is a metaphor. Park wants you to identify your top three audiences and prioritise them, because these are the heroes in the journey. You may have four, five, or six different audiences as most companies do, but Park only wants you to focus on the top three, because he finds that once you get those dialled in, the rest of the world flows through your audiences. Take one of those, take your backstory as the brand, and now, here's an audience that wants to do something, and that takes you to step number three, stakes, which Park breaks down into two different things: what do they wish for and what do they want? What do they wish for means emotionally, e.g. they wish to look smart, they wish to have optimism, they wish to get rid of that fear? What emotionally do they wish to achieve in their life? And then what do they want physically to buy to fulfil that wish?

For instance, in Park's world, people wish to become better, more confident, and compelling communicators. They want a proven system that they can deploy and measure the outcome of, so it becomes very physical, and the only reason why they do it is to fulfil that wish. Make no mistake, every business is in the wish-fulfilling business, and it's the problem everyone tries to solve. So, as you're setting the stage and the backstory, and as your audience is looking for what they wish and want, you are arriving at what problem to use successfully to help them overcome that, and that then launches you into act two, and that is the next couple steps of the Story Cycle System.

Park Howell talked about storification and the first few steps in his book, *Brand Bewitchery*. In the next article, he'll share the other steps involved in getting brands to excel through the stories they tell. Also, listen to Business of Story podcast, as it can also be really useful for entrepreneurs learning to communicate their business story to the world.

Taking a leaf out of Hollywood, Park Howell shares how to build a great narrative for the businesses.

How to Help Your Customers Solve a Problem

When you think about leaping into act two, which is where the conflict or the problem really arises, Park considers that disruption, which is part of Chapter Four. What has happened in the audience's or customers' life that has disrupted their world and has shaken them out of status quo? If they're in status quo thinking they're going to buy from the lowest price, that you're just a commodity, you want them out of that mindset. You want them to help them overcome that change. When you deliver on that, you can charge more, and you actually build greater loyalty. In Chapter Four of disruption, Park says your goal is to clarify what has changed in your audience's life. With that, it makes you get out of your own brain. Unless you demonstrate that you understand and empathise with what your customer actually wants, that'll remain a problem that you're trying to solve in that disruption phase.

The trick with storytelling is not just having a problem to overcome, but dealing with the universe that starts pushing back as well. Whenever you try to fix a problem, it actually gets worse quite often before it gets better, so use that dynamic, and that is Chapter Five, which Park calls villains, fog, and crevasses. What are the competitive forces that you're up against both externally and internally? This could be actual competition out there, or it could be not enough time, not enough money. You've got to think about all these things. And then internally, what's going on in their heads? What are they fearing? What is that voice that is telling them, "No, don't do this?" You do this to understand them.

The Story Cycle and the ABT Framework

As a side note, Park highly recommends that you use the Story Cycle System on yourself. Ask all these questions relative to yourself, and then use it on your business and on your customers too. You will find these worlds starting to meld together, and you will have a much better understanding and empathy for your audience. Words create worlds, and stories connect them, Park says. That's when you tell these true stories about the real world impact that you make a change in their lives. In act one, the protagonist, the backstory, and all that were introduced, and then boom, you pull the rug out from underneath them. What has changed that makes you the most dynamic, urgent, and relevant offering in the world? A really good example is with COVID, there's a global disruption that's created a massive disruption to everybody all over the world. Park then demonstrates the use of the ABT framework, which is a very simple foundational narrative framework. Imagine this, "We were all looking for the promise of 2020, AND what this new decade had in store for us, BUT COVID struck the world. THEREFORE, we are reassessing who we are, what we stand for, where our careers are going, and how we can be in service over sales." There, you have the setup, problem, and resolution. That is a perfect, three-act story structure that any marketer or any PR person can use to frame a point and then to go on. You literally are using the problem-solution dynamic algorithm of story of And, But, Therefore, where "And" is to set up, "But" is the problem, and "Therefore" is the resolution.

Then comes Chapter Six, which is where the mentor arrives. This is the person with the new app, product, or service who arrives on the scene. This chapter all about you and all about the brand and where you do your OOOH exercise, because everything leading up to this is all about your customer, what they're going through, and how you can help them. Now, you have to talk about how you are uniquely equipped to help them. You do the OOOH exercise to figure out those stories that are proof of what your UVP is and what your brand is all about. Boil it down to one word, and that's your brand promise. What do you promise that customers, partners, and staff will get from you emotionally by buying into your product or service? What is that one thread of emotion that they all get by buying in? And then you move on to the next thing which is, what is the intrinsic gift? What do they get when they go through this?

Brand Storytelling

Brand storytelling is not about what you make, but what you make happen in people's lives. For instance, Park makes the Story Cycle System, and he makes a measurable, proven training programme that you can physically take and teach people to grow a brand. What he makes happen is he helps leaders excel through the stories they tell. So, even though you're buying the system, what do you really want? You want to be smart and optimistic. You want to have the courage and confidence. You want to have all these emotional things that come with being a really good storyteller, and that's ultimately what he's selling to excel through the stories you tell. It's this journey of brand awareness, brand adoption, and then brand appreciation, and how you are going to level up people's lives in every one of these steps. What do you give them of unbelievable value that keeps them coming back in?

That leads, then, into Chapter Eight of victory. What are your success milestones? You've got to be strategic about what your audience's experience is in brand awareness when they first hear about you, brand adoption when they first buy into you, and brand appreciation when they come back for more and start telling their friends about you. You have to dial in like you're on a journey, so that they know when your story is progressing with them.

Chapter Nine is about the moral. When you're doing a brand story development, this is about your brand purpose. Why do you exist beyond making money? You can start the sentence by saying, "My brand exists to help people do what?" Park goes back to his moral, which is based off of his intrinsic gift. The Business of Story exists to help people live into and prosper from their most powerful stories. His job is to connect people with the power of story, so that they can connect their world with their audience's world for a better world overall. Use it for good, not for evil. That's what the moral is. That's high-level brand strategy thinking. This is what the brand stands for and what they believe in. Value, by the way, also appears through those nine one-word descriptors. As you are telling stories to your customers, you want to make sure you connect their shared beliefs and values with your beliefs and values, and that's where you use Chapter Nine to really understand what that is.

The last step focuses on a ritual. It's a metaphor for two things: building repeat business and word-of-mouth marketing, which is the most powerful form of advertising, because it's how customers tell their stories to the world, plus, it's free. When ritualising a brand, find out what your call to action is to get them involved. You're essentially inviting them into your story and making your story their story, so the magic is in understanding their story and determining where you can have a decisive impact on their journey. You invite them in, they purchase something, they purchase something else, and they share it with a friend. You want to be able to trigger that in your victory lap by showing them where they're having success with your brand, and then invite them to share that story and show them what to do online by giving them the tools and the story elements of videos, blog posts, or whatever it might be that they can re-share, because they have bought into who you are and what you're about. Now, they become a very active member in your story.

A Narrative Spiral, Not a Circle

It's worth pointing out that if you go to Amazon and search "Brand Bewitchery," the Story Cycle System is a spiral. Park's good friend Dr. Randy Olson, who worked with him on ABT framework, calls it the narrative spiral. Park calls it the Story Cycle System, a narrative spiral. It's different from Joseph Campbell's hero's journey because that was a circle. Your hero starts out in an ordinary world, and after a call to adventure, they go into this extraordinary world. They have trials and tribulations, they learn something, and then they return to their ordinary world, but they're elevated, and they are better and smarter. To Park, it's a spiral, because every time you go around this, you are actually elevating the customer experience and customer engagement. The moment you go through the story cycle once with a customer, that could be brand awareness already. Then, you start it all over again, but from a different spot, and they're now aware of you. Now, it's moving into brand adoption. And then you go through the same process again with brand adoption, and then it becomes brand appreciation. So, one can then see how those concentric circles just keep growing and growing as they become an active member of your story.

These were lessons on the story cycle from Park Howell and his book, Brand Bewitchery, which is on Amazon. Park shares how entrepreneurs can take the business and make it into a story, one that is empathetic to staff, customers, and partners. If you thought that was the last we'll hear from Park, you're wrong. In the next article, Park will discuss the impact of technology on storytelling and a couple of key case studies where storytelling has been great for business.

So, how can business owners create compelling stories that make them great storytellers?

When you think about the massive amounts of channels and the millions of messages that are being sent virtually every minute, if not every second, people are bombarded by content. The brain's cerebral frontal cortex has done a brilliant job of building technology that has evolved at the astounding rate of Moore's law that everyone's familiar with in technology, yet people are still walking around with their limbic system, the same brain that has not appreciably changed for over 90 000 years when ancestors were navigating and trying to survive the Savannah. It's the same system that people today are trying to use to navigate and survive the bombardment on the internet.

It's no wonder that people have a hard time connecting to stand out and be heard in this noisy world, because the masses have become the media. You don't just have a few TV stations and radio stations and print production in newspapers and magazines to choose from anymore to push your story out. Everybody's a TV station, everybody's a radio station, everybody's a different print production house, and they are live 24/7 with global reach from the privacy of their own kitchen table. It's almost like attention deficit disorder has become a communicable disease, and we are all the viruses, and the only way to hack through that noise and hook the hearts is with an anecdote, which is the antidote.

How to Get the Business to Stand Out

People don't operate in scarcity anymore, and because there are so many options to choose from, every company has immense competition. The only way to stand out is to be able to effectively use these primal elements and proven frameworks of storytelling to demonstrate what you stand for, why you are different and distinctive, and then how you tell that story. That's the power of storytelling and how it works.

Based on Watts' cascade theory, the goal is not to find one great influencer and hope that they will influence others, but to find many people who are easily influenced, because it's the masses with a low threshold to be influenced that will trigger a cascade; or what is commonly called "going viral." First and foremost, Park believes that going viral is utter luck, so he cautions to not expect it to happen. Instead, make a really powerful point with even just a handful of great customers that you can embrace and begin with an origin story. When you can reveal yourself in an authentic and vulnerable way, this humanises the business and will make customers more likely to enter into a long-term relationship.

With the proliferation of technology, people have, ironically, become more human oriented. Having previously relied more on big brand advertising through TV, billboards, and the radio, consumers are now facing a paradox wherein their personal technology devices are actually making them more separated from experiencing a brand within the broader context. In other words people are getting separated from the brand, which is reducing loyalty. The solution is to find ways to tell stories, and importantly to embed that person within the brand story so that they see themselves as part of that broader context. We need to rebuild the human connection.

Customers separated by distance want to hear more about the story of the business than the features, functions, and benefits of the product or service itself, because they need to trust before they buy. Customers want to know about the founders of the business – why was the product or service first developed? Moreover, they want to know what your service can do for them.

So lead with the stories. It could be an origin story, a quest story, a customer story, or a case story. It can be very simple too. You can tell an anecdote in under one minute that can have an unbelievable power. Since consumers are now buying things without actually even going anywhere, the story becomes even more important, because there's less brand infrastructure such as the shop, the office, or the showroom. Truth and trust are two of Park's nine one-word descriptors.

"Stories are the vehicle that delivers the truth that creates the trust."

In this sense, the business owner is the producer or the director. The audience is the hero. If you're talking to your employees, place them at the centre of the story, because it makes you understand who they are. Your role is to understand and articulate what they care about, to visualise the journey they're on, so that you, as the producer and director, know what kind of story to create. Your role is as a facilitator for the stories of others, and in the process, they will help you achieve your own story.

When it comes to serving customers, we have to think of the team as the cast in the narrative production of the brand or business. Everyone needs to know the play that they are creating for the customers, and their role in that. It's like an episode of a reality TV show. There is a production crew and infrastructure but the star is the member of the public who gets to fulfil a life's dream by winning a contest live on air. The contestants come and go but the show goes on season after season. Everyone has a role to play, but the customer is always the central focus of the production.

Proof of the Power of Stories

The first one is customer sales-centric, Park says. He was in Melbourne, Australia in March 2019 with his wife Michelle, and they were out there with one of her old childhood friends who had moved to Melbourne many years ago. That friend had a boyfriend who was a Swedish sailor, and he was talking about story and storytelling.

He was asking Park very sceptically how to "story," because he didn't understand storytelling in business. Park asked him, "Could you take me to a time like Tom Hanks in Castaway when you were at sea, and it seemed like all was lost, and something supernatural happened, like the whale came up and flipped water on you?" He laughed and said, "No, it never happened," and then Park just gave him a long pregnant pause. Then the Swedish man said, "Well, there was that one time I was sailing through the Galapagos Islands, and I came down to a channel I had never sailed before. The sun was starting to go down and starting to get dark. It was early evening. Back then, we didn't have GPS. We just had a sextant and compass, and dead reckoned our way through. I didn't really want to take on and navigate this water that I didn't know at dark. So I decided to weigh anchor and hang out in the mouth of this channel, and I would get up early in the morning and go. They next day, I woke up to the sound of dolphins screeching. I went up top on deck, and there were eight dolphins circling around my sailboat and screeching at me. I looked around, and I realised the tide had gone out much further than I had anticipated. In about another 30 minutes, me and my boat would have been impaled on these lava rocks. So, I pulled up anchor and successfully navigated the channel and made it to my destination."

Park then asked him, "Do you think they were warning you?" He goes, "What else were they doing there?" And then this sly grin came over his face, and he says, "Park, I just realised. Every big sale I ever made of a carwash came after I told someone about my sailing adventures. It had nothing to do with business." Park said, "Why do you think that is?" "I have no idea." Park said, "I'll tell you why. Because in the telling of that personal story, of your courage and your journey at sea, people get to know you. They say, 'I think I want this guy on my team. He's industrious. He can get himself out of trouble. He's willing to take risks. I want a guy like that to have my back if I'm going to spend a lot of money on a German carwash in Australia.'" That is the power of story, a true story well told.

The next case study is an event in which Park was speaking at Social Media Marketing World, the largest gathering of social media marketers in the world in San Diego every year. This was about four or five years ago. Park was invited to do the very first workshop on business and brand storytelling which ticked off the whole event, which Park enjoyed. As he was finishing up, a young man approaches him. Andre Martin Hobbs is his name, and he had this French accent. He said, "I loved your presentation. I want to talk to you about helping brand my business," to which Park replied, "Who are you and what is your business?" He goes, "Well, my business is selling used cars in Quebec, Canada to at-risk buyers," so he sold to people with poor credit. Park thought to himself, "I don't know if this is really the kind of brand I want to work with. I work with purpose-driven brands, and I could just picture the car sharks out there taking advantage of people that want these cars."

Park was so glad that Andre circled back with him, because once they started working on his brand story, he found out a whole other side to Andre's brand story. His thing is not about just selling a used car to an at-risk buyer. The purpose of his brand is to help people repair their credit. Andre said to Park, "These are people that have lost their credit, not because it's their fault. Things have just conspired against them. It could have been the global recession. Maybe they got a divorce. Maybe they had healthcare issues that drained them of their money. Maybe they lost a job. But these are genuinely good people that have had bad luck, and I want to help them repair their credit through the purchase of a car." That fascinated Park. Shortly after, the two sat down, and Park took him through the Story Cycle System and uncovered all these elements of it. It came down to his brand purpose, which is, "Your vehicle to financial freedom." In Canada, it takes you two years of dutifully paying bills, so this car is going to do that every month for you to repair your credit to where you can level up. Before you can buy a car at Andre's dealership, you have to go to a two- or three-hour financial planning session where you reveal completely where you are. Financial planners will help you figure out how much you can actually afford to pay on that car and then work with you after the purchase to make sure you do that, and that you're accountable to it. Today, they are the #1 car dealer in Canada for at-risk buyers, not because they're car sharks just selling them anything, but because they are helping them repair their credit. They have a bigger goal and purpose in life. That's why they are their "Vehicle to financial freedom." That's a wonderful story. It really shows that there are many hardships at the moment, but many great stories will come out of it.

Park's parting words were, "As your readers or listeners are becoming better storytellers and working through this, remember that the most potent story you'll ever tell is the story you tell yourself, so make sure you make it a great one." Park Howell, the world's most industrious storyteller and author of Brand Bewitchery, shared steps and tips from his brand story cycle to guide you on how to tell your own story effectively. With that, practise what you've learned from Park and you share your great business story with the world.

Chapter Four
Be Distinct or Go Extinct.

Interview with Los Angeles, California–based Gerry Foster; creator of the Big Brand Formula, speaker, trainer, and faculty member of CEO Space International.

One of the biggest challenges that entrepreneurs and business owners face is putting out a brand. It's something different from simply putting out a service, skill, product, or any other offering. When you put out a brand, you put out something into the world that people can be excited about. You can brand a company, a product, a service, a non-profit, and yourself.

Since 1985, brand strategist Gerry Foster has already coached around 100 000 entrepreneurs. In one of our podcast episodes, he shares tips on how you can build your own brand.

Unless You Stand Out, You're Invisible

There are around 1.7 billion websites in the world. With such a competition, it's getting harder for people to stand out and get noticed. However, you have to understand that unless you're standing out, you're invisible.

For Gerry, the first thing that you need to do to stand out is to have a mindset shift. Instead of being the fly that chases, be the honey that attracts flies. If you put out a brand that is distinctive and offers something fresh and original, you're going to attract people who want to work with you. It's because they know that you have something that they are looking for.

Brand, Market, Sell

As someone who helps people stand out and make more impact, Gerry advises people to follow the Golden Triangle: Brand, Market, Sell.

First, you have to nail your brand, then you market, and sell that brand. All these three processes are of equal importance; they have to work together to achieve the kind of impact that you're looking for.

The job of branding is to differentiate your business and get you known. The job of marketing is to get people to pay attention to what makes your business different – to get you found. The job of selling, on the other hand, is to get people to pay for that difference.

What Is a Brand?

A brand is more than a logo or a website. It's more than the aesthetics, pretty colours, and anything pictorial. It's more than what people can see. When you buy a soda and choose between Coke and

Pepsi, you won't be choosing the soda because it is in a red can or in a blue can. It's what inside the can that counts.

The challenge for you is to give people a reason to work with you; to put something out into the world and entice your audience to embrace it and purchase it. You have to make sure that you're swimming in the so-called untapped market space: Offer something that your audience hasn't heard or seen before. It's sort of identifying your customers' biggest complaint. What are they sick and tired of putting up with? What's not working? What's something they want to have worked better?

Part of your mindset shift as someone building a brand is to be an innovator. Many businesses fade into the background because they're not separating themselves from the rest of the crowd. This is why it's important to stand out and offer something unique so that you can be rewarded for your individuality.

The Role of a Brand Strategist

Gerry describes himself as a brand strategist and not a brand designer. He doesn't make logos and doesn't offer merchandise items. What he does is to help people become a standalone brand. And great brands are those that are built strategically – not visually.

The decision, however, comes down to you. There are different levels wherein you can play at. First is the me-too level, wherein you are only imitating. You're only another slice in the loaf. The second level is the so-called me-special, wherein you become an impersonator. You're putting out something different but people don't really find that important. The third, which Gerry wants you to play at, is the me-only level. This is where you become a brand that offers something unique and relevant.

Even if you're a small business that is limited on resources, you can still build a big brand around yourself. You can do so by making the decision strategically – that you are going to deviate and not conform, you're going against the flow and not with the flow. You are not adopting the me-too or me-special brand wherein you'll only become an imitator or an impersonator – you have to be an innovator.

What You Need To Offer

Once you make the decision that you want to be an innovator, you need to ask yourself: What are people looking for that they cannot currently avail of?

When it comes to branding, it's not the product or service per se that people are paying for. It's these things that make you different. And one of which is your ability to solve a problem that your target audience is having. Two is your ability to provide a better outcome for your market. Three is your ability to perform a miracle; to make the impossible, possible. This aspect is particularly huge nowadays given that we're living in the midst of a pandemic. You have to be able to make things possible or bring forth a future that your audience never thought could be possible.

The fourth ability is to provide your audience with an emotional payoff. Show people that you can stop them from experiencing negative emotions or from getting frustrated or stressed out.

Building a brand is being able to offer these four things to your audience. It's not simply offering some services or products.

Make Yourself Distinct or Go Extinct

If you want to become the go-to brand in your particular space or niche, you need to be different and be better.

If you're different, you're the only company or business that can offer something to your customers. And it's because of your superiority and expertise – your so-called secret sauce. If you have a system, a process, or a particular method, you can also leverage and monetise it through marketing and through offering courses and programs. This is one way of telling people that you're not only capable of delivering what they're looking for – nobody can duplicate, imitate, or negate it. You really have to stand out because unless you're distinct, you're at risk of being extinct.

If you already have a brand and you want to really establish your authority, you may need to rebrand. Re-engineer, reimagine, and re-tool what you currently have and make it more innovative. Back it up with your secret sauce and deliver what you're promising to your customers in a way that nobody else can. After all, no one else in the market has the same DNA as yours.

Gerry advises you to brand your brilliance and highlight those things that allow you to shine. Focus on what makes you admirable. Be distinct, brand your uniqueness, and believe in it.

Chapter Five
5Cs of Personal Branding.

Interview with Pensacola, Florida-based branding expert Michelle Griffin; host of "The Business of You" show and Certified Personal Brand Strategist.

Creating a personal brand is a subject close to Michelle Griffin's heart. However, even though marketing and branding are a part of her skill set, it was a challenge for her to brand herself. This is why she put together five easy steps that her clients can follow.

The 5Cs of Personal Branding

In one episode of The UnNoticed podcast, Michelle broke down the 5Cs of personal branding.

Confidence. Many people are afraid to step out because of uncertainty. They are uncertain if they're experienced enough or if there will people who will listen. However, if you won't step out to help others through your service or product, no one will ever know about you. This change in mindset to be more confident is almost a daily battle. And Michelle helps her clients out by diving deep into what can make them more confident about themselves – from message and mission to skills and expertise.

Clarity. If you're not clear about your identity, values, missions, perspectives, and the services you're going to provide – it is a huge issue. It's going to be a struggle to make sense of things and help others make sense of you. This is why you have to get clarity on your purpose internally first. After doing that, you can do external clarification: Who is your audience? What are their demographics? What are the challenges and desires? Part of this step is also identifying which platform should you use in getting yourself known. Michelle always tells that you don't need to do all things in all places to get traction. It's better to start small and build things up from there.

Content. The fastest way to attract more people and let them know who you are is with content. Content is at the heart of every branding endeavour. And when making content and conversation with your audience, you have to determine your strength. Do you like to do podcasts? Do you like blogging and writing? There are different ways to make your thought leadership and your brand get noticed. And all these can act as fuel for your brand; as a way of creating an online identity. To help you produce effective content, Michelle notes that choosing topics and themes and aligning your content to them is important. This will help you be clearer and more competent as a brand.

Consistency. Many people fail because they give up too soon. They're not consistent. However, Michelle emphasises that consistency wins the game. It wins the game for content, for personal brand building, for business. Keep in mind that you are doing things for a long haul. Look at it as a marathon and not a one-and-done thing. One thing that really propels people forward is consistently taking action. For instance, earlier this year, Michelle took on the 365-day challenge on LinkedIn wherein she had to post daily on the platform. This helps her ensure that she can consistently show up on her LinkedIn account.

Community. For Michelle, the most important thing is community. Start looking at your audience, clients, collaborators, friends, and partners as one big community – a community that's built to support one another. If you use this approach, you will experience a ripple and snowball effect. The more you connect and help people, the more that your brand will grow.

Michelle considers these 5Cs like a big circle – it all works around and it never ends. It's an endless cycle of constantly evolving, and growing a bigger circle.

Addressing Challenges

To address issues on confidence, Michelle asks her clients: "Why are you putting yourself out there? Why would people listen to you? What do you have to say?" After these are answered, she helps in spinning things around. Brand-building is not really about you; it's about how you can help others. It's about your audience. When you have this mindset, you'll be taking a huge burden off your shoulder and realise that you can do this. You can help others and even make a profit in the process.

In Donald Miller's *Building a StoryBrand*, clarity is emphasised. If you're confused, you will lose a sense of things. And clarity is not just for personal brands, it's for everyone, from entrepreneurs to big businesses.

One mistake that people make today is jumping straight into creating content for their social media platforms and websites without being clear of what their brands are. When you know who you are and what your strengths are, you can make your strategy aligned to it. And people will be able to sense that. As stated, it's vital to be internally clear first before extending the clarity externally. Based on her experience, seeing clients transform into a more clarified brand is the best part of her job. She also says that it is clarity that can further boost confidence.

Being clear – especially when it comes to knowing what your platform/s should be – further helps in saving time and money. If your audience is on LinkedIn, you don't necessarily have to be on Instagram, and vice versa.

Clarity also helps in being strategic about content. If you're internally and externally clear about your brand, you won't just be piece-mealing your content. This is why Michelle makes sure that she helps her client create a content strategy that's based on their goals and on their audience's problems that they want to address. From there, she assists in choosing about three to five pillar topics. Making content based on these topics will help things keep fresh and professional. If you are a personal brand, you have to create content that will attract your ideal customers in an organised manner.

However, content creation is not just about posting something on a certain platform like LinkedIn. You also have to comment and engage with your audience. You have to get a pulse of what your audience likes and what are the things that they resonate with. Track things and assess if your content is still relevant to your audience.

When producing content, Michelle advises having a mixture of video, live video, and graphic content. There are different tools such as Canva that can help you create these materials. In terms of copy creation, tools like Grammarly, Repurpose.io, and the Hemingway App can help. You don't have to be afraid because there are technologies you can leverage to help you grow your brand.

When asked about how to be consistent, Michelle points out that you should not be enamoured by "likes." While there are people who get an amazing number of likes, followers, and comments on social media, they're not getting any clients. This is why she always asks her clients: "Do you want likes or do you want leads?"

Consistency and content creation are not about posting something that will appeal to a lot of people — it's about targeting the right people. Michelle knows of brands that don't have a lot of social media following but are thriving in terms of clients and revenue. This goes to show that you don't have to give up if you're not getting huge social media statistics. If you're talking to your audience, they're going to see your value.

One reason to be consistent is to think of personal branding as a long-term thing. Success doesn't usually happen overnight. For instance, if you're on LinkedIn and you feel that no one is seeing your content, you have to know that about 97–99% of people there are mere lurkers. Even though they don't comment, you shouldn't give up because it doesn't mean that they're not seeing your content.

With regard to building a community, you can start small by simply participating first: Show up and show other people that you care. If you're on LinkedIn, bear in mind that you give what you get. Comment on other posts and be a helpful person, and you'll see that people will start to recognise you very fast. It's a way of expediting growing your community.

When building your community, it's also essential to start collaborating. As mentioned, by connecting to and working with other people, you will experience a ripple effect. This is based on what Michelle has personally experienced. When she got consistent on LinkedIn and she started getting connected and collaborative with other people, she started getting traction. Other opportunities like getting invited to Clubhouse, Zoom, and live events followed.

However, when reaching out to other people, she says that it's important to be genuine. You shouldn't talk in a hard-sell manner or appear sales led. For you to make a huge difference, you have to treat others as humans. Take note that networking and building relationships are about authentically connecting with like-minded people.

Chapter Six
The 8-seconds Pitch.

Interview with Taunton, Somerset-based Martin Barnes;
Crocodile wrestler, Founder of eightsecondstoconnect,
old China Hand.

Martin Barnes is a pitch coach and the founder of eightsecondstoconnect. He helps people enjoy pitching and presenting, specifically founders who are at the very beginning of their entrepreneurial or business journey. His target market are people who have amazing ideas that keep them awake at night and those who have seen a problem and have a solution, but can't seem to communicate it effectively.

For business owners to unlock the value in their business and enjoy telling the story of how their business can potentially grow, Martin helps them present and pitch their business ideas. He says cave paintings were the world's first ever pitch, and the cave painting is the slide for that pitch. His imagination is that these cave people are in a cave with a torch and a cave painting, and the community of tribe people is there, and they are telling each other how to survive. That was 65 000 years ago, proving that humans are storytelling creatures. That's how even the primitive people communicated, but it's something many today have forgotten how to do. Thankfully, modern technology has provided the opportunities and the tools for people to tell their stories.

The Perfect Tools for Pitching

Speaking of tools, Martin will make use of any tool for pitching: a whiteboard, a laptop, or even a smartphone, and he says ideas can be developed anywhere: on paper, on a whiteboard, on post-it notes, anywhere as long as you are thinking freely and can get into a creative flow state. Through a process of digitisation, organisation, and editing, you can then choose PowerPoint, Keynote, Prezi, or whatever software you want to share that message. It's very much process-driven, and it goes from analogue to digital, but the problem with that is people jump into creating a PowerPoint with half an idea and then hope the PowerPoint will help them organise their thinking.

Before writing ideas down, the challenge is finding the right words to articulate what it is that makes the business special, and this is all about discovery, listening, and asking questions. Martin has a long list of around 80 discovery questions that he goes through with his clients, and they're clustered within very tangible mechanical questions about what it is they're doing, and then there are more emotive questions around why they're doing it and whom they're helping. Martin aims to get clients to go through this discovery phase where they can explore the questions from end to end and encourage them to talk, because it is the job of communication people to listen and then to identify where the story is. One client of Martin's said that he is very good at helping people understand what they know, but packaging it in a new way. He is able to do this, because he has found that it's often the thing that someone will say on the edge which is the most important, and so he keeps his ears open and collects the edges because that's where the real insights are.

Martin focuses on helping founders overcome challenges in finding their voice and the narrative of the business more than other members of a company, because the founder is in the eye of the storm. Other team members of an organisation have their jobs, their goals, and their KPIs. Meanwhile, the founder is on the front of the ship with a compass, a map, and a destination, and he or she is in charge of figuring out how to get to where they want to be. Also, founders are able to see both the smaller and the bigger picture in terms of the business' potential and growth, which is why the need to be able to pitch convincingly to their audience.

One issue is that not everybody is comfortable or has the vocabulary to build their story, and so this is where the tools come in. Once you have a basic understanding of storytelling structure, you can then see the map. In line with this, Martin has developed a process called the three-beat mountain, which is a pitch structure, and it's very loosely based on the three-act play. All stories are generally told in the same way, in a structural basis, but it's the details of the characters in the drama that make it compelling. And so the three-beat mountain is a way of saying, "What do you want to say first? What do you want to say second? What do you want to say third? What's your call to action? And don't say any more than that."

Make Personalised Pitches

Technological advancements have propelled this generation into an era where AI can now do the writing for you, but the problem with AI-generated content is it can all end up coming across as generic. To personalise that and get the founder to stand out, aside from talking about structures and tools, another topic to talk about are the goals and the audience, because the biggest mistake Martin sees founders making is they make their pitch and use the same one for all audiences, but that shouldn't be the case. A pitch needs to be personalised for every single audience group, and that occurs as soon as there is an understanding of how the structure works.

When creating a different set of messages and a different pitch for each audience, the CEO or the founder is then tasked to remain a consistent personality. That can be done by taking a step back and realigning oneself, identifying the values, the vision, and the mission of the business. Once those high level concepts are clearly understood, it becomes easy to craft the message for each audience. Again, it's not about sharing everything. It's about sharing what matters to the audience in front of you that will move you closer to your goals. Before, Martin wanted to get as much information transferred down as possible, but then he over-pitched and failed, because his audiences would get overwhelmed. He learned that it's important as a leader to first develop the mission and vision and then pitch the key points of that to the different groups.

On the eightsecondstoconnect website, he shares the window of opportunity to persuade someone to either buy from you or invest in your business, because research suggests that you need to "pitch your pitch" or have a hook that grabs people's attention quickly. It might be futile to have a pitch and jump in with the best bits if people may have not tuned in yet. And so, this concept of having 8 seconds to connect was born. This also came as a result of Martin hearing about TikTok, social media attention span, YouTube video duration, and how people tune out very quickly. From that, Martin figured out a way for founders to hook people's attention before they deliver the main message.

Apart from the mainstream tools, Martin makes use of niche storytelling tools like Mmhmm which is a tool for making Zoom calls more interactive. It allows the speaker or the presenter to be bigger in the frame of their online pitch, therefore, they're no longer a postcard stamp-sized image, but they're actually part of the presentation itself. Martin's part of the beta testing group, and he can feel the higher levels of engagement through using this tool, which was one of many developed as a reaction to COVID and the fact that people are now pitching, presenting, and telling stories in very different ways than they were before COVID.

When people ask Martin what he does, he tells them he's a crocodile wrestler, to which he gets a smile and a confused look. He explains that he has twins under three and that his life feels like he's wrestling crocodiles, but when he's not wrestling crocodiles, he's a pitch coach. He's said this with the British Chamber of Commerce in Beijing, with groups in the southwest of England, and he always gets a smile. Talking about crocodiles is what he says during his 8 seconds to connect. He paints an incredibly vivid picture in the minds of his audience that they will remember, and that is key. Currently, he is working on an online course that will help people create an opening pitch that catches others' attention, because the whole reason of having 8 seconds to connect is that once you've got the attention of others, then you have a runway to sell. If you don't have that attention, you won't get anywhere.

Top Tips for Presenters

There are three things that a presenter controls as they pitch: they present what they say as their story, they control how they say it with their performance, their tonality, their eye contact, and then there's their slide design. Martin believes the most important is story, then it's performance, and then finally, it's the slides. It's a big help if the presenter is able to tell visual stories while the audience visualises it, and the background image is amplifying the main message and not conflicting with it. Many people make the mistake of having too many images on a slide, because they want to show everything, but then what they say doesn't really sync up with what they're showing, and so reducing the visuals and choosing one emotive image that really resonates is way more powerful.

Often, clients will want to include as much information as they can for fear of leaving out something important. This is a valid concern, because a pitch and a presentation are an incredibly high-value moments, because you have somebody's attention. A lot of people will pitch the same information they have on their website, but Martin advises not using someone's attention for what they could read much quicker on a website. Instead, use their attention to start building rapport. The presenter needs to have the confidence, the trust, and the bravery to say, "I do have more to say, but I don't have to say it now." You are allowed to leave things out. It's like if you're meeting someone at a networking event and they don't let you enter the conversation, you just back off. Those are the same rules. The point is if you've got a great hook, you create a level of interest, which means you don't have to dump everything on the listener, because your goal is to build a relationship first. This is something Martin learned the hard way. Now, he reminds himself that patience is a virtue. If you are able to identify what your customer is looking for, then the narrative shifts to thinking about what it would take to make them into a hero. It's not about you and sharing everything. It's about the solution you could provide to them, and it's given to them one piece at a time, so that they can have a sense of ownership over what you're sharing.

Chapter Seven
Case: Constructing a Story.

Interview with Pittsburgh, Illinois–based Chris Martin; President of Atlas Marketing, co-host of "Building PA Podcast," specialising in the construction industry.

Having worked in the construction industry for over two decades, it doesn't come as a surprise that Chris Martin would focus on providing marketing services for companies in this niche. He is the owner and President of Atlas Marketing, a Pittsburgh marketing agency that tells stories of people who build, make, and manufacture things.

Telling a Unique Story

At least in the US, Chris shares that every construction and manufacturing company always says three things: They're safe, on time, and on budget. However, if there are 20 million contractors that claim the same things, it can be difficult for clients to choose one among them. For contractors to get clients, they have to find a unique story that will differentiate them from others. Without those, consumers will be forced to simply use price as the deciding factor.

Through Atlas Marketing, Chris wants you to understand that there's a need to make it easier for clients to choose you. And that can be done by telling your story.

For example, he has worked with a contractor in Mississippi who agreed to take on a school construction project. The school owner requested to have the construction work done in the evening so that students can come to school during the day. In his over 25 years in the industry, Chris has never heard of a contractor who went the extra mile to work around the needs of the client. Though this cost a little more, the impact that it provided to the school and the community was immeasurable.

Chris job is to amplify unique stories like this. However, it doesn't mean that they will tell the entire story right away. As part of their strategy, they may first segment it through various social media posts, raise awareness, and build up the story and its impact over time.

Chris also has a client which is a labour group of iron workers. These people erect and set structural steel for bridges, buildings, and more. One interesting aspect that they have is that they hold an annual apprenticeship competition. Part of the competition is scaling 30–40-foot steel beams and climbing to the top of them within a few seconds. This event highlights the focus and athleticism that their job requires. What he and his agency did do was to build stories around how these workers can be regarded as superheroes – athletic men and women who can do extraordinary things. This eventually helped in their client's recruitment campaign.

Focusing on One Industry

For Chris, one of the best decisions that he made in terms of owning a business is focusing on one industry – the construction and manufacturing industry, in particular. This move helped them introduce themselves to the right customers and focus themselves on their and their clients' businesses.

Before this shift happened, his marketing company was no different from any other agency. Until three or four years ago, they were trying to be all things to everybody. Though he was nervous at first, them focusing on a certain market has become beneficial when it comes to decision-making. It has become easier for them to choose their clients, and identify which projects meet their core values and which projects can they pass on.

In the process, it also eventually helped them grow. Now, they are also working even with clients outside of the construction and manufacturing world. For Chris, it's not a matter of looking at things and saying that they're only going to work in this niche – it's a matter of defining who they are as a company. In Atlas Marketing's case, they're a company that tells stories.

During the transition from being a generic marketing agency into a more focused one, Atlas Marketing experienced challenges. However, it still worked out for the best as their company tallied a 20% growth in 2020. By 2021, their growth was projected at 25–30%.

Chris attributes this success to two things: First is the increased focus on business development and sales. Second, and more importantly, is having a clearer definition in terms of who they are and what they do.

Generating Content, Opening More Opportunities

Apart from his work in Atlas Marketing, Chris also started The Building PA Podcast with colleague Jon O'Brien. Jon serves as the executive director for Keystone Contractors Association (KCA) in Pittsburgh. The podcast, which they launched a year ago, did not only give them an outlet for their creative juices but also opened the door for more opportunities.

In fact, they recently commenced the publication of a digital magazine for KCA called *The Keystone Contractor Magazine*. In the interactive magazine, they talk about all things related to construction and incorporate links to relevant podcast episodes. For the magazine, they are using a tool called PubHTML5, which works similar to Issuu.

Tying both mediums together also provides Atlas Marketing more opportunities to assert themselves as an industry leader and to meet more people within the industry. While the relevance of newsletters and magazine publications has dwindled in the past years, Chris points out that now is a good opportunity to use content creation to raise awareness.

Through his podcast and digital magazine, Chris can also give back to the industry that he's been working in for the past two decades. And this is still in line with what his mission is all about: To tell a story and provide value.

You can find more about him and his marketing company on www.atlasstories.com. If you're looking for ways to get noticed, think about creating your own content – whether it's a podcast or a magazine – and find out what it is about you that makes your story unique.

PART TWO
Personalise

Chapter One
Introduction.

"Personalisation will be the prime driver of marketing success within five years."
— McKinsey Management Consulting

Building cars by hand one at a time tailored to a customer specification is the ultimate in personalisation, and in China where people will pay to express their individuality the Morgan offer was really compelling, but the principle applies to every business. Your product may be standard, a commodity even, but the customer experience does not have to be. If you take to heart the lessons from Chapter One, the need to craft stories for the people affected by your business, the logical extension is that we need to do the best we can to make each experience relevant to those people.

Personalisation is about understanding each individual person (sometimes called an avatar) who is going on a "hero's journey" with you and your company. The goal is to personalise their content experience so that it is as if they were saying it themselves. Personalisation is about identifying the characteristics of your audience so that you can serve them information which meets their needs. I say "audience" because personally I like to think of three distinct groups: those who work for you, the partners who help you deliver, and the people who buy from you.

It may seem strange to talk about public relations being personal, but the reality of it is that technology has once again changed the dynamics of marketing. Once upon a time, broadcasters and publishers spoke at us, and we had neither the right nor the ability to reply. As a media relations agency we competed for the limited space and time these power brokers held over the audience our clients wanted to reach. Today we can own that channel to our audience, and no longer have to rely on others to talk to our customers and potential customers on our behalf. Technology has democratised communication and made #gettingnoticed personal.

In these interviews, we are going to cover a lot of aspects of personalisation ranging from some platforms to some case studies. I've added in resources for media relations too because all work with journalists has always been personal, but what has changed is that the information relating to journalists is no longer the private preserve of the public relations agency. I spoke with a number of technology innovators who are showing the way that business owners can use each touch point with the outside world to build a brand so that we don't waste even one opportunity to #getnoticed. I also address customer service because acquisition is 5x more expensive than retention, and in this day and age customers who have a bad experience can make a harmful impact. In the case studies I show how tribes are being made of significant niches, and these are being built with personalisation of listening, content, and product.

Chapter Two
Teach Bots to Be Compassionate.

Interview with Andover, Hampshire–based Peter Dorrington of Anthrolytics.

Anthrolytics is a London-based company that uncovers the motivations behind human behaviour – why people do the things that they do and what they're likely to do next. According to co-founder and Chief Strategy Officer Peter Dorrington, they do this by looking at emotional motivation and adding that to other kinds of motivators. Why is somebody buying a particular product? Apart from factors such as price, convenience, and purpose, they ask: How do the customers feel about the products, and how does that work over the lifespan of them being a customer?

At Anthrolytics, data science is combined with behavioural science to answer that question. However, they don't only identify why people do what they do – they ultimately help businesses make better experience decisions, particularly when it comes to their digital channels where there isn't a human at the one end of the conversation. In sum, they turn motivation into action.

How They Help Bridge the Digital Divide

With COVID, the past 14 or 15 months have seen more businesses moving into a digital operating model. And this means that they often don't have a human talking to another human being. Many of the consumers have learned to self-serve and businesses have relied on bots. For most organisations, this is a very satisfactory, competent job: It does what they want them to do. However, there is this disintermediation – and it has really affected the experience economy.

Customer experience, as a discipline, has been around for about 25 years. It's not something new but what businesses have done are the easy aspects of it, e.g. listening to customer programs, doing customer journey mapping. However, what customers are saying is that they want empathy; they want compassion. They want to be more than a customer number. They want to feel that they're in a relationship with you. Once they feel that, research shows that business metrics will go off the chart. Customer satisfaction will leap up, and so does loyalty and economic activity. Your customers will spend more money more frequently – and they will enjoy doing it.

What Anthrolytics is focusing on is how to replicate or produce empathic experiences in digital channels. This one is possible and it can be likened to teaching a bot how humans feel. If someone says he's hungry, then the rational need is to eat. But if he wants a juicy burger and fries, then it becomes more emotional. Doing so will make him feel happy. However, it's not the only emotion that the customer wants to feel. He wants to feel less afraid and more certain during uncertain times. Therefore, at the heart of human-centered design (which is where a number of businesses are moving into), there's a need for empathy. You need to blend compassion with competence and once you're able to do that, business results will be outstanding.

The Process of Teaching Bots

Bots run automated tasks over the internet. But how do you teach them to be compassionate? How do you help them when they couldn't see the person on the other end?

According to Peter, it's a two-step process. And the first step is to use natural language processing or understanding technology to analyse what customers say. There's a specific kind of question that they'd typically ask, i.e. asking the customer to describe something, like their experience or a podcast episode, to a friend or a stranger. When customers do that, they tell you what's on top of their minds about the particular experience. In the process, they're leaking emotions. The first stage involves analysing those and figuring out which things do people remember and talk about and how they feel about them.

Now, when these are incorporated into a decision matrix (where you have all other factors like price or star ratings), you can then associate an event (e.g. listening to a podcast) with an outcome. Then, you can make decisions about what outcome do you want and what's best for both parties. So the bot has a decision-making algorithm that doesn't only tell about the logical side of things but also the emotional aspect – if a customer is likely to be feeling anxious or uncertain or unclear about what he does. Based on that, you can choose a different tone of voice or endorse a different product for that customer, something more suited to his wants and needs. These are things that can be taught to bots in any form of automation where there is a choice.

One reason why this can be complicated is that a lot of previous models over the last few years only worked when the customer had a completely free choice. Behavioural economics talks about free choices, but very few of us have them. For instance, if you want to buy an Italian supercar and you can't afford it, it's not a free choice. The operational part of the decision-making is to use these insights to let the system make better decisions on behalf of your business and your customers. When it does, you get something that feels a lot more humane.

The real trick is being able to do this proactively. Before somebody starts to exhibit fear or anxiety, anticipate where your customers might be right now. With that, you could reach out and offer reassurance before they have to dial in asking what they need to do. This is an incredibly human feeling and experience that everybody enjoys.

Understanding a Customer's History

If you try to model an individual person, you'd want to understand what his history did to put him to where he currently is. When you use traditional techniques, Peter says that it's undoable because there's not enough data and it'd take too much computing power.

A customer's history informs one's habits and opinions. It took Peter two years to figure out how to do that but what he found out was how you could extend that across an entire customer base of tens of millions of individuals – and update it every single day – based upon what has happened to a particular customer. Rather than trying to do regression (which is building a big complicated model), his company came up with a much more straightforward technique that's efficient and requires relatively little computing power. However, he points out that it's not going to be 100% accurate, as in any other behavioural model.

To make it clearer, take this as an example: You've probably gotten offers from a marketing department where they've used a predictive model. They've put you into a segment, let's say, Customer Segment A1, where there are a lot of other customers. Angry customers within that segment will respond differently from happy customers. If you treat them both the same, you'll probably irritate both of them. But, if you could tell the difference, then you could treat those customers differently according to their needs. And that's where the slight differentiation of the golden rule comes around: You're more focused on treating customers the way that they want to be treated – not the way that you want to be treated. After all, the customer should be at the centre of your thinking.

In this sense, you're using legacy data from that customer within your organisation rather than what they've done before they got to your organisation.

Everyone talks about customer journeys in customer experience. They plot the journey and see that there's a happy journey. Then there are derivations off of that. In reality, it's about "customer landscapes" because people's lives are messy. They are not sequential or linear – people have overlapping journeys and there are detours. When you take the approach that Peter and company have taken, your history will be a bit like dead-reckoning navigation. It's about where you are right now, what direction you're going in, and how fast you're traveling.

However, it doesn't really matter how fast you respond if you're taking the wrong treatment or direction. It's not necessary that you're making wrong decisions – you're not just making optimal decisions. And you can make a better one. From the human point of view, it's not about reducing choices or saying that certain people only get certain offers. It's about offering everybody the best possible choice that meets your customers' and your business' needs so that everybody walks away as happy as they could given the circumstances.

Hyper-Personalisation

If you've got everyone's data and you've got how they behave, you'll be able to personalise both the offer and the way you deliver it. In the digital context, the most talked-about version of that is what's called hyper-personalisation, which adds real-time context to personalisation. Apart from knowing what a customer wants, you delve into the emotional, empathic context of that: How is the customer feeling? Because this will influence his decisions. It's estimated that 98–99% of decisions people make on any given day are dictated by the subconscious and are influenced by emotions and habits – they don't follow logical rules.

This is one of the things that many businesses get wrong. When they're talking to their customers, they think that getting more facts helps. For some customers, this is true. But for others, the last thing that they need is more facts. What they want is help and guidance – something that is more narrative saying what is not right for them and offering a product or service that is. If an organisation could give a customer what he needs, he's more likely to trust that organisation even if it's too complex to understand intellectually.

There are tools and techniques to understand these things. However, these shouldn't be used to do dark psychology, which is to influence people to do things that are not in their best interest. These should be used to treat customers like human beings. And if you'd be able to address their needs – both emotional and rational – it will be a better experience for them. Subsequently, it will build a better business relationship. It would also be nearly impossible for your competitors to reverse-engineer because it's based upon a relationship that's unique to your business. Your relationship with your customer is not something that can be replicated.

Customer Relationship in the Digital Context

Establishing a personal relationship with a customer is more difficult to do in digital environments because there's no human-to-human relationship.

To be able to do that, Peter talks about two important aspects of empathy, the emotional side of things. With emotional intelligence training, you can understand what people are feeling and why they're feeling it. It's called cognitive empathy. The compassionate aspect comes when you take action as a result of recognising your customer's emotions. If someone is angry, what are you going to do about it? When you link cognitive empathy with compassionate, action empathy, you can display it through a machine. You don't need to be a human being to do that – it simply entails making the right decision that reflects what the customer values.

For big businesses, this one is easy because they'd only need to automate and operationalise for it to be done to millions of customers every day. For smaller businesses, on the other hand, there are a number of ways how this can be accomplished (e.g. customer feedback). However, the first thing you need to do here is to ask the right question – instead of asking how your customers feel, ask them to describe their experience.

As stated earlier, having them describe their experience will help leak emotions. If you have no infrastructure, you have to sit down with these verbatim and identify emotional words. If you've got a bit of infrastructure, you can use AI tools for natural language processing and let these tools strip out those words for you. You've probably seen word clouds where the most frequently used word is the biggest. That word can be associated with emotions, like anger and fear. Armed with that, you as a business can make better decisions. Whether you're a small business doing things manually or a big company automating the process, what's important is how you use the data. You should feed that directly to your marketing or customer service systems.

Keep in mind how important these interconnected bits are. Because when something goes wrong, your customer won't blame your delivery driver or your supplier – they are going to blame you. You are responsible for any failure no matter how unfair it might seem from your point of view. So, you really have to understand what your customer genuinely cares about and why do they care about it, and design your experience around that.

This is also where having a decision tree of templates becomes essential. Imagine if you're phoning with a complaint to a call centre and you get routed to a happy-clappy individual. If you're angry, a customer service representative that's upbeat is the last thing you'd want to hear. What you'd want is someone who's a bit more sombre, someone who's going to say that they're taking your problem seriously. You need to have a script, but it should be slightly different. You have to use certain words and tones depending on the customer. And for Peter, it doesn't have to cost your business more money. If anything, it can save you money if you do that in the right way. You're avoiding having a failure of process and a failure of thought.

Chapter Three
Finding the Appropriate Asia Pacific-based Journalist.

Interview with Matthew Law; Co-Founder and CMO of Telum Media.

There's nothing worse than spending hours putting together a press release only for it to not get the attention it deserves, and so this is the problem that Telum Media addresses for companies. Telum Media connects people, organisations, companies, business owners, and PR people who've got something they'd like to say and get out there with the right journalists, content creators, and earned media who are producing content in those particular areas, topics, or products. It's a platform to discover the right people to talk to, and it's also a community, because they encourage interaction between PR people, content creators, and journalists, and they do that in various ways. Fundamentally, it's an internet system where you can look up the media and journalists that you need to engage with and find out, through lots of rich content, whether that journalist might be the person that you want to talk to. At the core of their services is a platform where they provide newsletters for the journalist community and the PR community about journalistic and PR moves, as well as other media industry intelligence. They provide job news, and they work in multiple languages, including Bahasa, Thai, and traditional and simplified Chinese (to cover Hong Kong, Taiwan, and China).

Telum's Best Features

Telum Media currently has tens of thousands of journalists on its roster. Due to COVID and the significant changes that have taken place in media and in its structure, that's where the beauty of a business like theirs in Asia lies, because in the Asia-Pacific region, the media is extremely diverse. There are different languages and geography from Australia and New Zealand, which they cover all the way through to China and Taiwan, and it's really hard for a company to find the right journalist to engage with on their own. It's like looking for a needle in a haystack.

Matthew was only too aware of the difficulties of contacting journalists when he moved to Singapore from London, in 2010, as a Director of Bell Pottinger, the former British multinational public relations firm. As part of the team setting up the Singapore office for Bell Pottinger back then, it was a constant struggle to build and maintain these connections throughout the region.

Matthew shares that when he left Bell Pottinger in 2013 to begin building Telum, the PR agency was one of his first customers. Telum was a brand-new window looking into the Asia-Pacific media scene that otherwise would have been extremely hard for agencies and in-house communications teams to keep on top of.

Moving on to their client profile, Matthew says it's very diverse. There isn't a typical Telum client. It's the full gamut. They cover all sectors, and they've got small freelance operators, startups, MNCs, PR agencies, government organisations, and the like. Practically anybody who wants to engage with the media will be a Telum customer.

One of their unique features is that they have country teams or local language teams for each of their markets. Before, in the days of the little black book and Excel spreadsheet, you would literally have to have costly teams of people constantly updating information about journalists, and that would be just simply contact information. It wouldn't be what their preferences were, what they were looking to write about next, when to contact them. But at Telum Media, they've got teams for all of their main countries that are talking to the journalists every day. They've actually got KPIs, believe it or not, to network with journalists and PR people, and to make sure everything's not just up to date, but also actionable and useful. They're always keeping an eye out, like good PR people do, for information that somebody else might be interested in and helping them get a piece of coverage or engage better with that journalist.

How Telum Helps Companies Create Connections with Journalists

Over at Telum, they believe in meaningful engagement between you and the journalists. They don't exist to spam email thousands of journalists with irrelevant content. They want to make sure it's the right content. From a workflow perspective, they have very rich search information, right from the start when you're planning a campaign, to make sure that you're targeting the right media and putting together the list of the right journalists. Within that, they've got recommendation engines and multiple keyword searches. They also have a live list update, so that the next time you log in, it will tell you that this journalist has moved or that you might want to think about these journalists. It eliminates having to go through and manually check your list time and time again. Through the system, you can set up your press release to go out as a BCC or however you want to do it, but it comes from you.

The final component, which Matthew thinks is incredibly powerful, is that the whole ethos of their company is about networking and relationships, and you can track your relationships with the journalists that you're engaging with. From a compliance perspective, you might want to keep records of interactions if you're in financial services because you might want a record for when there might be a crisis or issue, especially if you have, say, a temporary person working on your PR and you want to keep a record of those interactions with journalists when that person's moved on. You might simply want to do it so that you have multiple people looking at the latest RSVP lists for a press product launch invitation. Essentially, they have that ecosystem within Telum. It's very active.

When you log in, you will see the latest media requests. These will be live opportunities where journalists announce what kind of stories they're looking for and how soon they hope to get it done. You'll see these in Telum's newsletters as well, so they take care of that component. What they don't do is some of the other areas like media monitoring, for example. They leave that to others, because they're quite focused on doing what they do and trying to do it well.

Why Telum Goes Hand in Hand with a Pr Agency

If anybody's thinking about engaging with the media, Matthew says that's the time to get Telum, and perhaps to get a PR agency as well if you have the money to do it, because PR agencies bring a huge amount of strategic value to their clients. It's the communications strategy that Telum can't replicate. Telum is simply complementary to that. When starting out, Telum should be a foundation stone, but you figure out yourself what you want to say, what you want to achieve, what the business objectives are, and then keep note of that. When it comes to whom you should be talking to and how to build relationships, that's Telum's forte. As anyone knows, relationships with journalists need to be built over time. That's often where some of the best coverage comes from, and it doesn't always happen overnight. It's a relationship and a long-term game.

The Telum platform is incredibly secure as all of their business is based on trust at the end of the day. For this reason, Telum encourages all their clients to create individual user logins for everyone from the Head of Communications down to the PR Intern. All Telum users are provided with in-depth training and onboarding by Telum's on-the-ground client services team. This also helps ensure that the information Telum provides on the media is respected and journalists are only contacted about relevant stories and opportunities.

They try to provide a lot of benefits to their two sets of customers: first of which are the PR people or business owners who are trying to market themselves, and their second set of customers are the journalists, content creators, bloggers, and podcasters. What Telum tries to do is create value for both groups, and in return, they place their trust in Telum, and Telum makes sure that everybody hopefully gets a better interaction out of it. The journalist doesn't get inundated with irrelevant pitches and requests they're not interested in, and the companies that are engaging with them are able to do so with a degree of insight, forethought, and information that really helps. Though they can't disclose the number of press releases that they sound out every month, they've made a deliberate choice to not send the actual press releases through Telum. This goes back to Matthew's point about media engagement. They firmly believe that the personal touch is very important. Within a few clicks of a button, you can have your distribution list set up, and you can send it. Most importantly, it comes from you. A lot of what they're trying to do and help people with is not so much the broad-brush press release distribution which can be done, but finding that one journalist, putting the pieces together, coming up with a great pitch, sending the message, and getting some publicity.

Telum Media gives you access to journalists' main contact details and anything business related. The main mode of contact, however, depends on the country. In China, it is done mostly via WeChat. In the Philippines, Facebook is what is used. In Australia and Singapore, communication is via email, phone, and WhatsApp. Twitter, Matthew says, is extremely important in Australia as well.

With Telum, you can even download a journalist's profile and share that with a client if the client wants to have a briefing book to see who they're being set up for an appointment with. If you're a business owner or PR agency, and you want to make sure that the CEO or spokesperson is fully briefed as they can be, then they can see the relevant biographical information, where this journalist has worked, what they've covered, video interviews with the journalist, and more, so that you can pick up snippets from that or they can explain what they're most recently interested in. There are media requests and surveys around the time of day a journalist prefers to be contacted, if they go out for coffees or lunch, if they're able to take gifts or not; those kinds of things. At Telum, they really try and put all of the good stuff in there, so that you've got plenty to work with, and so that you go into that interaction well-briefed.

What Makes Telum Special?

Across Asia-Pacific, Telum is the only company that does what they do. They are connectors, and they do that through their rich ecosystem that they try and provide everybody with. That means they give journalists newsletters on a weekly basis, where journalists can get job information and industry intelligence. They have PR news for the PR community, so they can see who's gone where and what. They do lots of webinars, virtual networking, and localised media mixers for their subscribers as well. If you subscribe to Telum, you join them as much for the network as you do for the information that they provide. It might be the connections that get you your next job or your next great employee, as well as, of course, helping you to reach out to the media.

According to Matthew, the pricing depends entirely on what you want to do with Telum, as it's pretty flexible. At its base, you buy regions, of which they have three main ones: Australia and New Zealand as one, Southeast Asia, and East Asia. You can buy a region, and then you can buy seats. If you've got a big company or multiple offices, you can buy more seats. Basically, for one region, it's around $500 a month, and you get an annual subscription for that, and then it depends what else you want to do. Within that, you get live journalists' data, newsletters, everything that you need from that one region. If you're in Asia and you're looking to project to the outside world to top-tier financial journalists or the top tech publications outside of Asia, or likewise, if you're in London or New York and you're looking at Asia, Telum can provide you with insight as to how to navigate this diverse, large, and vibrant region.

Chapter Four
Call in the PR Cavalry.

Interview with Manchester-based Nigel Sarbutts; Founder of The PR Cavalry.

The PR Cavalry is like Booking.com for clients in need of PR freelancers with a deep understanding of their market and relevant skill sets. It's somewhere between a search engine and a dating agency, Nigel jokes.

Nigel shared a glowing testimonial from a client about one of the consultants listed on The PR Calvary. This was a client in the Personal Protective Equipment (PPE) market, which is a very crowded market, and so they came to the platform to find a freelancer who could help them start a business. In only a day and a half of work, this freelancer was able to get them on national TV, get them impressive international press media coverage, and a huge number of specialist market titles as well. It was on the back of knowing the market, having great contacts in the media, and then, without any fuss or fanfare, just getting right down to it. That's what clients want. They want somebody to whom they don't have to explain how their market works. They want someone who understands right away what is needed to be done and can pick up the phone and speak to journalists that can make it happen. For the client, it was an amazing investment of a rather small amount of money for some amazing results in the media.

The Perks of Hiring a Freelancer over an Agency

When it comes to money, on the whole, clients and SMEs are really wary about agencies coming up with big-ticket consulting fees. Nigel's had clients who approached relatively small agencies, and those clients were told that unless they were willing to pay the agency a retainer of £3,000 or more a month, then there wasn't much they could do for them. Meanwhile, freelancers could be charging £400 a day, and that's five, six, or seven days a month of work from a freelancer who is experienced and also very invested in the results, because they can't pass the work on to anybody else. Freelancers will always give an honest appraisal of what's achievable, because only they are there to deliver it. For the investment of £400 or £500 a day, the upside is getting somebody with at least 10 years of experience in the market and has complete dedication to getting the task done and doing it well, and it's difficult for agencies to compete against that. Freelancers are able to benefit from low fixed costs, and while any business has overhead, a freelancer is an extraordinarily cost-efficient way to get an expert working for you with minimal overhead.

Nigel says that of the 1600 freelancers on their platform, around 95% are from the UK. Within that, as you can imagine, they have anything and everything on there. He reckons they've got about around 12–15% of the freelance market registered on their platform.

So, if you can't find what you're looking for in 1,600 people, then you probably have got a really unusual niche. They have had unique or very specific briefs that they've been able to match with extra diligence, but it's the algorithm that fuels the business. The matching algorithm between what the client wants and the skill sets of the freelancers that they've indexed is very accurate. They very rarely find that the client comes to them, searches the platform, and finds no matches. It just doesn't happen, according to Nigel.

What Can the PR Cavalry Offer?

When it comes to how a client would find a freelancer on PR Cavalry, the approach is similar to that of Booking.com where you input your criteria into the search engine and then the algorithm does the matching. A client would go on their website and say, for instance, "I want somebody who knows the DIY sector. And within that, I want somebody who has done blogger outreach, or event management, or copywriting, or has profiled a CEO." There are different types of PR work, just like hiring a lawyer. There are lawyers who specialise in divorce, property, crime, and so on; so for PR, it's not always simply, "I need a PR person." Quite often, businesses struggle with this. They say they want someone to do their PR work, but it doesn't have that extra level of narrowing down. Clients need to specify what they want, because The PR Cavalry has nearly 30 types of different PR and communications activities that a client can indicate.

The PR Cavalry makes it easy for clients to articulate their needs, which produces a much better outcome. When that first contact between the client and the freelancer takes place, it's a meeting of minds, because they've matched very precisely between what the client's got in mind through some simple drop-down menus on their platform and what the freelancer is able to provide. There are benefits to both parties in the way that they work, and it's all driven by a simple front-end on the platform. It doesn't take an expert in PR to work it, just as you don't have to be a travel agent to know what you want when you go into Booking.com to book your vacation. As long as there is a clear idea, The PR Cavalry makes it very easy for the system to understand that and match it precisely to find at least one in 1600 people who could possibly be the person you're looking for.

Nigel's background is PR. He's run agencies and he's been a freelancer, so he's been a buyer and a seller of freelance services. It was seeing both sides of the coin that gave him the inspiration for PR Cavalry as well as knowing that there is this huge talent pool of freelancers out there. But for most people, it's invisible. It's very hard to know where the talent is, and so clients end up putting a shout-out on LinkedIn, asking around, or fishing around for business cards that they may have. It's a very haphazard way, and Nigel thought, "In an era where we expect everything to be searchable and there will be instant results, there's got to be a way of matching the two sides, the need with the availability," so that's what they set out to do two years ago. They built the shop, and then they had to stock the shelves. They spent a long time building up that talent pool to the point where they were confident that pretty much any client search could be matched within their resources.

The PR Cavalry has been open to clients for searches for around a year and a half. And in that time, they've had around 300 assignments go through the platform, and they want that to increase. Everybody took a hit at the start of the year with COVID, but Nigel says it's surprising how much work is coming back to the platform now. They feel buoyant about the future, because they believe that as the economy feels its way back to the "new normal," people are going to take baby steps. They want to have flexible resources on tap rather than take the plunge. People are hopefully going to commit to a big investment in people as a resource, so having talent that you can dial up and dial down with very low risk and in a very cost efficient way positions The PR Cavalry at the right place at the right time. That's certainly borne out of the number of client briefs that are now coming back onto the platform.

In terms of their business model, Nigel says there is no mechanism in their model for them to charge a client for what they do. They are free: free to search and free to hire through the platform. The way that they make money is when the client pays the freelancer's invoice for the work, they take 10% from the freelancer, not the client. This way, they are creating value for the freelancer in work finding them possibly while they're doing something else, so they can devote more time to actually working and less time hunting for work which is expensive for a freelancer. And because of that precise matching, it's very profitable work, because it's right in their sweet spot of what they do best. For the client, they are an inversion of the traditional recruiter model where normally, a client would pay to be matched to somebody. But on PR Cavalry, they charge no fees at all to use their platform to hire anyone. Of course, clients love that, because they're getting access to a huge search for talent pool at no cost.

PR Is Not Only for Big Businesses

There's this perception that only big companies can do PR, but even SMEs and owner-operated businesses need the marketing support too. Nigel says that most of the work comes directly from SME business owners or SME marketing managers, because freelancers add huge amounts of value to their business. A very time-hassled SME marketing manager simply doesn't have the time or the resources to have a big black book of contacts or freelancers. These are the people posting on LinkedIn or looking around haphazardly for support, and they're in a position that is time-pressured. That can lead to a problem, and that's why they call The PR Cavalry. When people are pressed for time and trying to find an expert, those two things can be in conflict, and that can lead to hiring the wrong people.

A lot of clients can be dissatisfied with using PR, because it wasn't quite what they wanted. Nigel believes that the root of that problem is not speaking to the right person, or the right person wasn't available to them to hire at the time when they needed it. That's what The PR Cavalry is trying to solve. If 10 names are presented to you five seconds after you've hit "Search" on their platform, then they've solved that problem. They've given you a list of 10 people that are able to do the job, and then it's up to you to decide which of those 10 you want to have a further conversation with to dig deeper into their skills, and for that freelancer to dig deeper into exactly what you need, so that they can come up with a plan and proposal which is right for the budget, right for the task, and also right for human chemistry. The algorithm is great, but it doesn't replace human chemistry. They put human beings in touch with each other to determine whether they can genuinely work together, because Nigel says PR is a bit different from hiring a web developer or hiring someone to do your SEO. You need someone whom you have a deep understanding and good mental connection with, because there's a lot of trust and other variables involved. There are lots of tiny details that need to be oriented to get the right things in the right order in PR. That's why Nigel says they are very clear that the algorithm is great, but it's only the start of the process. It doesn't solve everything. And of course, no client would hire a freelancer on the click of a mouse, and probably no freelancer would want to be hired purely on the click of a mouse. There needs to be that human contact which is the second stage of their process once the client is shortlisted. In terms of testimonials, freelancers are free to place testimonials on their profile, previous work that they've done, and they do encourage them to do that, particularly with a named individual, because that offers the greatest credibility. However, they decided not to have a star rating, because things can go wrong. As TripAdvisor has found, people leave reviews sometimes for the wrong reasons, and AI is not a magician.

This goes back to the analogy of law. Simply hiring the best barrister in the city doesn't mean that your case will win. There are other factors involved. There is an element of risk. PR is a question of judgement and the risks involved, but when it works, it can do wonders, as with the mask supplier startup. They invested a day and a half, and they ended up with two or three minutes on the *Good Morning Britain* TV programme. They got an amazing spread of coverage for an investment which isn't even four figures. It was under £1000.

Chapter Five
The One Million Media Address Book.

Interview with Warsaw-based Joanna Drabent; Founder and CEO Prowly.

Prowly is a platform designed to help business owners find media contacts and manage outreach all using technology. It is a PR software that enables clients to win media attention in the most effortless way.

Thanks to this tool, business owners can easily find journalists and their contact data, build powerful media lists, create eye-catching press releases, and make the online newsroom a definitive source of information about a brand. They've simplified these processes for anyone dealing with PR on a daily basis, but it's not just for PR people. Business owners can also make good use of Prowly, as these entrepreneurs are a big PR resource for the company and the brand itself.

How Prowly Gets You Noticed

Prowly offers a free trial period, during which anyone can use all the features available. They are completely transparent on the matter of the product, allowing instant access whenever needed. An advantage of Prowly is that there is no lifelong commitment. You can upgrade or downgrade whenever you want. Prowly's pricing plans for their monthly and annual subscriptions are flexible and said to be more attractive compared to other PR software solutions available in the market, which is also very important from the perspective of a business owner. The monthly fee depends on the resources, such as the number of users on the account, the number of newsrooms to be created and managed along the way, and the number of media contacts or emails to get in touch with journalists. The starting rate is $210 per month, which is the plan most business owners subscribe to. Customers rave about the chat and general support they receive along the way, and these all contribute to making Prowly one of the most accessible tools in the PR space.

Prowly has over one million contacts available on their media database, and users can gain access to up to 1000 contacts per month, with Prowly giving you total control over which media contacts you want to use. For what would take a person hours of manual research, Prowly will find you the right journalists and media in only a matter of seconds. The way their system works is similar to a Google search but it is personalised and customised to the PR needs, as it identifies contact data using different sources available on the web. They've shortened the research process, and it's all a matter of technology. There are different parameters to narrow down a search, like topics that the journalists are covering, by region, by city, by country, and by influence score. Once you find the journalist that you're interested in, you will get all of his or her contact data, including email address, phone number or numbers, social media profiles, and the latest press publications. For companies in niches or verticals that Prowly may not be covering yet or for anyone struggling to get the proper search results, they can always reach out via chat. They always try to help, but they will also be transparent if they are unable to in certain cases.

Prowly is geared towards helping their users and so they provide tips and tricks on their app as well as via chat. They also offer consulting for any owners who want to speak with Prowly's PR team. Upon registration, there's an option to book a free PR consultancy call. During this session, they will try to help you get the most of the tool, considering your biggest challenges in PR. And like every software as a service tool, Prowly is available anytime from anywhere in the world, and while the interface of the app is in English, the content created can be in any language. Also, their media database consists of media contacts from different countries all over the world, so their clients are global too. They have customers everywhere, because the PR challenges are similar regardless of location.

Personalisation at Scale and Soon-to-Be Media Monitoring with Prowly

Personalisation is key when it comes to sending out emails, which is why Prowly offers what they call personalisation tokens, wherein different elements of the contact data can be used in the dynamic fields in the email. With one click, personalised emails can be sent to up to 1000 journalists, after which you can track the results or status of the emails, such as who opened the email, who clicked on the materials in the email, who went to the online newsroom, as well as general statistics like open rate and click rate. What's great is that there is no Prowly branding in the email itself. Journalists will only see your email address as the sender. During the email creation process, Prowly also provides suggestions regarding the email's content in order to help you get the best results, which can be compared with the general statistics.

Though monitoring was not one of the services that Prowly offers, thanks to Semrush's acquisition of Prowly, they have begun crafting their own roadmap for a media monitoring feature with the goal of launching this in the first half of 2021, making this one of their biggest product milestones. This will solidify Prowly as a complete all-in-one PR solution and enable users to track in real time all the effects of the PR campaigns through analysing media coverage, which is the end result of PR work.

In her own right, Joanna is a successful business owner, having built the business from Poland, and with Prowly now as a global business owned by an American SaaS company. They consider themselves a product-first company, meaning the product is always the biggest priority. Once they started to acquire their first customers from the US, those people would then recommend the tool to others, so the value for them comes from the word-of-mouth marketing from satisfied customers who would give reviews for others to hear and read about, and this naturally became the foundation of their brand.

Chapter Six
Prospecting on LinkedIn.

Interview with Montpellier-based Guillaume Portalier; co-founder of Waalaxy.

Waalaxy allows you to automate prospecting in one of the biggest business platforms today: LinkedIn. As many professionals spend more and more time on the platform – and with business leaders having very little time to reach out to these people – having a LinkedIn automation tool sounds really valuable.

The Goal of Waalaxy

Co-founder Guillaume Portalier, who hails from Montpellier in southern France, shares that lead generation is one of the things that business leaders have to accomplish. While there are plenty of ways to do so, LinkedIn and emails have emerged as the most effective channels in terms of generating Business-to-Business (B2B) leads.

Sending emails is something that has been automated more than a decade ago. However, a LinkedIn automation tool is relatively new. The principle behind this is similar to what email automation is – but instead of emails, you're using LinkedIn profiles.

This has two major advantages. First, you don't have to buy a huge email database. You just need to leverage the platform, which now has more than 700 million users with very detailed information about them. Second, you get response rates that are typically 10 times higher than emails. This is partly because people are receiving dozens of emails and only a few LinkedIn messages. Another reason is that LinkedIn is a more engaging platform than an email box.

The goal of Waalaxy is to automate your outreach on LinkedIn, with the tool requiring no technical skills. With it, something that is usually done manually – and in a time-consuming manner – can now be done automatically. And it only takes up less than 10 minutes per day.

How Waalaxy Works

When you prospect, Guillaume mentions that you have to make sure that you're reaching out to the right person. It's important to segment your campaign and your lists.

When you use LinkedIn Search (or Sales Navigator for those using the platform's premium plan), your first job is to identify who your targets are. You can filter by industry or by location. Once you have the results, you can use ProspectIn to export that list of profiles into their ProspectIn Customer Relationship Management (CRM) system. From there, you can now start your campaigns.

You can export your data in CSV format. However, you can make things more efficient through ProspectIn because this tool allows you to do so with just a click on a button.

To use Waalaxy which is a Google Chrome extension, you have to have Google Chrome as your browser. Simply download the extension and it will automatically sync with your LinkedIn account.

Setting up a Campaign

After exporting your targets' contacts into the Waalaxy CRM, you will have to set up a campaign next. A campaign is basically a sequence of actions. On LinkedIn, the four main types of actions are visiting a profile, following a profile, sending a connection request, and sending a message. One example of a LinkedIn campaign is to send a connection request; then one day after the invitation was accepted, you will send a message (and a follow-up message if the person has not yet replied).

If a sales manager uses the tool, he or she will be the one to set up the scenario and the message that will be sent. According to Guillaume, personalised variables can also be used, such as the prospect's first name or last name. Afterwards, he or she will simply need to click on a button to start a campaign. All actions will be carried out automatically – no additional work is needed.

With Waalaxy, all the actions you've chosen will be sent into a queue. And those actions will be accomplished progressively. Because one of the tool's goals is to simulate human behaviour (and not a robotic one), the actions are being sent with a delay in between. For example, after sending one connection request to a prospect, the succeeding connection request will be sent only after two minutes. Though there's a delay, all will still be done automatically.

Scope of Work

While Waalaxy is built to automate LinkedIn prospecting, the task of finding the prospects itself should be done by you. It's work that needs to be accomplished before you can use the LinkedIn automation tool. For instance, if you're trying to contact social media managers in the UK, you have to look for social media managers in the UK on LinkedIn through its search feature. Then, you will have to automatically export that list of contacts into the Waalaxy CRM.

Guillaume further shares that their tool is designed to prevent having duplicates. If the profile of one prospect is already in your Waalaxy CRM, it will automatically be skipped when you try to re-export that particular prospect.

They also have an enterprise feature wherein a whole sales team can use ProspectIn with several accounts. This feature has anti-duplicate protection that guarantees that one person who has already been contacted by one member of the team will not be able to be contacted by another member. Therefore, it's totally impossible to have duplicates within the ProspectIn CRM.

This is very useful for businesses like mine that manage LinkedIn for a company or multiple executives. In such a situation, there's this danger of having multiple executives contact the same person, causing disappointment and annoyance to the prospect.

The Impact of Waalaxy

Guillaume emphasises that Waalaxy offers help at the beginning of the funnel. Think of acquisition – because the goal of the tool is to help you generate leads; generate interest in prospects. Once a prospect replies on LinkedIn, you then have to take over. It's not ProspectIn that will automatically reply – it's you going forward.

In a sense, the tool helps increase conversion rates: The response rates you'll get are higher compared to email automation. But the conversation per se from prospects to clients will have to come from your part.

However, Guillaume notes that Waalaxy does more than just automating LinkedIn outreach. As he and his team have seen, their customers are utilising the tool in different ways. Some use it in a purely outreach way – in generating leads and having those leads reply to you. Others use their software to nurture their clients. Through Waalaxy, they send useful content to their contacts, including blog articles and white papers.

Sending content to existing customers is something that Waalaxy can automatically do. Again, you simply have to import those contacts into the CRM, then set up a sequence and a message. You can choose to send a white paper, for example, to your contact base using the software.

To track your results, Waalaxy has a dashboard that can be filtered by campaign or by date. With this, you will have an overview of your response rates and you will see which campaign works best. You can also perform A/B testing on the notes or the messages that you send. This will help you identify which one helps increase your acceptance rates.

Chapter Seven
Website Personalisation at Scale.

Interview with Amsterdam-based Sander Nagtegaal; CEO of Unless

Unless is a platform that accomplishes personalisation at scale for websites in a unique and interesting way.

On the internet, the attention span of people is very short, the result of that being that most people who visit a website will probably leave without making a purchase or doing whatever you want them to do. Data reflects that, because globally, the conversion rate sits at approximately 1–2% for the average e-commerce venture. That's a terrible number, because it literally means that only one out of 100 people will do whatever you want them to do. So, the assumption is that face-to-face interactions with people will produce better results. If you ask the average sales person who does account-based marketing, their conversion rates are more likely at the scales of 30–40%, which is a healthy conversion rate.

Another fact is that, on the internet, people will leave a website in less than seven seconds if what is on there does not interest them, but when it comes to human interaction, people are much better at this and would not end a conversation in seven seconds, because they adapt the narrative to whomever they are talking to. They personalise that pitch, and so for the team at Unless, they developed an idea to make websites behave like humans. That became their goal, to change the internet from the static publication medium that it is today into more of a conversation-like medium, similar to talking with a friend or a favourite salesperson.

What Unless Has to Offer

How they transform the web experience into conversations and engagement begins with people's empathic skills. Accordingly, people have the verbal capacity to be flexible enough to change whatever they want to say, to make it shorter, to make it longer, or to use different words. Think of their product as putting empathy into a machine and then building a structure that could change the content of any given website into something that would be more relevant to the visitor. That's what their product does. They use machine empathy to figure out who sits in front of the keyboard, and they do this in several different ways. Like what A/B testing platforms use, they gather contextual details such as your location, what time of day it is there, if it's the weekday or the weekend, if you came through a certain campaign, etc. It also involves behavioural factors like, "What did I click? What did I view? What am I interested in?" After determining those details, they offer profile segmentation based on CRM integrations, where one can add additional details to a visitor profile or everything to know about your prospect. It's possible to connect platforms like Salesforce or HubSpot and then sync this information to Unless so that they will also know what a visitor looks like in your database.

What makes Unless stand out among other platforms is the fact that they add qualitative empathy to it. They do predictions and try to figure out what the attention span of a person is, what the engagement factors are, the "stickiness" of the session or whether a person is going to leave the website or not, and they estimate the lead score if it's a hot lead or a cold lead, and whether that person will buy or not. This can be used the same way as in a sales conversation. If you, as a salesperson, look at the person who's sitting in front of you and you know that he wants to buy something but he's also looking at his watch, what do you do? You quickly make him a good offer that he can't refuse and one that he has to accept it within 10 seconds, and the team at Unless believes you can do the same on a website. If they have figured out that this high-profile lead that's now visiting your website has enormous probability to buy something and is a very hot lead but, at the same time, has a very low attention span factor, they can simply add content components face that will encourage him to make a purchase immediately, for instance, by offering an additional discount if they do so. That's what they can do with these kinds of audiences.

Why Empathy Matters

They are able to classify the traffic, which is the role machine empathy plays, and then they create experiences that are slightly different or more relevant to each person. They do this in technically clever ways through changing existing content like pictures and headlines, configuring components like popups and bars, and even adding additional feature blocks in the website like industry-specific recommendation blocks on the homepage if you figured out that your visitor comes from a certain industry.

They believe in loosely coupled applications, and that's a technical term for something that can be thrown away at any point. They feel that it's better to not intervene with a user's existing systems, because if they will do that, then their implementation cycle would be very long and they wouldn't be able to serve that many customers. Also, it's much safer for their CTO to try something out if he knows that he can take it out at any point in time. To put it simply, Unless is just one JavaScript snippet in a website, and that will give you the entire power of their service offering. If you want to integrate a CRM system, all you have to do is go to the backend of Unless itself, press the Salesforce button, click "Connect," authenticate it on your server, and then it will work.

In terms of the technology, because they are developers, they've built something that practically anybody can use. Because of that, their typical users are either people who are very interested in optimising the user experience of their own websites very quickly or marketers and salespeople who do account-based marketing or conversion rate optimisation themselves. The idea is that if you have a little bit of qualitative knowledge about how you want your website to look and behave, you should be able to use it.

In terms of the content or blocks the user would have to input about their website visitors, they've made easy. How they've managed to pull that off is through personalisation at scale, meaning that without a lot of work, one can create an almost unlimited amount of variations of a website catering to specific people, because their system works with audiences, even ones that are not even very large. They can be very small subsections of traffic, for example, people belonging to a certain industry, coming from a certain location, or behaving in a certain way. In the end, website visitors, like real people, can fit within multiple audiences at the same time. So, if you fit multiple audiences at the same time, it may well be that on the page that you're visiting, multiple experiences that are only suitable for those audiences will trigger at the same time. That means that if you only have one specific audience with one experience, you need to make one experience. But if you have 10 different audiences with 10 experiences, then your homepage is already a million different perturbations in theory, because it's two to the power of 10. With only 10 experiences, that create an almost unlimited amount of different variations, because you don't need to create an entire page variation. It's a single experience that fits in the page that will be shown or not, depending on the audience definitions, and so they've simplified the creation of a highly personalised website that doesn't require a lot of time and effort.

Unless is entirely focused on web user interfaces, so using other tools like those for personalisation of email outreach is a specialisation in itself. For personalised outreach on other platforms, they integrate with it in the sense that they will provide the tools to make sure that a personalised outreach will also lead to a personalised website funnel. For instance, if you send out an email to a specific person, you can add a dynamic code in there which will allow Unless to recognise this person specifically, which means you can hyper-personalise your narrative towards this single contact if you'd like to. This is an optional feature, but it works well. Especially for very high-profile customers, it becomes worth it to create a specific funnel for them. For high-level companies, you may want to create a picture on the website that shows their office and only highlights a specific product that's suitable for them and not the other products that you have that may not be suitable for this particular company.

In the Netherlands where Unless is based, when the COVID situation got out of hand in March, some of their customers had to implement COVID notifications depending on the local situation, and using Unless, they were able to add those notifications to their websites, to the checkouts, and to everything they had online. The fastest way their users were able to do that was to simply use one of their add-on components or inline blocks with notification blocks to add it to the website in an instant. Their clients suddenly saw that they could use Unless to quickly do those things. Now, they're using it as their primary way of releasing new features or notifications in general, testing its efficiency, and then possibly adding it to their structural roadmap. It's allowed a lot of people to increase the time to market any change on their website, including COVID notifications.

Unless' Global Reach and Cost

In terms of its reach, they first aimed to test as many customers as they could to make the best product possible, so they did several marketing campaigns a few years ago for people who would be willing to be early adopters, and for that, they were given a lifetime deal. These people from all over the world took the plunge even without a product, and thanks to them, Unless was able to sell 5000 accounts in a matter of days. From this initial batch, over half of the companies are American, and then it's more or less normally distributed. Behind the US which has 50%, there's about 20% of users from the UK, 10%, from Germany, 5% from Russia, and so on. Since then, Unless has been building their system based on this initial customer base and they have distributed their computing capacity across 75 endpoints across the world to make sure it's available equally anywhere. People from places like Russia and China use their systems, so it's safe to say that it works in different languages.

It's amazing what technology has now made possible, that machines can read empathy and use that for personalisation at scale. With that, consider using a great tool like Unless to help you do that with your website.

Chapter Eight
Auto-Signature to Trust.

Interview with San Francisco-based Helga Zabalkanskaya, Chief Marketing Officer of Newoldstamp.

If you didn't know, there is power in email auto-signatures, and founders of small companies, business owners, and marketers can improve brand visibility by using email signatures as a marketing channel.

Statistically, billions of emails are sent and received everyday around the world, and at the end of the email, most of them don't have contact details or branding, so it's definitely something people can improve on, since a common instinct when receiving an email is to scroll to the end and find out who is the person behind this email before even reading its content. Imagine seeing a photo at the end. Now you know what the person looks like, and that email automatically builds a bit more trust with a company. So, it's important to add banners or calls to action to visit a page, check out an offer, or book a demo. People often miss out on this part, but it's really helpful, and it increases replies and trust.

Newoldstamp's Useful Features

When creating an email signature on their platform, they make sure that all the signatures look consistent regardless of the platform or device. One signature can be sent from your iPhone's Mail, to Gmail, to Outlook, and more, and it will all look the same. Even if you send or receive emails from different email clients, it will be consistent. They also have a central management system that can be integrated with your Exchange Server for Outlook as well as for GSuite and Office 365, and they can create standardised signatures for all the employees in the company too. Basically, anyone who owns a Newoldstamp account can make changes on their platform, set up an integration, and then just with a click of a button, they can make all the updates and have it go out to all members of staff. For individuals and small companies that don't have GSuite, Exchange Server, or Office 365, they can simply copy and paste. Most of their email clients allow them to make updates using their system, even if you just copy the code of the signatures.

Depending on the organisation set up and brand requirements, the auto-signatures can also be used on platforms like LinkedIn, Facebook, Instagram, etc. With their integration, all these resources would be stored in the GSuite organisation or in the Exchange Server, so you can create one signature template, and their system will automatically update all the elements that need to be updated. For smaller companies where the work would be more of a manual process, you can upload a CSV file with the necessary information, and then their system will create signatures for all employees based on the master template. They can also set up rules for replies and forwards for internal and external communication, so you can have different signatures for each employee. GSuite and Gmail recently added this option for having reply and forward signatures, so they are now automating this.

Why Newoldstamp Is Special

Most marketing emails are used for cold outreach to quite a lot of people, so having the signature there will be more than beneficial, because you can add value your marketing message in your outreach through the email signature by adding a banner or clickable information that can lead to a landing page. They support CRM systems, so they can easily set up signatures in them. What makes Newoldstamp unique is that they are the only solution that works in Pipedrive properly, and they can also be integrated to Salesforce, HubSpot, and pretty much any CRM system that supports HTML.

When you have special promotions in your email, you can add a promotional banner at the bottom of the signature. You can even use it to drive subscribers to your email newsletter by adding a call to action button that will add a link to the subscribing page, so that when someone clicks and goes to the landing page, they can easily subscribe. You can opt to add a promotional banner to draw a bit more attention and add a link too. Moreover, you can also schedule signatures, and their system will update it automatically, especially when it comes to banners. For instance, you want to set up a signature only for the duration of Black Friday, after which it will be a holiday season auto-signature. Thanks to automation, they can make that happen.

No Need to Worry About Your Online Safety and Security

Another great thing about Newoldstamp is that they don't track emails; they only track the signatures. They track clicks and signature impressions, and they also calculate the click-through rate, because in marketing, changes always need to be done to see what works better for the audience. They found that the average click-through rate increases by 2–3% simply from using their auto-signatures, and if you think of that increase as attributed to a simple email signature, then that makes it quite significant. If you're not maximising this seemingly unnoticeable feature of your emails, you're actually missing out on a big opportunity. Apart from the click-through rate being important, the brand impression is as well. When you reach out to somebody you don't know, every time someone opens an email from you, they will see a log of it if they've been emailed multiple times, so this is definitely about the brand awareness too.

With their signature generator, they have customisable templates which allow you to reproduce any type of signature you may need. You can move the fields around, and you can choose the layout of the icon elements. The best part is that you don't need to be a designer to stylise your auto-signature. Even if you follow their template, it could be enough to get you noticed.

Newoldstamp Is for Companies of All Sizes

If you're wondering about their pricing, it's accessible even for small business owners. They currently have a package system. If you need one signature, you can buy one, and the more signatures you buy, the cheaper it will be, but the price generally begins at $1 per signature per month. They are now changing it up a bit though, because they see the value in it and they see that users sometimes don't want to have access to all the features. They started Newoldstamp, because they saw the need to educate people who were unaware of the potential clients they could have by adding something as simple as an auto-signature. In terms of security, they access only the signature settings. Unlike other extensions that read emails and email addresses, they don't do this. For bigger organisations using Exchange Server, they don't integrate deeply with the server. Most companies' IT departments would set up specific rules for using their tool. That makes Newoldstamp very secure. And though they are based in Ukraine, they work globally. In fact, the majority of their customers are from the US and the UK. Their target market would be small companies, as they provide a simplified solution for them, but they are also used by small teams from big companies such as FedEx and Vodafone.

Chapter Nine
Inbound Marketing for Sales.

Interview with Montreal-based Laura L. Bernhard; host of the Marketing Bound podcast.

To begin with, inbound marketing is a strategy to get an audience to come to you. It's putting out free content that builds trust with an audience, because as they are searching for a solution to a problem that they experience on a daily basis, they stumble upon your content which helps them out. An example of helpful content, Laura shares, is googling something and one of the top results being a blog that's a few years old. That's the perfect example of an inbound marketing blog, because it's still helpful and it's still popping up, since it is useful. This is called evergreen content, because it is long-lasting and serves a purpose to the audience.

Why You Should Focus on Your Inbound Marketing More Than Ads

A lot of people think that inbound marketing is very time-consuming, and there is some truth to that. It is a long-term strategy that one has to constantly put effort into. However, the long-term benefits outweigh all the time and effort spent on it. Experts actually say that it's more cost-effective to be working on an inbound strategy than Facebook ads, a billboard, or a commercial. Although Facebook, LinkedIn, and Instagram marketing can also be considered inbound marketing since they are also non-destructive, when you speak about inbound marketing in terms of blogs, email nurturing, and social media, those have a longer life than a Facebook ad. Take, for instance, a magazine that you're promoting. Once people flip through the magazine and see your ad, that's it, and eventually, it will be thrown away. However, a blog stays on a website and on the internet forever. If that is a good piece of evergreen content, that will keep popping up on Google and it will keep working for you and for others.

In terms of the kind of content to create for inbound marketing, it depends on what's best for the audience. If your audience is listening to podcasts, then that's where you want to be. If your audience is watching videos, then that's what you want to create. There is the luxury of having many options and then picking the most optimal one that's going to reach the audience at the right time. This also applies to content scheduling; what's best depends on the audience. Generally, it would be good to put out content on a weekly basis. Laura emphasises "putting out content" rather than "creating content," because of the belief that a strong inbound strategy requires batching one's content. This means creating a handful of content all at once and then slowly releasing them throughout a period of time.

Finding the Best Content for Your Brand

For the average business owner or entrepreneur who may not be confident in their writing skills, or prefers not to hire a freelance writer since it could take just as long to brief someone as it does to writing an article yourself, rethink the kind of content that you are producing. Maybe it would be better to do a podcast or video instead, and then later on turn it into a blog, an audiogram, or convert it into other types of media. This will still be helpful, and it is still considered inbound marketing. Now, to break through the content block many people experience, start with what the audience is asking and then address those questions. So then, when they are typing it into Google, you're popping up. Getting into the workflow, once a great piece of content has been created and the next problem becomes figuring out how to turn this into different pieces of content and the process for that, for Laura, with her podcast, she uses Otter to transcribe it, Headliner to create audiograms, create short clips from the video of her podcast, and create captions for it.

At every point in the visitor's journey, you can identify what is actually going wrong. You may be getting people to a website, but then people are not converting on the website, and there a few reasons why this is happening. First, the call to action may not be strong enough. The form or the text of the form may not be attractive enough, and this is something that can be corrected by using clear and compelling words, such as "Sign up to get free inbound marketing resources right to your inbox once a month." That attracts people because it's not often, it's only monthly, and instead of people having to go to the website and reading blogs or listening to the podcast, it all gets sent straight to their inbox. If that's something that is going to be helpful to them, they're going to sign up for that. Having a lead magnet is another great way to get people to sign up to, for instance, your newsletter. Something like "Top Five Ways to put PR into your company tomorrow" could be the lead magnet, and then you say the only way that you can get this is if you sign up. So, having a lead magnet is one way to do it.

How to Get Customers Through the Sales Funnel

Inbound marketing is on a journey to customer acquisition, but it definitely doesn't end with someone subscribing to a newsletter. The goal is for them to move down the funnel, but with all the free content available on the internet, give people a good enough reason to go down that funnel. Once people are signing up to get that lead magnet, the next step is converting them. If you're not thinking about that, then your lead magnet is worthless. The whole point is to get your audience to engage with you. You want to build a community. You want people to get involved, and one effective method is directly asking the audience questions. For anyone that was wondering whether Facebook and having a Facebook group is a necessary part of the inbound marketing strategy, Laura is here to say that it is not. Finding an alternative to Facebook is easy as long as the goal of creating an engaged community is at the centre of everything. It's always about making sure that there is a dialogue with the audience.

Chapter Ten
Personal Service Earns Praise.

Interview with Singapore-based Irishman Paul Hourihane; Principal of CX Vision and Founder of ReMark Asia Pacific.

At ReMark APAC, the team brings the best solutions they can find and have trust in from other parts of the world into Asia and points them in the direction of businesses that need them the most. One of the first brands they brought to the Asia market was a business out of Ireland called the CX Academy, which is an enablement and training product to help businesses up their act in terms of customer experience excellence and drive better outcomes for the interactions they have with their customers on a day-to-day basis.

Very often, there is confusion between customer service and customer experience, so Paul differentiates customer service as what you do, how you do it, how quickly you do it, how effective it is, and all that stuff that is measured quantitatively, while customer experience, on the other hand, is all about the emotional outtake after an interaction with a brand or company. Airlines are a great example. People don't tend to talk about how the check-in was a disaster, how the air hostess wasn't very nice, the flight got delayed, etc. They tend to talk about the entire experience, if it was awful, if it was wonderful, if it met a person's expectations. It's all about people's expectations and then meeting those expectations which results in an emotional outcome. The most positive results about the effectiveness of a customer experience and how it integrates with PR is what can be called a remarkable experience that people will talk about, and one of the key objectives of PR is to get people to talk about you.

ReMark's Service Offering

ReMark helps companies evaluate where they're at and how they can improve, and it's done through actions, not ads. The overpromising done by marketing folks is a hard act for the actual business to deliver and meet those expectations, so ReMark gets them to align that. They also try to determine what emotional outcomes the business is trying to drive and having to deal with on a daily basis. Some of them are more quantitative. Some are qualitative.

Paul enumerates six outcomes that any business is going to drive to. Trust is the first and most important. It's the hardest to earn and easiest to lose. Second is what they call drivers of excellence. The word that everybody wants to hear most often in the world is their own name, so it's important to get a person's name right and to get to know their business situation, purchase situation, or emotional situation. Making it easy to transact or complete the business within the desired timeframe is another outcome. Empathy is next, and it's about understanding the situation and what it's like to be doing business with someone if they're stressed, in a hurry, or disappointed. For instance, casinos have got a very interesting empathy play. With gambling, people are happy, sad, excited, and stressed. The next outcome is a really important driver which is called "You fix things." If someone bothers to complain and say there's an issue with the business, it means they care. If you fix it heroically, you'll get rewarded with an enormous amount of positive energy, emotional outcome, and remarks from other people.

For CX Academy, what ReMark did was they educated the staff at scale, and that was key. CX Academy offers certificate and diploma courses that are endorsed by trade associations in a university. The whole point is to give businesses a management measurement framework of the outcomes that they're driving to as a business, and then give them the ability to enable their people (senior, middle, and front end) to execute and drive those outcomes.

COVID has actually made things interesting for ReMark. Some frontline staff have become lions when they were once lambs. Talking to brands about investing in their frontline staff became a very different conversation than it might have been a year or two ago. Business owners are now appreciative and telling their staff how wonderful and good they are when they're in difficult situations, and they're looking after them. Investment in staff has become a priority for good, well-run businesses. And so, ReMark offers 6- and 14-week-long courses to the same structure, to the same measurement delivered by experts in the field and professional educators. It's all done online, so it's COVID-friendly in how it's executed, and it's been done in a very visually rewarding way. It's a great experience. Basically, that's what ReMark gives to businesses and adds value to, and there are many businesses taking it up, and the timing for this given the current atmosphere is interesting to say the least, Paul shares.

How ReMark Ensures Long-Term Success at an Affordable Price

The investment of companies makes it sound like quite a holistic approach, and it requires almost the entire organisation to go through it as opposed to only a few people within the organisation. When it comes to pricing, the operative word is scale. There are not many products like theirs in the market. A certificate from ReMark is €500, and it is equivalent to about 17 hours of learning over a six-week duration, and the diploma is about €2800. These are not normal sums of money, and it's a very sensitive and competitive topic. ReMark's services are absolutely available to small to medium businesses at that kind of scale. It's not outrageously expensive. It is hundreds and small thousands of euros per person trained and executed, and there are even government incentives too for acquiring services like ReMark in terms of it being a skills upgrade. They have those available in Ireland, Singapore, Malaysia, and Hong Kong. What Paul tells people is if they don't think it's worth the money, don't go and look for the government subsidy. This is the value it's worth, and that's how you should really look at it.

Many programs or productivity initiatives within companies are developed but often fail to get implemented. In terms of the success rate and how they ensure the follow through once a company has completed their course, there are three levels to it. They hold continuous training programs after the formal training is finished which keeps the skill levels up. Secondly, they stitch this into an HR approach to make sure that the skill levels are maintained, meaning if other people join, they go through the same level of enablement to achieve the objective. Thirdly, there's no point in doing this if it's not taken seriously. It has to be incorporated into a fundamental strategy for the business. Otherwise, it just simply won't work.

Sometimes, they tell larger businesses that there's no point in taking two or three people to do this and explaining the material to them. It requires a whole department or office to demonstrate it at work. Once it's piloted with a degree of success, the retention rates go up very dramatically in terms of it as a strategy, so it depends on how serious the business is strategically about its customers and what sort of competitive edge they want to build. Though ReMark is a young business that has only been operating for close to two years, they do have statistics on that. There's a lot of research on CX in terms of project failures and the like. There are numbers, and they've definitely seen more people complete than fail their course. In terms of ROI, clients will eventually notice reduced staff turnover or attrition. In other words, it increases staff retention. It decreases the cost to serve as people become more self-enabled and happier to deal with you. It can increase margin with people paying a little bit more money for easier access for the things they want. These key measures are all boardroom-level measures of what's important to small, medium, and large businesses.

ReMark's services work well for businesses that have a few people serving many people, or a lot of people serving very many people. That's when it comes into a zone and things can be done at a scale that's appropriate to the business. It's meant for any business that has to serve a number of clients or customers at a fair count in commoditised areas, whether it's airlines, restaurants, or hotels, etc. Financial services, companies, telcos, utilities, transport, government, where service and the outcomes of making people happy and satisfying their needs are important, that's the sweet spot for ReMark, and it comes down to smaller chains and restaurants. They've got customers who run hotels with 100–200 people. This is where they can really use this to make the personalisation of their business world-class, so it typically goes down to that size of a business, from really big business to people dealing with a lot of people effectively.

Within the CX programme, Paul's team found the entire thing to be particularly effective for them, and he emphasised the importance of a good reputation. He believes it's the strongest marketing tool in almost any business. Particularly for his business which is quite young, they've been utilising social media and LinkedIn heavily, and that has helped get their profile up and get them into conversations they may not have been in a lot faster than perhaps some of the more traditional methods of marketing. So, word of mouth and well-run business social media have worked really well so far for them.

Chapter Eleven
Case: A Virtual Village for Parents.

Interview with Gurgaon, India–based Nitin Pandey; the founder of the Indian parenting network Parentune.

People say that it takes a village to raise a child. Nitin Pandey, the founder of the Indian parenting network Parentune, revolutionised the game and created a platform that has now become a virtual village comprising more than 5 million parents.

What Is Parentune All About?

Parentune was created to offer information and advice on how to raise a child at various stages.

What parents typically do is search for things online, only to find millions of answers and solutions. It has become a challenge with regard to pointing out which topic is relevant for them and which source is trustworthy.

With Parentune, parents can find results and content coming from fellow parents. It's a platform where you can also create your network of like-minded parents who are always available to help you with your parenting concerns. This eliminates the tedious process of trying to find people or reaching out to friends and family members just to validate certain information.

Over the years, Parentune has grown bigger as parents share the content they found on the platform. When other parents find the content valuable, it prompts them to join the network and contribute something relevant as well.

Parentune's Beginnings

According to Nitin, the idea of establishing Parentune started back in 2012. He had this idea that parents need support and real-time validation on parenting information; they need to have a trustworthy report that they can use on how to raise their children. Given that families have started transitioning into open nuclear family setups during that time, the need to have a platform like Parentune became more urgent.

Having worked in an education company, Nitin says that he has seen a huge gap between resources and parents. This all the more drove him to establish Parentune as a credible, real-time advice centre for parents After initial beta testings were made, the network went live in 2013. However, it was only in 2014 that it started getting results.

Throughout establishing Parentune, Nitin realised that three main things are important for parents looking for advice online.

The first is that they want to be in a safe space: They want to be in a closed network, not on social media. Second, they are looking for personalised, relevant, and specific content – not just generalised ones – because this is content they will use to make parenting decisions. The third is that parents look for support and not judgement. They don't want to be looked down on and talked about.

With these in mind, Nitin and his team built Parentune to become a platform that can safely and effectively cater to various parenting concerns.

Parentune Today

Today, Parentune has over 5 million registered parents. It is considered the most used parenting network in India capable of providing pieces of advice and information in a matter of minutes. It's accessible via a website (both desktop and mobile) and a mobile progressive app (it's currently only compatible with Android). Around 97% of their users access their platform on mobile.

To cater to as many Indians as possible, Parentune is available in five languages. Because English alphabets can be used to speak or type in a certain Indian language, it has helped the platform to be more utilisable in a country like India with different languages.

While the platform is largely India-based, around 11% of its users are foreign parents. They have users from the UK, Africa, and Southeast Asia, and other parts of the world.

Tapping and Welcoming Experts Into the Platform

Parentune is not only a network of parents. It's also a platform with an expert panel on parenting. For the education frontier, Nitin is offering his expertise. He also tapped experts in gynaecology and paediatrics as well as professionals specialising in children with autism, attention deficit hyperactivity disorder, and other special needs.

Initially, he and his team reached out to the top 20 doctors representing different fields. These experts are carefully handpicked because they believe that quality begets quality. This panel is assigned to answer questions coming from parents. However, as more questions came in, they saw the need to reach out to more experts.

At first, they put out their application form on LinkedIn. However, they did not receive much response. This is when they incorporated a form on their site and app where interested experts can input their details (e.g. their curriculum vitae, their degrees and specialisations, the reason why they want to join Parentune). This made the panel bigger, with two to three more experts applying daily to be part of the network.

Apart from applicants enquiring through the form, Parentune is also expanding its expert panel by asking for recommendations from their resident experts.

A Freemium Model

Parentune utilises a freemium business model, which makes it accessible to anyone without having to pay anything. However, the platform requires users to have a verified account to mitigate bots and the like.

Once you have a verified account, you can now reach out to other parents on the platform. The first question is free of charge. Accessing the content in different languages is also free. However, if you want to ask more, clear doubts with experts, attend workshops and live shows hosted on the platform, you'd have to pay a certain amount (around £1). If you want to have 24/7 access, you then have to pay for a subscription, which can be monthly or annually.

Because of the COVID-19 pandemic, Parentune offered discounts on their subscription fees: For the monthly, the original £3 was cut down to £1; for the annual, the original £12 to £15 fee was now down to just £5. It's a flexible pricing system that allows you to stop or get a refund in case you won't be satisfied with the experience.

Payments are done using online payment wallets (In India, internet banking is now enabled by the Unified Payments Interface, which is "an instant payment system developed by the National Payments Corporation of India.") Parents outside India are typically paying through their credit cards.

Parentune in the Time of COVID-19

During the COVID-19 situation, Parentune was charged the same fee regardless of the user's location because, in times of need, they wanted to be as helpful as possible. But just as how it was before the pandemic, their pricing would change in various geographies after the pandemic.

In terms of content, Parentune has also allotted a dedicated cluster to address topics related to COVID-19. In the form of videos, they provided information on how to stay calm, how to know if your child is facing anxiety in these tough times, and how to take care of your family among others.

Promoting Parentune

Search has really been important for Parentune. After all, the platform was created as a response to the need of people who are looking for help with parenting. This is why they continue to incorporate search marketing in their efforts to promote their platform.

They also utilise two of the most popular networking platforms in India: Facebook and WhatsApp. Now, they are also on LinkedIn and Instagram to get Parentune discovered by more people.

Chapter Twelve
Case: Building a Toothpaste Tribe.

Interview with Howard Kaufman, Scottsdale Arizona: Co-Founder and CEO at ORL.

ORL is a two-year-old company that offers organic oral hygiene products. Though it took them around six months before they were able to break into the market, co-founder Howard Kaufman and his business partners consider their journey as a labour of love.

The idea behind ORL began when Howard went to a grocery store and noticed a certain toothpaste brand's warning label: The toothpaste contains sodium fluoride that, when swallowed by children (six years old and below), can be harmful. The irony is that the product is being advertised as a children's toothpaste.

Howard thought that if there's a harmful ingredient with a warning label for children's toothpaste, it can also be the case for other oral care products. As he researched more about these ingredients, he felt compelled and motivated to create ORL.

He worked with a number of dentists, a food scientist, and a pharmacist for this venture. They started with the idea of creating a natural and organic formulation for oral healthcare products – products that contain vitamins, minerals, and certain plant-based essential oils that have been previously identified to be beneficial for oral health; products that don't have any of the 100 ingredients that were found to be hazardous. Their group used PubChem to get access to scientific reports on ingredients. Through the reports, they learned about health and safety issues as well as the different aliases for the toxic ingredients.

Creating Awareness

At the end of the day, businesses aim to be profitable. But for Howard, it's more of an outcome; it should not be your focus when you're starting. The real focus should be to create awareness in the right target market. Then after gaining modest awareness, you should do a trial for your product.

Howard's mantra is to think big, start small, then scale. Though there are other brands that have entered their respective markets successfully from the get-go, they should be considered as more of an exception than a rule.

As someone new to the oral healthcare market, Howard and his team at ORL focused on their belief in the customers that they are serving. But apart from knowing who their audience is, they also challenged themselves to become active listeners. Listening is important because it's the marketplace that will tell you what they like and what they don't like – and what are the things that they don't understand about your product. What may seem important to you might not be for your audience. Citing leading advertising agency Leo Burnett, he points out how vital it is to test your internal paradigm: Is it true? If so, does it matter to your audience? As a marketer of your brand, you have to build awareness and figure out if what you offer matters to your marketplace.

Overcoming Challenges as a New Player in the Industry

Back in October 2019, ORL's goal was to introduce eight stock-keeping units to the market. They have two product lines – a toothpaste and a mouthwash – and each has four different flavours or formulations. They offer a fresh mint flavour that captures the sentiment of bubble gum for kids. They also have a formulation that includes cannabinoid (CBD) oil. CBD is a non-hallucinogenic part of the cannabis plant which offers dental benefits (e.g. it addresses gum irritation and slows down jaw bone loss).

However, they ran into a production issue: They were tallying a high failure rate (about 70%) when labelling their glass containers. Their production supplier was only able to provide them with their CBD oil-containing products. As there's still no national guidance from the Food and Drug Administration (FDA) regarding CBD, ORL only worked with CBD boutiques and distributors, and a segment of dentists who believe in the benefits of CBD, in the beginning.

In February 2020, right before the pandemic hit, they were able to solve their labelling issue and introduce the rest of their product line. Their main channels of selling include retail groceries, boutiques, apothecaries, and dental offices. They also sell directly to consumers online (For Amazon, they only listed their non-CBD products as the platform doesn't approve selling CBD products until a guideline from the FDA is released). For ORL, Howard and company used an omni channel approach to enter the market. Though they don't have resources as big as what multinational companies utilise, they focused on winning with what they have. Because they're small, they can be more responsive to their customers. They can also make decisions faster and can be more generous with their products. Basically, they are using their advantages to set foot in the oral healthcare market.

Hearing Feedback from Consumers

Howard knows that ORL, as a brand, caters to consumers who want to lead a more active and healthier lifestyle. They don't have grand ambitions like being a dominating force in the market.

What he acknowledges is that 18 months after they first introduced their products, they are now getting validation for the research that they have done. And it doesn't end there, because they continue to look at consumer behaviour and get insights from their retail partners – a group that Howard calls the tribe for their brand.

Gaining feedback and input from their tribe has been vital in improving their products. For instance, when they learned from their customers that one of their ingredients is sourced from a shellfish which may cause allergy concerns, they modified their formulation and eliminated that said ingredient.

For Howard, it really matters to hear your audience and determine what you can do based on their feedback.

Adjusting Own Strategy Using Insights from the Market

Part of building a brand is having a plan – a business strategy – ahead. However, as a brand grows, it's inevitable to have product iterations based on customer feedback.

ORL engages with their customers directly and through their retail partners. Furthermore, they are not only open to hearing from their customer base. They also receive and use insights from a segment of consumers who haven't purchased yet but have shared opinions through email.

For example, in January, they introduced a travel set as part of their product development roadmap. For this offering, they got feedback pointing out that their product is quite bulky to travel with (their mouthwash is 500 ml while their toothpaste is 120 ml). Taking that into account, they changed their travel set inclusions into a one-ounce toothpaste and mouthwash packaged in mess-free containers. Getting feedback early on from their tribe has helped them swiftly improve their offering.

It's also part of their goal to earn more loyal consumers – consumers who wouldn't just buy once or twice, but consumers who will make ORL their oral healthcare product of choice. Howard sees taking immediate action based on consumer insights as an advantage that they have over bigger market players.

PART THREE
Engage

Chapter One
Introduction.

"These days, people want to learn before they buy, to be educated instead of pitched."
— Brian Clark, entrepreneur and founder of Copyblogger.

Placing that British racing green Morgan roadster into the central square at the Forbidden City in Beijing was the ultimate piece of content marketing; I placed a new and exciting product into a space rich for my audience in contextual history and aspiration. These opportunities may not be quite so obvious for you, but they always exist and we have to keep looking for them to create engaging content. The old adage that content is king is true, but it is now joined by context as queen. In other words, the audience have to be able to understand how and why our message will make a difference to them, content which sells is seen as pure play advertising, but content which looks as though it could have been created by your heros themselves will be watched, read, heard, and shared.

The engagement stage is about creating content which is novel, useful, and easy to understand. People, as a consumer or a business buyer, have a reluctance to change existing behaviour. And therefore, any information that you provide needs to be accessible. And when we look at sharing information, people only share information that they can understand. The content we create needs to deliver new information and yet be easy to understand, which means moving away from a reliance on one dimensional text and using infographics, video, and audio. Public Relations is aimed at asking people to believe something and possibly to change behaviour as a result of what they have come to believe as a result, and it becomes really powerful when a cascade of behaviour changes take place.

In the series of articles coming, you will learn different ways and examples of creating engaging content. I talk with a voice coach and voice-over artist, look at the format of podcasting, take you through a simple five-stage process for your own media relations, and address what to prepare for a crisis. I look at different ways to source content, including surveys and impact analytics, and harnessing the power of artificial intelligence. In this section, I have two case studies; both of which illustrate the importance of creating content so that it is in the format the audience can engage with. These are particularly powerful because they address the needs of the legally disenfranchised and children who otherwise would have their issues unresolved.

Chapter Two
Your Voice Performance.

Interview with Jimmy Cannon, UK; Voice and Performance Anxiety Coach.

Jimmy Cannon is a UK-based voice coach, singer, and saxophonist who helps people get heard – literally. Whenever he talks to people, including his clients, the first thing he notices is the sound of their voice and how they're engaging. For instance, when he was featured in one episode of The UnNoticed podcast, he noticed that my on-air voice had higher energy and a more expanded pitch range and dynamics compared with my off-air voice.

Your Voice Should Depend on Circumstance and Environment

The way you modulate your voice should depend on the circumstance and environment.

If you're pitching or selling a product, you need to create some energy and engage with the audience. If you're speaking to around 500 or 600 people, you have to use your voice as a core instrument and inject an element of performance. When you're presenting, there has to be a variety in dynamics, pitch, and tone of voice so you can express yourself and communicate your message better.

Whenever you go on stage, Jimmy emphasises that you have a responsibility to communicate with the audience. There's this expectation that you have to meet what your audience needs.

Proper Preparation

Before doing a talk or taking a Zoom call, you have to prepare and warm up your voice – get the gears in motion and get the oil moving around the engine.

One of the first things you need to do is to drink water. Hydration is key in activating your vocal folds, which are folds of tissue (about 2 cm in length) in the throat or larynx whose vibrations produce sound. If you put two fingers just above your Adam's apple, and you transition from a "sh" sound to a prolonged "zh" sound, you will feel what is called resonance or your vocal folds moving together. If you put too much air over these folds, you will end up straining your throat.

There are people who drink coffee and feel a certain narrowness in the throat. The same sensation is felt if you get nervous before speaking. By warming up your voice and using the correct muscles, you can keep the throat more relaxed and open. This is why it's important to let the air go.

Exercises to Try

To warm up your voice, there are a couple of exercises that you can try. One is called the lip trill, which helps take the energy away from your throat. You can do this by putting your lips together and producing a horse-like sound (a prolonged "brrr" sound).

Another is the tongue trill, which helps in increasing your vocal range. This is done by continuously rolling your R's, putting the middle of your tongue to the roof of your mouth.

You can also use your fists to give the bottom of your cheekbone a massage. This will help loosen up the jaw and the surrounding area.

Breathing Is Key

When Jimmy voice-coaches a client, the first session is spent on breathing. Breathing is key in making your voice heard more effectively. However, the majority of people are not doing it correctly. Though we're breathing correctly when we were still babies, things change when we get about six months of age when our body starts to change the way we breathe. If you observe babies who are lying on their stomachs, you will notice that their lower back raises when they're taking a breath in.

To properly breathe in, you should let your belly out (instead of tucking it in). Let your diaphragm drop and contract to allow your lungs to expand. When you exhale, your diaphragm should relax, pushing the air out of your lungs and through your windpipe.

When speaking, think about how much you'll need for each phrase. As much as you need to control the amount of breath that you're taking in, you also have to control the breath you exhale. Doing so will help you control where the breath goes and which parts of the body it will resonate with. By resonating different areas of the body (there are seven areas of resonators, with head, chest, and throat as the most common ones), you can produce different tones and emotions when you speak.

As mentioned, these changes in dynamics, pitch, and tone can help you keep your audience engaged.

Take Your Perception Into Account

When you're speaking, it's vital to think about your perception: What is your self-observation about your voice? From there, we can do exercises to correct your speaking.

During my interview with him, Jimmy asked me to share what I think about my voice, to which I mentioned that I am speaking too much through the nose – not from the chest. He shared that I'm resonating with my nasal passages. However, the actual phonation is coming from the throat.

In this case, if you don't allow your throat to relax and you don't breathe properly, your vocal tract (a passage in the body that starts from the upper part of the vocal folds to the edge of the lips) will narrow, making it more difficult to speak. To widen your vocal tract, access a bit more phonation within that area and allow your jaw to relax a bit more. You can use your abdominal muscles as well to create more pressure and open up areas of resonance. Knowing how to breathe in and out correctly will further help you access these areas.

As a pro tip, Jimmy recommends focusing on the inhale. Put your hands on your belly and breathe in very slowly through your nose for about eight seconds. Then let it out with a "ha" sound. This will make you feel more relaxed and subsequently give you more resonance and a wider dynamic range of voice.

Chapter Three
The Engaging Voice.

| Interview with Melbourne-based Ant Bohun; Owner of Sound
| Please.

Ant Bohun is an international sound specialist who does voiceovers for companies large and small. He believes hiring a professional to do a voiceover is worth the investment in getting the right voice for the brand. As they say, "If you think it's expensive to hire professional, hire an amateur first." There are some voices that when you hear them, you automatically know the brand they represent. A good voiceover has a pleasant voice yet gets the message across, and that requires skill and practice in taking direction and delivering the read that suits the brand.

When deciding on what voice could best represent a brand, it depends on the industry and the company being represented. For instance, a corporate bank could hire someone with a prestigious-sounding voice, a voice that commands attention and a professional feeling that this company is very successful. If it's a bank that's appealing to the general public such as families, it's going to be spoken in such a different way. It could need a warm voice that speaks directly to the listeners. Whether the spokesperson should be a female or male or needs both a female and male, it depends on the campaign itself, and these decisions would be made by an advertising agency or a creative director. The client would choose the best option out of the ones presented, and then the campaign is developed from there.

How to Find the Right Voiceover Artist for the Job

Years ago, people would need to contact a voiceover agency that would have many people on their books. But nowadays with the world being on the internet, there are many voiceover agencies online that represent major actors and people who do voiceovers for a living, and there's a distinction that needs to be made to that. Voiceover actors might not necessarily be screen actors, but there are people who make their living from doing purely voiceovers and taking direction from directors and advertising agencies or wherever the session is being recorded. There are also people like Ant who run their own voiceover businesses online. A simple Google search will provide anyone with many options to choose from, whether male or female or with a specific accent, and the beauty of this is you can deal directly with voiceover artists without having to go through an agency, although it's not always going to be the case if you are thinking of hiring specific actors. Nevertheless, there are many websites to choose voiceovers from and have a listen to see if they'd be the right fit. Voiceover artists will normally display a compilation of past work for prospective clients to have a listen to, and these can be downloaded and sent to other staff members for a second opinion.

In terms of pricing, it depends on the location. There are different rate cards around the world, and ideally, these are preferred because it works better for everybody in the industry. However, more often than not, direct negotiation with the voiceover artist can be done too. In terms of the license, because the client has paid the fee that was negotiated with either the voiceover artist or the agent, that audio is the client's property. For something like a telephone on hold message, there is no need to pay for residuals or rollovers, but for a television commercial, licences are usually valid for around 12 months and then the artist would need to be paid for the next 12 months, although again, it varies from country to country.

Professional Versus Amateur

Companies sometimes turn to their own staff to do the voiceovers, but there are many reasons it could go bad. That person who isn't a professional could clam up and may sound not appealing when trying to represent a business or product. Whereas with a voiceover professional, this person who does it for a living will look at a script, find out exactly what the client wants the listeners to feel, and nail that message. That's the value in hiring someone who does voiceovers for a living rather than hiring an amateur or just anyone in the company.

Anyone knows that winning an award is a big deal, and in fact, Ant won an award in 2019 for a documentary that he did a voiceover on. The documentary was about bushfires and wild fires in Australia, and it was for the Country Fire Authority, which is the Volunteer Fire Brigade. Ant's voice for this was serious, because it was dealing with a pretty bleak subject matter, but at the same time, it kept the viewers interested and got the facts across.

Choosing the right voice to get the message across is the main thing. Certainly, with radio and TV commercials, people will choose a voice appropriate to whether it's direct advertising or whether it's something that needs to be warm, sentimental, and heartfelt. Those are two different reads. While some voiceover artists are not actors, they are essentially actors as well, because they are acting. They are taking the script and then bringing it to life by interpreting what they are given. Another benefit of working with an experienced person is they'll be able to provide tips or work out a better way of saying a sentence or getting a message across. Ultimately, hiring a professional like Ant is worth considering when you want to make sure the brand is represented by the right voice.

Chapter Four
The Power Podcaster.

> Interview with Paris-based Sabrina Scholkowski; host of "Pretty Sure" podcast, and podcast coach.

Half-Mexican, half-German, and a full-time podcast coach, and speaker living in Paris, Sabrina began her journey as a podcast coach when more and more people started asking her for advice on how to do a podcast. As having her own successful podcast gave more credibility to what she advises, she made a living out of it. In one The UnNoticed podcast episode, she shared key pieces of advice on how you can make your podcast successful.

Be Confident and Passionate

Although podcasting has been around for over 10 years now, it was only two or three years ago that it became mainstream.

One of the things that hinder aspiring podcasters to start their own is a lack of confidence. Sabrina shares that people think of themselves as a nobody: Why would people listen to me? I don't have this fantastic business idea. I am not an influencer.

The statistics may also sound intimidating. There are about 3.12 million podcasts* out there. But compared to blogs (there are around 500 million blogs online, yet people still continue to launch their own), it is a relatively small figure. Furthermore, of the 1.5 million podcasts, only half are active. Many stop producing content after about 5 or 10 episodes. In reality, you don't have that much competition.

Sabrina points out that it's because people don't start podcasts for the right reasons.

The most successful podcast hosts are those who have a passion for them to keep their podcasts going.

When someone consults with Sabrina, she always asks about her client's passion – the topics that they can talk about for 20 minutes without getting bored. From the list of possible topics, she helps select the best one.

Topic selection is important because people can tell if you're passionate about what you're talking about. For instance, if you're a marketing person but you're passionate about sports, launching a podcast about your main job – which is marketing – might make you less driven to produce content. As you put less effort, it will reflect on your content and people can tell.

What Sabrina advises you to do is to actually merge marketing and sports on your podcast. You can talk about sports marketing or interview people that work in the sports industry. This will allow you to get ahead in business while being able to discuss what you're passionate about.

---

* **3 122 629** podcasts and **167 604 547** episodes in the world. Source: Listennotes.

Don't just start a podcast about a topic that you're good at. For Sabrina, it's one reason why many companies fail to sustain a podcast. They typically talk about corporate-related things (like how they run their business). If companies would feature their own people and let them talk about their products or humanise their CEO, that podcast will be more successful.

Choose a Production Schedule that Works for You

Podcasting has a wide range of production schedules. There are successful podcasts that run for five minutes daily. There are those that run for around three hours. Whether it will be a monthly, bi-monthly, or weekly podcast, Sabrina says that it boils down to choosing a schedule that is manageable for you – something that you can sustain.

When Sabrina was only starting last year, she aired one episode per week. She would only do twice-per-week podcasts during special events such as Social Media Week or Mental Health Week. When she did the twice-per-week schedule, it opened the opportunity for her to have more guests wanting to be on her show. This prompted her to consistently do two or three episodes per week.

If you are to do your podcast more frequently, you have to consider several factors, including bandwidth, the energy to release more episodes, the capacity to hire a team member, or outsource production or guest-booking. You also have to consider your goals and the speed at which you want to grow. Again, it's all about having that deeper why.

Find Your Level of Comfort

Unlike Instagram or other social media platforms, listenership statistics in podcasts are not publicly available. Sabrina mentions an article that she read and it talked about how some people fake their figures. While it's certainly unethical, the point is that podcasting metrics are not really regulated and not yet well-established.

To a degree, it's advantageous for people because it lessens the pressure.

There are podcast hosts who don't like talking to themselves and get a co-host. There are those who are comfortable talking about themselves and do solo episodes about their lives. There are also people who only do interviews. In the case of The UnNoticed podcast, interviews are being done to feature guests who can use our five-stage methodology to grow their brand.

Then there are those who do a mix, including Sabrina. Recently, she found herself receiving requests from listeners to talk more about herself. She realised that the audience can have that desire to hear more about you as much as they want to hear about your guests.

The format really depends on the level of comfort that you have and the number of things that you want to talk about.

Get Feedback from Listeners

When getting feedback from her listeners, Sabrina heavily relies on Instagram and other platforms.

On Instagram, she has one account for her business and another for her podcast. She uses her podcast Instagram account to constantly do stories and live interviews. Every Thursday, she goes live and encourages people to give their comments and forward any questions. She also assures her audience that they're free to message her on Instagram because she always responds.

Another way she gets feedback is through her friends and acquaintances, who send her text messages sharing their thoughts on her podcast episodes.

· The key is letting your audience know that you're open to having communication and getting feedback.

Set Aside Enough Time for Production Work

The basic rule in podcasting is to allocate editing time that's twice the duration of your podcast episode. For instance, if you have a 20-minute episode, you'd need 40 minutes up to an hour to edit that episode.

Additionally, you'd need to allocate another hour thinking, researching, and planning your topics. Then, you'd set aside 30–40 minutes per week to promote on Instagram, Facebook, LinkedIn, or any other platform of your choice. Another hour will be for booking guests and checking if their schedule fits yours.

All in all, the bare minimum for a 20-minute once-a-week episode is about four to five hours. That's 40 minutes to an hour per day per week.

Promote, Be Proactive, and Monetise

A lot of people have this misconception that the only way to make money through podcasting is by getting sponsorships, advertising, and getting picked up by a network. While these three are great options, they're actually the hardest to accomplish.

For a network to pick you up, you must have a certain number of downloads. They have to see something in you and that's subjective. Sometimes, it's also all about having contacts. For sponsorships, there's this notion that you need 10 000 downloads to attract sponsors.

If you're counting on that, Sabrina advises you to go back to the drawing board and think of another idea. The truth is that you just need to have your things together. Create a media kit that talks about your audience and shows some results that you've had (e.g. you've entered the charts). Then, contact brands whose products you'd love to feature and review on your podcast. You can start doing this for free and once it gets traction, you can start charging. The amount is up to you but the common beginner's rate is $150 per episode.

Another way to monetise is to promote within your platform. According to Sabrina, this method is not talked about enough but is actually effective.

For example, if you're a podcast host that talks about marketing. In one episode, you can talk about the value of marketing and then include information about how your audience can hire you or avail of your marketing course. You can put links in the description and redirect your audience to those links so they will know how to find you or purchase your offering.

There's also this so-called PR currency. Though you may not get money directly, you can be offered PR opportunities such as speaking on a summit or an online event or teaching a masterclass. PR currency can also create a ripple effect: An audience member from your previous speaking engagement can recommend you to a friend or acquaintance who would then hire your service.

By promoting within your platform, you can earn money by offering a product or service, and get PR currency, which is similar to word of mouth.

Choose Tools and Equipment that Suit Your Goals and Capabilities

There are free platforms for podcast creation such as Anchor, which was recently bought by Spotify (with this acquisition, you can guarantee it's a quality platform). Though it doesn't offer many metrics, it's still user-friendly and free.

For headphones, Sabrina says that beginners can start with what their mobile phones already have. Whether you're using a high-end microphone or not, you'd still need to edit anyway. It's your skills as an editor that matter. You can produce a high-quality podcast with basic headphones.

For editing, she mentions Audacity, which is a free audio editing tool. She uses Adobe Audition because she's already familiar with the Adobe Systems due to her background as a magazine editor.

You can start a podcast with $0. Once your podcast grows, you can spend around $300 – set aside $100 for a microphone and spend the rest for your hosting platform. From there, you can go as high as you want. You can go big and invest in equipment and tools that you think will give you your target Return on Investment (ROI). Again, it all depends on your goals.

Chapter Five
Five-Stages to DIY PR.

*Interview with Santa Rosa Beach, Florida–based Brandon Watts;
Founder and Principal of the PR agency Wattsware, which focuses
on helping seed-stage tech startups.*

The Five-Step Methodology

Brandon loves working with early stage startups as these are companies that are fresh and still trying to figure out who their audience is. Because their budget is still modest, most of them wouldn't really be interested in working with traditional PR agencies. With Wattsware, he offers do-it-yourself PR strategies to help these companies make their first successful pitch to the press.

His five-step methodology starts with meeting the client to understand their goals. Then he and the client work together to create and review their strategy. After the final strategy is presented, he conducts training on how the client can effectively execute it. After three months, he does a review call to check and assess the progress, see what works and what needs to be tweaked, and offer advice. This methodology, which productises PR service, aims to help small companies do their own PR successfully.

Eliminating the Middleman

Brandon still considers Wattsware a normal PR agency. If there's a good client that he can help full-time, he will accept that client and assist him or her.

His DIY PR methodology is born out of the separate need that he saw for a certain type of customer, which is the early stage startup.

If you own a company, you are the best messenger for your product or service. As said on the Wattsware website, reporters and journalists don't want to talk to an agency – they want to talk to you. Here, PR professionals are considered eliminable middlemen as they bridge two different entities that, in the first place, want to talk to each other.

Through Wattsware, he teaches you how you and your company can handle it yourselves. You can learn the ability to talk to the press – the proper way and at the right time. You can establish a closer connection to them and create your own success because of that direct relationship. Once your company scales up, that's when you may need to hire a full-time agency.

This approach offers you a way to be lean and be productive through realistic and implementable strategies.

The Efficient Way to Do It

Many companies, including startups, don't have the time to build and implement their PR strategies.

To efficiently do it, Brandon advises you to start with identifying who your priority contacts are. There are thousands of people you can communicate with through PR activities, so you have to find who has the most impact and best deserves your time and attention.

After identifying them, utilise Twitter. Follow them on the said platform, spend about 15 minutes a day reviewing what they're saying and what they care about, and interact with them. Being a listener on social media can help you land your pitch better to your target reporters.

Another thing that hinders companies from directly getting in touch with the press is the technicality of it. When articulating a message, Brandon advises that less is always more.

After figuring out what your competitors are doing and what is it that makes your company unique, you need to sum it up in a boilerplate. It's a short paragraph that clearly, comprehensively, and appealingly states what your company is all about. In the book *Building a StoryBrand*, StoryBrand CEO Donald Miller shares principles of storytelling and communication. The storytelling framework that Brandon uses is the problem – solution – experience – results framework.

According to data, 37% of journalists prefer an initial pitch composed of two to three sentences. This debunks the common notion that you have to tell an incredible, long story and incorporate different elements to attract the press. In reality, journalists have time constraints. As they receive hundreds of pitches, you have to make yours interesting as quickly as possible.

Wattsware helps you make your initial contact with the press straightforward, simple, yet attractive. Once you're able to secure a meeting, a briefing, or a request for an interview, you can now flesh out your story, make it more verbose, and relate it to your goals.

Structuring Content for the Media

Brandon uses a data-focused approach when it comes to structuring content that's effective for the media. Based on surveys about journalist preferences done by companies such as Muck Rack and Cision, he creates a structure that the press can appreciate. This also covers applying what format they want and what kinds of images appeal to them most.

He also uses such data to improve a company strategy. From that data, he will help you develop quarterly PR strategies, map out the goals you want to achieve along the way, and teach you how you can communicate effectively.

While formatting pitches and communication pieces may be reporter-specific, Brandon advises you to first follow the best practices in the field. After over a year of dealing with reporters, use the feedback that you get to adjust what you're already doing.

Avoiding Being Internally Focused

Many companies tend to talk about themselves to the point that most of their content becomes internally focused.

Instead of merely doing long blog posts, Brandon encourages you to try out different formats such as video series and podcasts. Citing The UnNoticed podcast as an example, he shares how it has become effective: It's not only about advising, but also presenting ways how things are done by actual companies and organisations. Featuring other people and getting other voices also help provide balance.

When you as a company always talk about yourself, it can make your audience and the press becomes unresponsive. This is why it's important to get other people in your industry involved. An interview with an expert, for instance, could be a blog post or a 10-minute video content. This way, you can also foster a mutual relationship with other businesses – you get validation from them while they can promote their own content.

This process involves a lot of creativity and being open-minded to the different formats of storytelling that exist today.

Meanwhile, with regard to crisis management (which can be a sensitive topic for many clients), Brandon tries to incorporate it in the process of strategising for his clients. He helps determine possible weak spots and improves them. Crisis management is also about planning for different scenarios and preparing different options or responses to what might occur.

Creating Content Using Different Tools

Different tools can be used to accomplish different things. If you're trying to create quick visuals for your content, Brandon recommends Canva, which is an easy-to-use online design platform. If you want to develop professional-looking marketing videos, there's a tool called Biteable. In terms of media monitoring, he relies on SAS tools.

When he works with clients, Brandon tries to cover all the basics so that they won't need to use different tools. When PR efforts increase, he steps in and instructs them on how to use other tools to make things easier and more efficient. For instance, Newswire can be used for PR distribution.

Giving Voice to Small Startups

Sheryl Sandberg, Facebook's Chief Operating Officer, previously said that the media aren't really interested in small companies. For Brandon, however, these businesses have a lot of hope. This is why he likes working with smaller startups. After all, it still boils down to having a good story and the willingness to tell that good story.

Many startups today get ambitious when talking to venture capital firms and raising funding. When it's time to talk to the media, they aren't quite as ambitious. What Brandon does is help clients realise that they have to tell a big story. It's about the quality of your work and how you talk about it. Though it will be challenging, PR agencies such as Wattsware can come in to give you advice, find the most appealing angle about your company, and get the attention it deserves.

To kick things off, Brandon recommends focusing on your own media channels first. For instance, plan for quarterly content themes. Then create pitches, share your content on social media, and do some advertisements.

As a fan of Spin Sucks' Jenny Dietrich, Brandon follows the model that she proposed. The PESO model – which stands for paid, earned, shared, and owned – emphasises that these four media channels should work together for you to get the most mileage for a piece of content. For instance, you can start creating a blog post on your own channel. Then use earned media to pitch it to the press. Then you share it on social media and amplify it with paid advertising.

Chapter Six
The Media Interview.

Interview with Alex Greenwood, Kansas City Missouri; host of the "PR After Hours" podcast, "The Mysterious Goings On" podcast, and Principal of AGPR.

Practise and Prepare

For many people, panic arises when they get invited for a media interview after their project or PR effort becomes successful. Part of Alex's work is offering tips on how to help people make the most of their appearance.

One of the first things that you need to do is to practise – especially if it's your first time getting interviewed. Come prepared even though your segment will only run for a few minutes. Alex has seen many professionals zone out and forget what they're talking about simply by not practising. Making sure that you have your thoughts down is more important than how you look or what you wear.

As a rule, he recommends preparing three points. Have three salient points – three good anecdotes – to talk about. Bear in mind that people mostly learn through storytelling and hearing about others' mistakes or experiences. If you can find entertaining anecdotes that get your point across, tell those stories during your interview. You won't only get more engagement from the interviewer, you can also send your message across more effectively – and even get asked back.

Talk About Something Relatable

If you're going to get interviewed on a local television station, consider it a golden opportunity. It's an opportunity that's not simply handed out to anybody because TV show producers can only allocate a certain amount of time for a feature for every episode.

When appearing on any local media, one of the first things that they will ask is if your topic is going to be local. They have to know if your story is relatable to their local viewers. Then, they'd also make sure that you can speak and present your story well.

If you're pitching to the press, show proof that you can talk effectively and be confident in front of the camera. Ready some tape or a YouTube video (think of it as some sort of an audition reel) and take it from the media's perspective. They wouldn't want to have someone who looks unpresentable or someone who might freeze during the interview. The key is to demonstrate ahead of time that you know what you're talking about and you won't leave them hanging.

Alex points out that you have to know that news presenters, producers, and reporters don't really know much about the subject matter you're talking about. So on your part, you have to come off as someone confident and well-prepared. You have to look good on camera and know how much time do you have for your segment. Take note that your job is to make sure that you fill in all gaps for them and answer their questions.

Know the Program Where You'll Be Featured

Researching is also vital before guesting on a show. Watch the programme or listen to the podcast where you will be featured so you can get the tone and the flow of the show. For instance, before Alex did his interview for The UnNoticed Show, he shared that he listened to a few episodes to get an idea of what the podcast is all about.

If you watch a programme, read a reporter's column, or listen to a show beforehand, you're going to know what to expect. This will help in taking off your tension. In other cases, like with The UnNoticed, yours truly and the guests have a little conversation first to establish good rapport before the recording proper. For Alex's part, it has been helpful in bringing the temperature down because he still encounters anxiety even though he did interviews a lot of times already.

Once in-studio features are also back after the lockdown, Alex also points out it's important to have a little talk with the host during commercial breaks. Bring up something he or she has previously talked about in the show. Many hosts will appreciate you knowing that you've taken the time to watch the programme and know their work better. Again, it helps in establishing good rapport immensely.

Be Mindful About Audio Quality

In one of Alex's articles on Medium, he shares tips with people who will be featured on podcasts. For a medium that relies on audio, it's vital to have spot-on sound quality. You can achieve this by maintaining a three-inch distance from your microphone.

When people get featured on his podcasts, he makes sure that his guests have good audio quality (apart from requesting them to promote their feature on social media before and after the episode). One of the main reasons that audiences stop listening to podcasts is poor audio quality. If people continually hear a dog barking or children playing, or someone typing out really loud, they'll be turned off. If you do something that's distracting (like eating, which Alex has encountered in real life), it can also leave a bad impression on the interviewer.

Alex doesn't expect all guests to have a fancy microphone. However, it's something that's worth the investment if you're consistently getting interviewed. If you have less frequent features, using less expensive USB microphones or a microphone with built-in earbuds can already suffice to have good audio quality.

Take note that podcasting is an intimate medium. And many people who listen to podcasts use headphones. If there will be a creak or fraying, all these noises can be heard. In Alex's experience, people who don't invest in good sound quality are those that don't get invited again on podcasts.

Tell a Topic Suitable for the Program

As a PR professional, Alex knows how important it is to not waste clients' time. If you're getting featured on news media, this applies just the same. This is why it's vital that you and the media person should agree on what you will talk about.

For instance, he had a client who was into negotiating with the Internal Revenue System. And that client was delving more on the heavier side – like getting behind in arrears of taxes for several years and having the risk of getting jailed. Such a heavy topic is not fit for a 9 o'clock show whose audiences are morning people drinking their coffee; it's more apt, for instance, for a business radio outlet.

Alex has also worked with a national pest control company and what they do is provide ingredients for do-it-yourself pest controls via mail order. Their services helped save money and were timely during lockdown wherein delivering commodities was the trend. This is an example of a topic that can work well in every kind of media outlet.

As stated, when choosing a topic, it also pays to have a local angle to it. If you can, it's also better to feature another resource person. For example, if your product is being used by a local restaurant, you can have the restaurant owner talk about it himself or herself. The show can also get B-rolls featuring that restaurant using your product. Localise things as much as possible. This way, you can offer free publicity to your client while injecting your feature with third-party credibility.

Put Yourself in the Media People's Chair

The biggest tip that Alex can give to people getting interviewed is putting themselves in the chair of the people behind the programme. Think of all the potential objections that they may give and knock them down beforehand. Prepare video materials that can be played, refer them to other relevant people who can be interviewed, and give free samples of your product.

You can also remind them how local and timely your offering is. In the industry, there's this so-called newsjacking. It means riding along to a certain big phenomenon (e.g. pandemic) and finding an angle where you can inject your own story.

Chapter Seven
Crisis Communications.

Interview with Anthony Hayes, New York; Proprietor of The Hayes Initiative.

As a public relations professional, Anthony Hayes says that half of PR work is about crisis management. Communication in times of crisis is essential because you need to shape stories, manage the impact of the crisis, and reach out to reporters and convince them that there's no issue that needs to be written. Anthony runs The Hayes Initiative, an LGBTQ+-owned and operated public affairs firm that has worked with different clients including Bloomberg L.P. and a major league soccer team in New York. Currently, his company works on a game-changing major infrastructure project that involves congestion pricing.

In issues like pricing schemes, wherein a lot of stakeholders are included, PR firms like his help provide support to bigger agencies such as the Metropolitan Transportation Authority in terms of implementing the plan that they want. The PR work includes mapping out who are the people who will be affected and figuring out the best road to meet with them. Discussions with these people can happen through one-on-one conversations, group meetings, and community outreaches.

It's Better to Be Prepared

Though it may sound ominous, Anthony believes that if there's going to be a crisis, then that's when there's going to be a crisis. Realistically speaking, there will always be a bump in the road; there will always be a disruption to the flow of your business. This is why it's vital to have a basic communications plan.

One of the key elements of a crisis plan is knowing who your team is. If you're a small business, everyone's going to be in the war room to get your business get through the crisis. If you're a bigger organisation, you'd need to have a core team – it should include someone from the legal team, the human resources team, and the communications team. Everybody in the core team should also have a clear and defined role and know the hierarchy of decision-making.

Apart from having a core team, you also have to have a list of internal and external stakeholders. Many people tend to overlook the importance of having an internal list. When there's a crisis, your sales team will be the one to field phone calls and they will need to have talking points to help you get your message out to your investors. These internal people are significantly instrumental in getting the message known once the message is decided.

Another important thing is to know *when* you're already in a crisis. Many people get crisis management wrong because they wait too long before they respond to the situation and get their message out. While there's no one-size-fits-all answer on how to manage a crisis, one thing you need to do is to acknowledge that there is a crisis happening.

Handling a Crisis Remotely

Now that the workforce is not gathered in one place because of the pandemic, messaging and videoconferencing platforms such as Zoom are critical. However, as people shift into cloud-based systems, Anthony notes that it's still important to have a hard copy of contacts and other pertinent information. This will come in handy especially during times of natural disasters where there will be power outages.

One upside of the COVID-19 pandemic is that more businesses have become familiar with working remotely. A lot of teams have gotten excellent when it comes to pulling things together even when they're not physically together. Anthony points out, however, that you have to limit the duration and frequency of your conversations. Having quick conversations will make things more efficient because time is of the essence.

Communications Plans Are a Breathing Document

Businesses should have a template for media advisories and press releases. These documents should include a boilerplate about your company at the bottom, and contact numbers at the top.

When you have these basic templates, it can help you make press releases even when your main communications person is not available. However, you still need to be careful because every crisis is unique.

As not all crises are the same, Anthony recommends for crisis management teams to meet at least once a year. This is to keep the plan updated, including the phone lists. Doing these administrative things proactively is a big help because these are things that you can't do in the middle of a crisis.

As we're still collectively facing a public health crisis, businesses should look back at the previous year and make adjustments to their communications plan. The crisis management plan should be seen as a living, breathing document.

Apart from making sure your document is updated, you also have to prioritise your press lists. Know the people who are more friendly, those who are going to be adversarial, and those who are neutral. Then, contact those who are more friendly first. Especially in this age of social media, reporters are really instrumental in informing the public that they will be getting a statement from you soon. This will also help you buy time to get your full plan in place.

Trusting Your PR Firm

In times of a crisis, businesses often don't know who to trust. Depending on the structure of your organisation – if you're a large institution and you're the leader – you may not have even met your PR firm. The barrier also comes from the notion that PR people are initially seen as the "no" people, which can be a point of friction.

However, take note that your PR team needs to know pertinent details. This will help them help you push through with the plan, game out scenarios, and handle the crisis better.

When it comes to telling the media what not to write about, Anthony points out the importance of maintaining a relationship with reporters. As mentioned earlier, it's easier to deal with reporters that you are on good terms. Another option is to trade it for a bigger story. While this may not always work, it is part of the *magic* that PR people do.

When you have a business, it's best to have a better plan for the worst.

Chapter Eight
Surveys as a Source.

Interview with Brighton, Sussex–based Chris Robinson; the founder of Boost Marketing Ltd.

Chris Robinson, the founder of Boost Marketing Ltd. (a.k.a Boost Awards), has been helping companies with their awards entries. He has centred another part of his business on evaluating what customers think about their clients – a service that they offer through their subsidiary, Boost Evaluation.

When Boost Awards began in 2006, they found out that for a company to win awards, they had to research and conduct well-designed surveys. You can't simply win an award with lovely purple prose. You have to back up your claims with evidence of satisfied customers, staff, suppliers, and community.

As they started before the recession, they found that a lot of people in the industry didn't want to be seen hiring a marketing agency. This market trend led to the birth of Boost Evaluation. It's a new legal entity that marries up what their people specialise in: working on award entries and conducting surveys and research.

The Importance of Listening

Traditionally, for companies to prove their worth, they do a survey and cherry-pick and focus on the best news and testimonials. They package it up without distorting the truth and then compile it into a narrative, which can be a case study or an award entry.

However, what people often forget to do is to listen. An important aspect of evaluation and especially relevant on podcasts about marketing and PR; listening helps in improving strategies and making important decisions. But as companies become so busy reflecting on how awesome their past was, they forget to improve their future.

The entire awards industry has been doing things the conventional way, guessing and firing from the hip. So when Boost Evaluation ran a survey (they got 330 people who entered awards and asked them to state what they really want for the awards industry; they also got several award organisers on a call and relayed what the respondents said), it became an epiphany for the award organisers and to the whole industry.

Boost Evaluation then worked with a recruitment company that stopped entering awards. Instead, the company focused their energy on a customer survey. They got out, worked with training departments, and assessed what people wanted to do (e.g. digital learning). Chris found out, in the process, that companies have to reinvent themselves, come up with entirely new propositions, and learn from the process – they don't need to merely go back to the status quo.

How Evaluation Is Done

Sometimes, people tend to use the telephone by default – an evaluation mechanism that is actually quite intrusive.

An easier way to begin evaluation is through a digital survey like Laser, Qualtrics, and Survey Monkey. With these platforms, you can be less intrusive by starting with a survey and then enquiring if the respondent is available to be contacted by phone.

To get as many responses as possible, incentivising a survey is key. When you incentivise, you won't just get a higher response rate but a more balanced response. When you don't offer incentives, you will end up experiencing the Maritime effect, wherein people respond prompted by a strong view (either they love you or hate you). In the end, you will get an imbalanced response.

Forum panel conversations are great as well. Zoom meetings proved to be helpful in hosting individual telephone calls.

However, it's important to always bear in mind that a survey has to have two aspects: Qualitative, which are stories and anecdotes that add colour to your research; and qualitative, which are numbers and figures.

When evaluating, you must also be familiar with these two more jargons: objective measurement and subjective measurement.

The latter is composed of questions that can only be measured through a conversation or survey. It focuses on feelings, emotions, and the respondents' sense of the future. Meanwhile, the former are objects of data that defy interpretation. These are data that can be obtained from Google Analytics or Trustpilot scores.

If you're coming up with an evaluation strategy, start with a discussion of your hypotheses (What are you trying to prove? What is something you don't know that you need your responders to vote on?). Then, divide your list into qualitative, quantitative, subjective, and objective. These are four jargons that must be incorporated into the evaluation process. Otherwise, if you simply dive in and write a survey, you might get responses that would make you think that you should have asked a different question or have phrased it differently, or have asked through a vote or a scale.

Countering Survey Dropouts

In conducting surveys, dropout is a major problem. There have been questions about some sort of magic number of questions or the duration of the survey.

Bain & Company once published a book called "The Ultimate Question" and their philosophy is that it should be just one popular question. For instance, "On a scale of 0–10, would you recommend us to your friends?" This is called the net promoter score.

However, asking one question is overdoing it a bit.

For example, if a huge survey will be done by facilities management on thought leadership, they would have the respondents say whether they have done it or not. If they did not do it, they will be answering questions about barriers, excitement, and ROI. If they did it, they will be reflecting on what worked and what didn't. It's a multi-path survey that's 10 minutes on average.

When doing such surveys, Boost Evaluation recommends setting expectations. For instance, your respondents will have a 10-minute survey but in return, they will have a chance to win an iPad. Instead of offering a small chance and a big prize, you can also provide a high chance of a small prize, such as 10 x 30-pound Amazon vouchers or free cups of coffee for everyone.

Business-to-business companies, including a lot of The UnNoticed podcast listeners, tend to fall into the annual and bi-annual surveys.

This different approach to evaluation is called continuous customer monitoring.

For instance, if you have a massive call centre in Dublin and you want to track daily the net promoter score on a call-to-call basis – by call centre agent, by department – then you would need to send out text messages to consumers featuring a question or two before asking if you can ask a few more. Typically, there will be a 90% drop-off rate. But what's important is that you've captured the critical 10%.

Making Surveys More Accurate

When determining the correct sample size, mathematical models can be used. You can input the variables and it will tell you the degree of accuracy or the sample size required to hit your target degree of accuracy.

In statistics, whether your sample size is 10 or 10000, you're going to get a wobble – the response will wobble on what was and what wasn't and it will become smaller and smaller over time. If you have a binary question (e.g. Will you recommend our product to a friend?), the wobble will last longer because one person can influence it.

In B2B, the common sample size is 50. The trick to making it more accurate is to have a 10-point scale. If you use this scale, such as a net promoter score, the wobble will settle down a lot faster and will stabilise quicker.

If you want to split the data into new customers and long-term customers, you must look at the smallest group. A survey wouldn't be sound unless you get at least 10 responses. However, in PR principles, a magazine or a newspaper would not be interested in publishing such statistics. In the end, the techniques you can use to make surveys more accurate depends on the context.

On Anonymity

The UnNoticed podcast has three different audience groups: the external customers, the staff, and the suppliers. When conducting surveys in these groups, anonymity is a point of debate.

One Swiss telecom company is quite upfront and says that their survey is not an anonymous one. It's part of their culture. However, in a lot of organisations where there might be a union, anonymity is essential. If you're doing a compliance-related survey (which Boost Evaluation is doing on behalf of a client), you wouldn't want to give that impression that the respondent's supervisor will know if he or she talks about the company at a dinner party. In staff surveys, anonymity is indeed a big thing.

For customer surveys, it's a different thing. Boost Evaluation encourages people to include a box that asks respondents for consent for their testimonials to be quoted on a company homepage.

At Boost Evaluation, you can be confident that your responses will not be shared with anyone within the business because they're using a third party.

Still, anonymity remains a debate. If you don't do anonymity, you lose the ability to send out reminders or attribute problems correctly. There's also this grey area wherein, for instance, in a staff survey, you can know which department your respondents are from but not their names.

The Cost of Surveys and Evaluations

The pricing for surveys is flexible. In Survey Monkey, you can avail free licences once you sign up. But it will be peppered with advertisements and there will be a few people you can send your surveys to.

Meanwhile, a whole grading scale is also available. If you're happy to pay £200–£300, you can get a decent licence wherein you can lose the Survey Monkey branding and input a lot of questions. As it is an American System, you also have to adhere to American CAN-SPAM laws and avoid spamming thousands of people, and there are other more economical alternatives.

If you're in business, it's important to listen to and evaluate your customers. Equally, you're also encouraged to sit down with your team and your partners to get some guidance on what you'd do moving forward after getting out of lockdown.

Chapter Nine
Content from Social Impact Analytics.

Interview with Catherine Griffin; Philadelphia-based
co-founder and CEO of ImpactableX Analytics

ImpactableX Analytics is doing some really exciting things around measuring the economic impact of sustainable activities, and Catherine Griffin, the co-founder and CEO, was able to share some insights behind the platform. Before ImpactableX came to be, Catherine was the Managing Director at an accelerator for early stage social entrepreneurs called Good Company Ventures. They worked with the Obama administration's Climate Data Initiative, Bloomberg Philanthropies, Wharton Social Impact Initiative, and others around supporting new innovations to solve old and challenging social and environmental issues. Over the course of that time, many of the founders were grappling with how to verify and validate their aspirations for impact, how to differentiate themselves both to impact and traditional venture tech investors, and how to legitimise what were otherwise anecdotal experiences of impact on final beneficiaries.

They looked around at some of the other approaches to impact quantification and verification and found that they applied to later-stage companies or corporations, and they evaluated supply chain and operational footprint as opposed to measuring the products and services of a company. They were strictly retrospective. In the meantime, the entrepreneurs they worked with were trying to engage investors around their potential. They had new innovations, they could solve massive challenges, and they needed to engage investors around that possibility. And so, they needed an approach to impact quantification that captured that future potential. It was out of this personal experience with entrepreneurs and seeing their struggle with this issue for years that Catherine and her team developed an approach to quantifying social impact and projecting it over a given term.

Catherine says many entrepreneurs struggled with the data piece, especially on the social side, which often is viewed as subjective or anecdotal. And so, they operate with founders on a unit level. They take a unit of sale, think of one thing sold or one buyer sold to, and identify the impact on a unit level. Where a company is lacking primary data, which is often the case with startup companies, they are able to draw from comparable companies, and the efficacy that has been proven there or through third-party research that says that this kind of an innovation can do or generate this kind of impact. Generating that impact on a unit level really makes it much more manageable.

At ImpactableX, they have a three-step process, which is very simple and straightforward. The first step is they define the metrics.

Take, for example, a ton of carbon as the first impact metric. Then in the second step, they identify the unit level impact, so for each thing sold, how many tons of carbon are abated or saved or, in one case from a current client, actually pulled from the atmosphere to generate a new product? They relate a unit of sale to a unit of impact and by operating on an individual basis, they then allow entrepreneurs to have a dynamic future-looking projection. Because if they know the impact of one thing sold, then they know the impact of 50, 100, or 10 000 things sold over the next five or 10 years.

Case study: Reducing Recidivism

A case study she gave was that of a company that participated in a project with Bloomberg Philanthropies in the city of Philadelphia and Wharton Social Impact Initiative, and it was addressing recidivism. When that company worked with ImpactableX, they were very new. Their idea was that by selling certain types of tablet technologies to prisons with educational content built-in, they could reduce the likelihood of recidivism, of an inmate returning to prison within a certain period of release. Step one was identifying the core metrics. For that company, it was a reduced three-year re-incarceration rate and sustained employment one year post-release. In the second step, they talked about that unit level impact. They looked at how many prisons the company expected to sell to over the next five years, how many prisoners in average are in each prison, how many active users then per prison will use their product, and then of those, how many will be released over a given period and won't return to prison based off of what the research says. Sure enough, the RAND Corporation had published a report that said that this type of educational content can reduce the likelihood of returning to prison by quite a substantial percent. They typically discount that percentage to engage stakeholders and operate as conservatively as possible. Now, they have a rough number of prisoners who, based off of the research, won't return to that one prison over a given term. They can then apply that across all of the prisons that the company expects to sell to over the next five years, so that's an impact output or KPI.

In the third step, they look at economic valuation of impact, at new value created and costs avoided as a function of the impact. In that example, they looked at what it costs a state every time an inmate is released and returns to prison within a period of time, and it's expensive. The costs to the state are astronomical. They often discount it and look at averages over the entire country. They are then able to multiply this economic value of one prisoner returning to prison within three years of release by the number of prisoners that the research says will be impacted by this technology over the same period of time. From that, they get the social impact projection for that one metric, which represents the total impact value that this company can generate over a given period of time, pursuant to their sales and revenue projections.

Clearly, what they're doing over at ImpactableX is not just an environmental index. They focus on lots of different metrics in which you are making an impact, so they are able to cover many of the UN Sustainable Development Goals. This follows the theory behind their approach, which is that social entrepreneurs are solving massive problems. And by doing so, they create massive value, but they can only monetise a portion of that value that they create.

If you look at a company's revenue model, you're missing all of that additional value that they're creating. But with their approach, they really try to capture all of that external value, whether that value is experienced by the buyer or by the commons, and whether it is social or environmental. That's why getting clear on what the metrics are in that first step is very important, as well as aligning with global standards like the Impact Management Project of IRIS+, and notably, the Sustainable Development Goals. Their indicators and targets are so important, because it's not standardised. The kinds of impact that different innovations and business models and technologies can have should really be acknowledged, Catherine thinks, on a case-by-case basis, even though they can roll up into more general categories or impact verticals.

What It's Like Working with ImpactableX

For business owners who are curious about ImpactableX, Catherine says that when you work with them, they start by having that conversation about your company's impact metrics, they understand your business model, and then you get access to software that walks you through the data collection process. This includes all of the different input you need in order to generate these analytics. You get access to the methodology, and you get guidance through it, customised for your specific innovation and business model.

Once they have all of the baseline data collected, they generate a company report, which shows all of the high-level data points that they've uncovered. This is your impact metrics, impact outputs, impact evaluations, and impact multiples. They generate revenue to impact multiples and capital to impact multiples, which Catherine finds particularly fascinating and interesting for investors. They generate a company report that has all of that clearly laid out. That is also supported by a data validation page, which shows all of their work, their assumptions, if they make any calculations, citations, etc., and then they generate a certification mark. A founder can say on their website, pitch deck, or marketing material that this data has been verified, it is third-party certified, and you get a core logic model, which is essentially a stable formula with variable inputs.

You can play around with your revenue and sales projections, or you can play around with your impact percentages, capital requirements, or various data points that feed into their analytics within a stable formula. That allows you to be a startup founder, to play around with their assumptions and expectations of how your business will grow over time.

From there, they check in with you every three months, just to make sure that your data is tight. If you've pivoted, they update their analytics. They support you with office hours, with investors, and with marketing advisors and experts who can help you integrate some of these data points into your marketing and branding. Their mission at ImpactableX is really to help founders deliver their impact at scale. They want to see social impact scaled far and wide. They want to provide all of the value, practical and theoretical that can help you do that, and they think that impact data is the right place to start.

The reception from VCs or the finance community to ImpactableX's offering and formula was resounding, Catherine says. Increasingly, impact investors are beginning to really require impact data. Investors have been trying to figure out what kinds of impact or reporting to expect from the founders they invest in for quite some time, and they're very wary about placing undue burden. But with ImpactableX, this is intended to only take a couple of weeks to a month. This is not a lifecycle assessment or one that takes years and requires piles of primary data.

What they do also streamlines ongoing impact reporting. Once they certify the relationship between revenue and impact, impact reporting becomes a function of financial reporting, which they're doing already. This adds credibility and legitimacy to the impact claims of entrepreneurs. By converting it into a dollar value, it allows impact to integrate into traditional fund management practices. Investors can actually understand impact performance against financial performance, and they can see what kind of ownership stake they and their LPs have in the impact generation of their portfolio companies. It generates tremendous new insights for investors, while also offering a really user-friendly approach, and therefore the response to what they are doing is overwhelmingly positive.

Chapter Ten
The AI Content World.

Interview with London-based Dr. Stylianos Kampakis; CEO of the Tesseract Academy and Data Science Advisor at the London Business School.

Dr. Stylianos Kampakis, or Dr. Stelios for short, is an expert data scientist on a mission to educate the public about the power of data science, artificial intelligence, and blockchain. He is a member of the Royal Statistical Society, an honorary research fellow at the UCL Centre for Blockchain Technologies, and a data science advisor for the London Business School. He is also the CEO of Tesseract, an organisation with a vision of making data science available to everyone, even non-technical people. On top of that, he is an author, with his book, *The Decision Maker's Handbook to Data Science*, currently selling on Amazon.

AI works in multiple ways in marketing, and Dr. Stelios shares that one of the main ways is in analytics and trying to answer traditional marketing problems, from improved ways to performing A/B testing to understanding execution in a better way as well as content generation of articles, titles, images, and even videos. A large part of Dr. Stelios' work over the last few years has been around explaining to decision makers from startups and bigger organisations, and helping them understand how they can implement AI in the best possible way, how they can get the most value out of AI and data science, and strategies on designing it. That being said, many of the marketing tools are more focused and easier to use, because the idea behind these tools is that you can use them for very specific purposes. For instance, when it comes to AI generating titles, there's less risk in terms of implementation because the purpose of this is clear.

Let AI Do the Writing for You

Companies have their own style, and so one of the best things about AI in marketing is that AI writers can craft content with personality. The AI can be taught these skills so that the content doesn't sound generic. Dr. Stelios says it's not very difficult to do because in natural language generation, there are models like GPT-3 and GPT-2, and these can simply be fine-tuned so that the model learns how to speak in the language of those texts. If you want them to make the network speak like Shakespeare, all you would need to do is feed it some of Shakespeare's work, and then it will learn that language and start speaking in that manner. That is a problem which AI can solve.

Generative models in AI can create fresh content, eliminating possible issues of plagiarism or copyright lawsuits. Research and development in this area have advanced a lot to the point that algorithms can now write pretty realistic content, albeit with minor improvements needing to be made. Nevertheless, copyright is not considered a major issue when using AI to create content. Realism and writing relevant content might probably even be bigger issues than plagiarism. The network can also be trained in any language or even multiple languages simultaneously, so it can be used multinationally. Training a network does require resources, so if you want to train a network on a language it's not familiar with, you'll need to spend time training it but also collecting the data set, which is where the challenge presents itself.

The state-of-the-art model in natural language generation is GPT-3, which is a model developed by OpenAI, unlike GPT-2 which was developed by Open Source AI. If you type GPT-2 and Python, you will find some implementations in Python, and it's fairly easy to use. The GPT-3 model is pre-trained, so it knows English, basically. Dr. Stelios actually fed his book called *The Decision Maker's Handbook to Data Science* into this algorithm, and because he had a certain manner of speaking, the AI generated sentences which sounded like his tone of writing and were somewhat realistic. The text that was produced was factually correct, although there were no deep insights, and it uncovered the relationships between AI as a subfield of computer science, databases, and more.

There's a certain humour and nuance in advertising that isn't in a long-form article, but with AI, that's no problem. One can use similar technology, and it'll work just as well. The technology is there; it's just not as refined yet to be used generally. Another thing is that the models are big, so they may not necessarily be easy to sell to users, but it won't take long before AI content generation becomes widely available. That's not to say that humans don't have a role. AI learns from humans, but for now, it won't be able to come up with novel ideas. In the near future, one can expect to see great content generation services based on AI for content, which is largely "vanilla."

When it comes to technical write-ups like brochures, manuals, or handbooks, which are a big body of work as well for most companies, AI may not be the best approach. These are facts and systematised knowledge that is built-in and put into boxes, and when you're reading a guide, you want it to be very precise. Whereas when talking about AI, it produces content which looks as if it was created by a human. The blurred lines to using AI, too, are in intellectual property rights. If you use AI to create an article, technically, you didn't write it yourself, so do you own the copyright, or can you copyright content that wasn't generated by you?

AI Is Universal in Its Usage and Its Reach

AI is great at reaching out across various bodies of information, compiling synthesising, and generating a narrative. From the three main data formats, text, audio, and video, it's possible to create an article from which a video or an audiogram could be made from that same piece of content. And these days, AI is increasingly being used by companies big and small, as it's not just about efficiency. With the pandemic still going on, it's also about using technology in domains where humans might not be able to work because of a virus.

The impact of AI on marketing would be lower barriers to entry into the game for smaller agencies and companies. AI tools for marketing would become cheaper, making it easier for a smaller company to do the job that a bigger company with a marketing department is doing. This is going to level the playing field, because problem that smaller companies have is the continuation of content, because people are trying to do so many things at once. But with AI helping them out, they are able to focus on other important aspects of the business. There will also be more and more tools as well as better ones continuously being developed to go out into the market. The first step to this is creating cheaper tools, because currently, some of the solutions out there are meant for big companies, but eventually, they will get cheaper and more accessible.

AI is proving to be a global innovation, with it taking place in many countries. The world leader is the US, and China is a close second. People are witnessing a global arms race around AI and data science, and over the next few years, people will see many different pockets of innovation as more countries realise the hidden value in these technologies.

The Tesseract Academy

Dr. Stelios' Tesseract Academy has a goal to serve the content needs to help decision makers, and these decision makers can be anyone from a CEO, to an entrepreneur with a startup, to a company manager to help them better understand how they can implement data science without having to go through the all the technicalities and details, which can sometimes seem obscure or esoteric. The Tesseract Academy has worked on topics like data strategy and scoping out AI projects, and they worked with the US Navy and Vodafone.

A recurring theme in this line of work involves explaining to stakeholders how AI and data science can be used and helping them achieve their goals because, quite often, people lose sight of the big picture. They make poor decisions, or they might not have the right plan in place, and so they teach them about building the right culture for data science adoption, because these are the things that the decision maker needs to deal with early on to get the most value out of their data. And as data science and AI become more and more widespread, it's also a question as to whether you can do this as a competition.

Sooner or later, everyone will need to make the change and implement AI if they haven't already in their organisation. So, the Tesseract Academy has been helping decision makers get the most out of this technology in the simplest way possible and in the most efficient way possible.

Chapter Eleven
Case: Legally Content.

Interview with Denver-based Mauricio Duarte; Justice Entrepreneur and Chief Operating Officer at Access2Justice Tech.

Originally from Guatemala, Colorado-based Mauricio Duarte gave up his life as a lawyer to join A2J Tech as its Chief Operating Officer. A2J Tech is a social enterprise that builds technology to improve access to justice.

Access to justice is a worldwide problem, with 5 billion people having unmet justice needs. These range from lack of access to courts down to simple legal services and information. Even in the US, a market that is relatively more robust, around 86% of the population still doesn't have access to justice.

As attorneys, in general, have expensive fees, many people can't avail of such vital services. This inaccessibility also renders many people unknowledgeable of their rights when they get caught in a conflict.

Legal Services Made Accessible and Affordable

A2J Tech uses two approaches to make justice more accessible. One is to leverage technology to provide free do-it-yourself-style legal solutions. For instance, if you need a legal document or a form, A2J Tech offers an automation technology that can provide you with just that. The second is to make solutions and legal services that cannot be provided for free, more affordable.

In their effort to make justice more accessible and affordable, Mauricio and his team encountered two big challenges.

Coming from the legal industry, attorneys are used to using sophisticated words when speaking. They use complex words to explain something that is rather simple. In reality, those who lack access to justice are those who probably don't have access to the internet, or those who didn't go to college or have dropped out of school because of some circumstance. The challenge, for them, is to translate legal information – such as those in the statutes that the Congress passes – into a more accessible language. This will allow people to understand their rights better.

Another challenge is the lack of access to the internet. In today's digital age, there are still people who don't have access to a desktop. Some are even lucky to at least have a mobile phone or a tablet. For Mauricio, access to justice has a strong and direct correlation to access to the internet. With this in mind, he and those at A2J had to create solutions that don't necessarily depend on the internet.

Addressing Challenges

Looking at the bigger picture, A2J needed to make legal information more communicable and come up with offline solutions to provide a bigger impact on the population.

Addressing the first challenge, Mauricio mentions how working with other professionals such as copywriters has helped their company. They work hand in hand to achieve, for instance, a sixth grade-level reading: He researches and gives the content; the copywriter makes it more understandable.

He considers working with other professionals game-changing for the legal industry. To be more effective, you have to think that you don't know everything; you have to rely on other professionals who can provide more value and bring more to the table.

A2J also uses tools to ensure that their wordings are apt for their readers. Combining these human and technology elements helped them create solutions and content that are understandable.

To resolve the accessibility challenge, A2J uses this vision: When creating a product or a solution, you have to build it for a mobile phone first – not a desktop. Today, the odds are more people will have access to a mobile phone than to a desktop. In the process of creating a mobile-friendly solution, you also have to perform tests and make product iterations. Once you're satisfied with how your solution looks on mobile, you can then move into creating a desktop or laptop version.

For them to cater to people without mobile phones, A2J created what they call legal kiosks. Instead of having people rely on an internet connection, they can simply go to the kiosk (which can be located in a public library or a governmental office) and access the legal solution that they need.

Automating Eviction Forms

One of A2J's projects that proved to be helpful to many people is the COVID-19 Eviction Form.

When the pandemic hit last year, the US Centers for Disease Control and Prevention (CDC) issued an order to prohibit tenant eviction during these tough times. For tenants living in a housing project to not be evicted, they would need to meet some eligibility requirements, fill out a declaration form, and submit it to their respective landlords. The legal letter must adhere to the language that the CDC uses.

Considering it an opportunity to make justice more accessible, A2J focused their efforts and resources on creating a solution that would automate making eviction forms. Within 48 hours – just in time before the order took effect back in September – Mauricio and their CEO gathered the whole team and worked hard to come up with a platform wherein users can generate their declaration letters.

Even without getting third-party or angel-round financing, they were able to launch the project. Now, they have already helped around 40 000 people.

What Mauricio observed was that within the 48 hours that they worked on the solution, everyone involved was passionate. They know that what they're making is something impactful and meaningful. The product ended up achieving growth organically. A2J didn't need Google or Facebook advertisements or press releases. They simply posted on their main platforms (LinkedIn and Twitter). Then, they launched COVID-19 eviction forums in English, Spanish, and Portuguese to make their effort more inclusive.

As things progressed, they noticed that the usage of their platform peaked in October through December. These spikes can be attributed to referrals. Even without a marketing budget, their solution was able to reach more people through users simply recommending it to other people who may need it. Now, even non-profitable organisations tackling housing issues are using their solution. Getting featured in different media platforms also followed.

Mauricio's takeaway in this is that you don't need to have a big budget and grand marketing plan in order to make your product successful. You just need to make a good impression. And it involves testing your product, making sure it has a good user experience and user interface so that your users can refer it to someone else. Now that the CDC extended the effectiveness of their order until 30 June, 2021, A2J expects their users' tally to reach 50 000.

Making a Positive Impact

If you're creating a meaningful solution – especially if you're in an industry wherein accessibility is an issue – your target audience will see the need to use it and start referring it to other people.

Mauricio advises not to simply build things and expect people to come and patronise them. You have to offer something meaningful; something that will have a tangible, positive impact on people's lives. If they will see a need for it, they will come naturally, especially if you're providing it for free.

Furthermore, you shouldn't think that being successful means having big expenditures on online advertisements or on hiring a digital marketing agency. You also don't have to be an expert on social media (Mauricio, for instance, is only an attorney who uses Hootsuite to post content on social media platforms). As long as what you offer is meaningful, you can achieve organic growth.

A2J's COVID-19 eviction form is a good example of the so-called cascade theory. It states that if you share information that is new and easy to understand, people are more likely to cross the threshold of reservation and share it with others.

Chapter Twelve
Case: Edumercials Shine on Millions of Kids.

Interview with UK-Based Dr. Shelley James; Lumenologist and Founder of the Age of Light Innovations Group.

Dr. Shelley James, an internationally recognised expert on light, started the Luna Golightly project during the lockdown. It is a series of "edumercials" or educational infomercials that explain the impact of light on human well-being (e.g. getting exposed to sunlight can lower your need to wear eyeglasses by 40%).

Learnings Worth Sharing

The Luna Golightly project – which has now garnered over 1.5 million views on social media and has earned sponsorship from major lighting industry players (including Fagerhult, Seoul Semiconductor, and Signify) – began with Dr Shelley reaching out to experts in the field. She spoke to scientists, education specialists, and manufacturers, and recorded them as a series of interviews.

As it started to build an audience, she invited her resource speakers for a panel debate. It was a rare opportunity to have these experts from different disciplines come together and share precious and powerful information about light. But while these learnings are vital, there was no way for ordinary folks to find them out. This urged Dr. Shelley to take on the challenge and share them with more people.

How Luna Golightly Came Into Fruition

The aforementioned manufacturers, who were previously involved in the interviews, agreed to sponsor the project. With Dr Shelley at the helm, they came up with the idea of creating the fictional Luna Golightly and other characters to serve as the hosts of their edumercials.

They also identified the teens as their target audience. The reason behind it is, first, they are affected by the topic; second, they are the sort of people who will act upon something once they learn and understand the need to do it.

To make sure that this project will be independent, Dr Shelley chose sponsors from different sectors to avoid having competition. This approach also helped ensure that all who are involved are after the same thing: to shed a light on human-centric lighting.

She also brought in scientists to take part, making the project solution-driven. Luna Golightly is not about selling products but making a difference.

Having identified the audience and enlisting resource persons, Dr Shelley next created a focus group composed of teens. The goal is to learn what these people are interested in and which method would work best in terms of delivering the learnings that she wanted to share.

Getting Help from Online Tools

Dr Shelley used online design tools to create the project's avatars. For the main video content, she tried creating hand-drawn cartoons and storifying them using various online applications, before settling with Lumen5. Lumen5 is a time-efficient platform that allows you to create videos with a poppy aesthetic.

Based on feedback from her focus group, Dr Shelley learned that their initial idea of doing a narrative took too long to deliver the message. This prompted her and her team to opt for a more straightforward formula.

Another learning that Dr. Shelley got from her focus group is that the topics that the teens wanted to know are also in line with the products of her manufacturer sponsors. Though this isn't part of the agenda, it's a good coincidence that she was able to get after having sponsors onboard that are really passionate about light.

Using feedback from the teens, Dr. Shelley and her team were able to come up with impactful content – one that uses visual language, has the right length, and features topics that really sparked the interest of their audience.

Boosting Video Performance

Currently, Luna Golightly has a presence on Facebook and Instagram – platforms which they identified as where their target audience is. The project has videos that are 40 seconds long and 1½ to 2 minutes long (the latter covers practical solutions). The campaign also features interviews with scientists to tackle underlying concepts.

Dr Shelley observed that their 2-minute videos discussing more technical topics such as flickers and headaches are getting significant attention (they comprise about 49% of their project's total watch time).

They also obtained week-by-week data from their social media platforms and adjusted their content elements based on them. For instance, when they changed the title of one particular video, the click-through rate went from 7.5–13%. When they replaced one of their thumbnails into a photo of a dad, the post became one of their top-performing content. With monitoring social media analytics, you can quickly get feedback, adjust certain things, and spend on advertisements to improve your content's performance.

In terms of advertisement campaigns, they initially placed ads separately on Facebook and Instagram. Then they tried placing Instagram ads via Facebook. With this, their Facebook videos got 12–20% click-through rates while Instagram reached 6–9%. Though they tallied lower reach, they garnered higher click-throughs and engagement. The key takeaway here is that fine-tuning your campaigns and content can make a massive difference.

Having Confidence in Your Ideas

When Dr. Shelley was only starting the Luna Golightly project, she first went to a couple of big agencies to help her out in the production (She previously had stints working in big agencies). She also tried reaching out to smaller agencies. Either way, she learned that she'd need to spend thousands of pounds to turn her ideas into reality.

If you cannot go top dollar to produce the content you want to share, you need to look for other ways. If you have confidence in your ideas, use the available tools online and go out there. After all, you're in the realm of things where you can take a chance. When Dr. Shelley started sharing the content that she created using online tools with her sponsors, she was still able to get a positive response.

What also helped her is the very movement where her project falls into. When the pandemic hit and companies got money that they needed to mop up, they reallocated their budget and pivoted them to meaningful causes, such as Luna Golightly.

Building Relationships Goes a Long Way

When it comes to negotiating with sponsors, building a relationship is key. When Dr. Shelley first began Luna Golightly, she didn't even know the people who eventually sponsored her project. All she did was to reach out and offer them a platform. Through offering interviews, she was able to speak to them and introduce her cause in the process.

Taking inspiration from her experience, she advises meeting people who are passionate about the topic you're talking about or promoting. Give them the benefit of the doubt and set expectations. These will help you convince them that you're working altogether for the right reasons.

Also, you have to be clear that you're a team. Offer an environment that fosters collaboration and resource-sharing. For instance,

Dr. Shelley, for her part, offers content that her sponsors can use during their own sales pitches, trade fairs, and other similar events wherein they have to break the monotony of a PowerPoint presentation. She shows that she and her stakeholders are collectively on the same journey of shifting people's attention into human-centric lighting.

PART FOUR
Amplify

Chapter One
Introduction.

"Most people create content first, then think about content promotion as an afterthought. You're much better off flipping this on it's head – thinking about who would help amplify your content and why."
– Larry Kim, Founder of Wordstream

I knew that the best way to conquer a market of 1.4 billion people with my one-man PR machine was to get the Chinese to share images, videos, and anecdotes about this British hand-built sports car with their networks. When content goes viral, it is benefitting from the cascade effect; when people like and understand the content sufficiently to overcome their inertia and to share it with their network. I made sure that every time a Morgan was stationary or in transit it had a quick response code stuck to it which led to our social media, and I encouraged customers, staff and bystanders to take photographs of themselves with the cars and to share them. It worked – within five years we had over 250 000 unique visitors to our website. This was simple amplification.

Amplification is more than just a fancy modern name for marketing, it is the process of placing content across multiple platforms so that your content works as hard as it possibly can for you. As more and more content gushes onto the internet every day, Facebook alone has 2.79 billion users, we all have to keep up to avoid being diluted. As search engines and social platforms rate content based on links and authority, amplification isn't a choice but a necessity for all of us.

In practical terms, the challenge is creating more content and proactively publishing this across more channels, whilst still being context sensitive and relevant. Publishing content across many channels must enhance, not dilute the message, it must enrich the brand whilst reaching out to new audiences.

We are all in luck. Sir Tim Berners Lee is the modern equivalent of Johannes Gutenberg, and the internet is the digital typesetting apparatus to replace that of the 1440s printing press. My guests on The UnNoticed show covered a range of topics from the impact of data on building a content plan to the law of reciprocity on LinkedIn, to building your own web TV station. The exciting message overall is that public relations is no longer guess work, that we are gaining greater and greater control, and the window for communications with potential clients is now open 24/7. Within this though is the recurring theme of the need to reach out to people with relevant content, and as you'll read in the case studies it's possible to be listed on Amazon and Apple TV, and to build a global audience for a niche community which becomes self-funding.

Chapter Two
Pitching to Journalists.

| *Interview with Justin Goldstein in New York; Founder of Press Record Communications.*

Press Record Communications uses a very targeted approach when helming their clients' media relations. First, they find what their clients' goals are. Next, they search for media outlets, reporters, and other press contacts that they think will be a fit for their clients. Then, they work with these reporters, coordinating and telling them their clients' stories.

Ultimately, it's about getting *that* media coverage that will support their clients' sales and marketing goals.

The Changing Media Landscape

For Justin, the difficulty of getting media coverage for a client depends on who you're working with.

Over the past years, the media landscape has changed: Newsrooms and their staff are getting smaller; a lot are also getting acquired by holding groups or larger media organisations. With this, the opportunity for traditional media has diminished. On the other side, this has also created new opportunities. Reporters who have been laid off or have left their previous publications have started their own podcasts and newsletters. Sites like Substack have also emerged to make it easier for people to become a reporter.

The definition of what's considered "media," in the traditional sense, has definitely changed. Getting covered by the media now comes down to the effort you put into finding the right press people.

The Press Record Process

The process of getting media coverage for a client depends on the goals of their client.

According to Justin, there's a challenge when it comes to putting together public relations programs for firms with 30 000-foot goals. Somebody might say that they want to get on national television. However, this could entail different meanings. Do you want to be on more of a CNBC Squawk Box kind of show or do you want to be on more of The Today Show? Therefore, you, as a client, should have to really go around and dive deeper into those goals. You have to have a good understanding of who exactly you want to speak to and what kind of coverage you want to see.

After identifying those, Press Record then helps the client come up with a roadmap for developing pitches, identifying who the target media are going to be, and then actually going out and reaching out to reporters and other media contacts. Though they try to get those opportunities for their clients, it really does start with understanding their goals at the micro and macro levels to make sure that they're getting the right coverage.

These so-called 30000-foot goals are typically from the media perspective. However, it does play into the business goals as well. For instance, If you're looking to talk to more of a business audience, it won't benefit you to go on *The Today Show* or a local TV or radio station. If you want to drill down and reach a specific audience, you have to be on platforms like Bloomberg Radio, CNBC TV, or Fox Business TV. In the end, the media and business goals can be tied together. It's a matter of understanding who your audience is and who you're talking to the most.

Putting a Practical Roadmap

There are a lot of firms out there that create detailed presentations for proposals and roadmaps. Press Record, on the contrary, tries to keep it as simple as possible. Justin notes that they do it as such because they know that their clients are going to be busy.

According to him, what he puts together is an action plan that essentially goes over the key metrics for the campaign. It also includes the target media that they're looking to approach. It's more of sampling so that the client will have a snapshot of what the campaign might look like. Some initial pitch ideas that could potentially work well are also being included.

Once the action plan is signed off, they build the campaign and start developing pitches. They then send it to their clients for review. After the pitches are signed off, that's when they start on their outreach. After that, they try to taper off sending pages to their clients – they don't want to be a bottleneck or to make their clients feel that they have to put in more effort than they need to. It's really about getting on the same page as early as in the initial plan and then moving forward from there.

What's an Effective Pitch

Creating an effective pitch document depends on who you're pitching. But for Justin, one of the key things that you have to keep in mind is this: In this day and age, brevity is key.

When you're making a pitch, the subject line should be straight to the point. Though you can put a little bit of creativity there, you shouldn't go too far. You should aim for your contact to easily understand what it is that you're pitching. The body of the email should also be the same. For instance, Justin always starts with an upfront note that says, "Hey, so-and-so. I know you'll cover XYZ and you've been reporting this kind of story over the past weeks. I'm curious if you're working on some additional coverage and if so, I have this client that I think would be a great fit."

Apart from brevity, it's also about making sure that you have the right information in the pitch. This is actually going to get reporters to keep their eyes on the email.

Then, you also have to understand what kind of assets do the reporters need – Do they need headshots? Do they need a video or audio content? If you can mix and match and put all the necessary information in there, you'll have more chances of winning your contact's interest.

Another important aspect is email personalisation. But, again, it really depends on what you are pitching. If you're inviting reporters to an event, a mass email is fine. Based on Justin's experience, reporters would understand that you're trying to get as many attendees as you possibly can.

However, when it comes to pitching a story, you really have to personalise. The last thing a reporter would want is to see that they're not being paid attention to. If you think about it, it also doesn't feel real when you receive a marketing email or a LinkedIn message that is generic. This is why you have to take the time to do it. Justin recommends following the 80–20 rule: Focus 80% of your time on personalising emails and the other 20% on mass emails.

Let Your Pitch Stand Out

Media people are getting hundreds of pitches per week. To make your pitch stand out, Justin reiterates that you have to make your pitch brief. Brevity will help set you apart from other people who are essentially pitching essays.

You also have to focus on your call-to-action (CTA). If you want to have a reporter respond to you, frame up your email in such a way that it solicits an answer – tell that you're looking for something in return (e.g. Would you be interested in connecting with so-and-so? Can we schedule a call to discuss more?). This puts into their head that there's an action that they actually have to take. If your pitch doesn't have a CTA, reporters would think that they don't have to do anything about it. They'll simply flag it for later or, worse, just move on and not even care.

When it comes to setting deadlines for reporters' responses, Justin shares that it's dependent on who you're pitching to. If you're pitching a story to a publication like *The New York Times*, you have to give a leeway because *it's The New York Times*. If he's the one pitching it, what he'd do is to send it a month or two in advance so there'd be a buffer time. This helps avoid having a deadline issue in the first place.

If the pitch is non-exclusive, pitches typically don't have deadlines. On the other hand, if you're offering an exclusive, you have to give a first-come-first-served notice. You could say that you'd need a response within 48 hours. This gives them a day to read emails and think about their response. To avoid putting too much pressure on the reporters, you could simply inform them that you just need some feedback or some kind of direction on whether they'd pursue the pitch or not.

You also have to keep in mind that journalists also often have to get the approval of an editor before pursuing a story. If you're looking to get a story opportunity, it's still better to go to reporters than editors because they will do a better job of selling it than you. If an editor hears from a journalist why they should pursue your story, it becomes a totally different conversation. You should only go to editors directly if you're pitching an op-ed or a byline.

Proper Follow-up

For Justin, hitting the phone is still the most important manner to do a follow-up after pitching. Some reporters are going to have an adverse reaction but some will be fine about it. It's much like sales in the sense that you really don't know who you're going to get.

In this day where reporters are getting many emails, it's very important to do just that. If you really want to get that media coverage opportunity, calling can give you quick feedback at the very least. This will help guide you about the next steps that you need to take.

However, as not every reporter has a phone number, the next thing that you can do is to reach out via LinkedIn. Unless a reporter puts on their social media profile (like Twitter) that you can direct-message them, it's still better to contact them via LinkedIn, which has a more professional setting.

Traditional broadcast media are typically harder to reach on email than print and online journalists. The nature of a 24-hour newsroom is that they're constantly sending reporters to the field; they're fielding calls from everyday people about certain stories.

They don't have much time to respond via email and they tend to be less apt to fully committing to something – unless you get them on the phone.

On Storytelling

Doing storytelling on your pitch is effective depending on the kind of media coverage you want.

Personally speaking, Justin considers storytelling overrated. For him, it's more about effectively communicating the kind of story that you want to tell. However, it's important to do so as a brand because reporters have to understand who you are and what you do. And these details are essential in sealing the deal – in moving the media coverage to the finish line. But when it comes to getting a reporter's initial interest, you have to consider brevity. Going into an entire, detailed story in an email pitch isn't going to work as well as just giving the facts of the story.

In terms of delivering the rest of the story, or more details about your pitch, the timing depends on what the reporter's request is. If you're working with a broadcast outlet, there's typically a list of assets that they'd require, such as headshots and B-rolls. Some also need suggested questions, because many broadcast producers won't have the time to think about it due to their tight schedule. Some even send a booking form where you need to fill out questions.

This is a little bit different from print and online publications. Reporters on these platforms are not keen to do those as it will make it seem like you're doing their job for them. For these journalists, it will depend on how exactly your conversation is. Typically, unless they ask for something in advance, you don't have to send something. For instance, if you're the spokesperson and during your conversation, you happened to bring up about a certain study that relates to the story you are pitching – if they'd tell you to send that study after the call, that's only when you should send that. So, typically, the assets that need to be sent only come after you're done with your conversation.

Handling Journalists Who Can't Make It

There are instances wherein journalists won't be able to make it to a scheduled interview opportunity. For whatever reason, they may postpone or cancel on you. In this situation, Justin emphasises how essential it is to communicate to the client that this is something normal. Ultimately, if you want to build a relationship with a reporter, you have to let it go. Complaining about it will only create friction and it's not going to lead to a productive conversation in the future.

To handle this scenario, ask the reporter if it can be rescheduled. Find their availability or vice versa: Get the availability of your client's spokesperson. Most of the time, if a reporter has committed to a conversation, he or she is going to reschedule.

When Press Record books an interview, they always ask the reporter's schedule first. This will lessen the chance of having them postpone or cancel the interview. But if it does happen, you have to be understanding of both sides. Be calm with the client and understand why they're frustrated. Also, understand the situation of the reporter (e.g. he or she may have been pulled into a time-sensitive coverage). If the reporter doesn't want to have the conversation, he or she wouldn't even commit in the first place. If he or she has committed, it's because he or she has found some value in your pitch. It's not like it's being postponed because he or she just feels like it – there's usually a good reason behind it.

This is why you really have to coach your client and let them understand that, while it's understandably frustrating, they have to accept the consequences of building a relationship with the media. This is akin to when you're building a relationship with a customer. You're not going to go and tell the customer, "Why did you do that?" Instead, you're going to try to smooth it over and make it as good of a situation as possibly can.

Chapter Three
Dreaming of Being on TV?

> Interview with Eric Mitchell, Portland Oregon; Co-Founder of LifeFlip Media, Forbes Agency Council, On-Air media talent.

Getting on TV

The year 2020 brought forth new trends such as working from home and opening remote studios. We're able to watch Trevor Noah do his shows straight from the studio at his house. Taking inspiration from this concept, it's also now possible for you to be on TV, too.

The first thing you need to do is to have a plan. Then, start local. Across the globe, there are different local television stations that cover news and happenings in different communities. One common mistake people do is that they immediately want to go for the biggest shows such as *Good Morning America.*

When contacting press people, Eric recommends Twitter. It's a great social media platform that many journalists around the world use. The majority of the reporters also include information on how to get in touch with them in their profiles.

With this platform, you can see what they report about and even have a glimpse of their personal life. For instance, Eric has a good friend who's an anchor on a national TV show. He happened to know that that person is a huge fan of the basketball team, Arkansas Razorbacks. Based on that knowledge, he decided to send him gift boxes whenever March Madness arrives. Similar to that, with Twitter, you can learn something from your prospective journalists. You can leverage that and give them something that they want to talk about; something that will make them realise that you're paying attention to them. You can use direct messaging to commence a conversation with them. As DMs are available on Twitter and other platforms like Instagram, it's now easier to reach out, talk to, and engage with reporters. Getting yourself on TV is really more mental than anything else.

Being newsworthy is a whole different topic altogether.

In 2020, the world saw an increase in people who claim to be digital marketers or word entrepreneurs. However, a number of them are only "wanna-preneurs," and they're different from authentic entrepreneurs. What spells the difference is how you make yourself newsworthy, how you tell your story, and how you separate yourself from the bunch.

Why Bother Being on Radio and Podcast

If you will ask Eric, he would recommend you to never turn down a podcast or a radio feature. If the show is talking about a topic that you know a lot about and you can provide value for, say yes to that show.

This is what most people tend to forget about: the similarity between TV and radio. What a TV network wants is for you to have a story that resonates with others. If you simply pitch yourself and your product but it won't provide value to their audience, you won't make it on their show. They want you to have something valuable for their millions of audience (or hundreds of thousands, if they're local) because it can help drive up their engagement.

The same goes for the radio. However, this platform has an advantage: You can have a longer talk time (radio shows and podcasts usually last from 15 to 30 minutes; TV shows only offer around five to seven minutes).

Also, when you look at data consumption, digital audio like podcasts are now getting bigger more than ever. Radio shows also have their own share of audience, including those who are on the road.

Unlike TV, you'll also be rarely affected by breaking news on radio and podcasts. Furthermore, you can guest on a show, do a radio tour, and get quality media mileage without letting people know that you're having a bad hair day. This is why Eric recommends to not just aspire to be on TV, but also to target podcast and radio show hosts as well.

Trying Out New Platforms

In the era of live chats and live streams, many apps continue to emerge. One of the apps that grow rapidly nowadays is the audio-driven Clubhouse.

Based on his experience using the app, Eric shares that it has been a helpful platform in his pursuit of giving back and providing value to people, especially to those who are unknown and unnoticed. In his rooms, which he does every Tuesday night, he hosts question-and-answer portions featuring industry leaders, fellow PR professionals, producers, on-air hosts, and other media personnel. This gives his audience the chance to converse with these people and learn something from them. Some of the topics they discuss include knowing where and how to start, making a pitch, and assessing brand direction among others.

Setting up Your Home Studio

Setting up home studios shouldn't cost a lot of money. If you're just starting, you can start small. If you will use your laptop, Eric recommends you make sure it's clean (especially your web camera) and levelled.

You shouldn't also oversimplify what you're doing. Put things behind you, like fancy lights. If you want to know more about proper lighting techniques, you can go to YouTube and learn from YouTubers. While they're not on traditional media, these people have become experts on the matter and are willing to engage with their audience.

If you will use a green screen, you have to do it right. Secure yourself to your seat so you won't have that motion glare when you move or you won't have your hands appear as if they were cut off. As an alternative, Eric uses a 75-inch TV and frames it properly to serve as his backdrop.

Staying Relevant

If you're pitching yourself to the press, Eric recommends freshening up your talking points on a weekly basis. Pay attention to what's happening around you to make sure that your pitch is relevant.

You can also rely on subscriptions and news sources such as The Associated Press, Wall Street Journal, BBC, Daily Mail, and Scoop.it! among others. There's also Morning Brew, a newsletter that rounds up the news of the day. For instance, if you found that a news story on a Tuesday fits your needs, you can grab it, send it to a producer, and tell how it relates to what you want to share. Even if what you're targeting is a local producer, if your story is compelling, it can entice those on the national level to invite you to their shows.

If you want to affect the masses, to get on TV, the key is having a catchy story.

Chapter Four
Speaking at Events.

Interview with Zachary Nadler, New York; CEO of VaynerSpeakers

Reinforcing the Power of Purpose

VaynerSpeakers was created to build a speaker Roster which includes people who can inspire others and give the best tactics and strategies. While they can't help every single person in the world through representation, they aim to set an example on how to get a particularly positive message out there; to give an idea of what they do and the effective way that they've done it.

So how do they do it? As Zach has mentioned in one of his other podcast engagements, it's all about focusing on the purpose and sort of removing the "transaction" aspect from the engagement.

The founders of VaynerSpeakers started the business with the idea that they want to be different. They don't want to be just another speakers bureau because, really, there's enough of that out there already. For every event that they provide a speaker for, they consider it different and unique. They see past the business and the money-making side of it. Because for them, focusing on those won't give much chance for success and won't be able to build long-term relationships. "Transaction" is perceived only as a small piece of what actually goes down.

Breaking Into a New Market

Trying to break out into a new market, according to Zach, is about creating awareness. So if your product is yourself, the speaker, you've got to make your prospective audience aware of yourself. And that will entail marketing yourself in other languages.

But what's more crucial is targeting a smaller market. It brings forth a more beneficial relationship, something that is more advantageous. By establishing yourself in that kind of market – a market wherein there are fewer speakers – you can create lasting relationships with groups and audiences that will want to bring you back.

Another trend is finding more territorial topics. Now, themes about resilience and grit are going global because, with the pandemic that's happening, everyone is dealing with the same situation. The key is to delve into certain topics that are more exclusive to an area.

But if you really want to build a market for yourself anywhere, you have to have a message that is useful to anyone. With the internet democratising information, anyone could build a marketplace for anything, in any part of the world. In this case, you have to put more time and effort to do that and impart a message that people would actually want to hear about.

Why VaynerSpeakers Remain Tech-Agnostic

At a time when more and more virtual events are taking place, VaynerSpeakers remain pretty tech-agnostic when it comes to sharing their speakers' messages worldwide.

Zach points out that technology is fast-changing. Ten years ago, people were all on Skype. But now, no one is using the platform anymore. Zoom, which is a video conferencing app that gained skyrocketing traction because of the pandemic, as I mentioned, has already reached its threshold when it comes to interactivity and connectivity.

According to him, there still isn't a technology that comes even close to replacing the atmosphere set by face-to-face interactions. Nothing can yet replicate the VIP experiences and the after-parties.

And with that, they opt not to stick with one particular platform to get their speakers' stories across. In fact, last year, the group utilised 10 to 15 different platforms. That's how malleable they are – they use whichever is most preferred by their customers.

It All Boils Down to Authenticity

VaynerSpeakers recognise that they have a platform to offer for the unnoticed. With it, they can help broadcast and amplify those unnoticed people's messages. So it all boils down to finding who they are going to offer that avenue to.

Zach emphasises he is proud of the people they currently represent. They are all very individual in their way and they all have varying messages to tell – the kind of messages that they're excited to broadcast with the megaphone. This is why they do their best to overexpose those underexposed.

Feeling privileged to work with such a roster, Zach and the rest of his team at VaynerSpeakers take their responsibility seriously. They make sure that their customers know what their options are, and connect the dots between a speaker and an event. They figure out who the audience is, who the company is, why they're being brought in, in the first place. They do their best to create a custom message, something that you don't get to see every day.

If a speaker has an understanding of his or her cultural relevancy and can turn that to his or her audience, VaynerSpeakers will give a platform for that speaker to be heard. For instance, this summer, they have an American-born client who's supposed to go to Singapore in person. But because of the pandemic, it will only be virtual. But the idea is there: to bring a speaker to an international crowd. To overcome language barriers, they are working on being able to simultaneously translate it into about 20 different languages.

This is why, right from the start, they make sure that the speakers they represent have a message to share, not just a mere speech. The speakers they're looking for must have a way to connect with a crowd. For instance, if the speaker will talk about working with business owners and entrepreneurs and he or she comes in as if they're all employees, they're going to have a very difficult time having a conversation like that. He or she should have that ability to connect and be authentic – be able to speak to the audience in a way that's going to be powerful and meaningful for them.

While they provide information that speakers need to perfect their craft and make sure that every presentation is custom, they don't necessarily coach or write speeches for them. Again, it all goes back to authenticity.

If you know your message, then you should be able to understand how to connect it to a different audience. And that demands more research than otherwise. For example, if you're sharing your message to teachers, a very special audience, you have to know how to be able to speak to them. There has to be that value of adaptability. You have to know your audience, be able to craft your message, and own the content. Zach says that if you can't stand on a soapbox and talk about the thing that you're most passionate about, then you shouldn't have been out there in the first place. You're like a musician who has his style and own form of composition but has to think of something new to stay relevant.

Leveraging the Internet

In the process of being a successful speaker, a lot of work goes on. It's not an overnight success. So how do VaynerSpeakers help their clients move from one stage or level to another?

It's leveraging how the internet democratises information. The internet can be a platform that can expedite success. In this age, for instance, anyone can be a Kim Kardashian quickly. Somebody can release a song on TikTok and two weeks later, that somebody could be playing at the Grammys already.

Zach advises that if you have a great story, tell it – and find people to hear it. Remember when Justin Bieber became a phenomenon and to think that he just played a song on YouTube and someone saw it? Well, the rest, as they say, is history. But that was 10 years ago already. Today, things are a lot easier than they were during that time. The good news is, it just keeps getting better. Take advantage of the technology available and grab the opportunity to share your message.

Just don't lose that self-awareness, he shares. Know what message people would want to hear. Don't just tell stories; share information in a way that can benefit someone else. Just like how a client of Zach told him all sorts of crazy experiences he encountered and was able to impart lessons in the process – even if Zach did not necessarily find the experiences fun for him on a personal level.

Indeed, great stories become even more effective when they're told the best way to tell them.

It's Not About Fame, But the Ability to Share

At VaynerSpeakers, Zach and company try to be as open-minded as possible.

They are looking for people who are different. It's not exactly fame or following that they're looking for – it's the ability to serve and to share. And, of course, good people. They don't want to bring anyone too much to handle.

Their prospective client need not be this successful or should have this many followers on social media – any sort of periphery numbers and things that don't really quantify success in the world of speaking engagements. They need authentic speakers who can put the whole package together and simply be themselves.

Chapter Five
The Law of Reciprocity.

Interview with Cory Warfield in Chicago; Waiter-turned-tech entrepreneur followed 280 000 on LinkedIn, Chief Connection Officer at Cory Connects.

Cory spent about 20 years of his adulthood working in different restaurants as a manager, waiter, and bartender. Out of his frustration with the erratic nature of his work's schedule, he created a platform – a scheduling software, specifically – to help restaurants and their employees manage their work shifts better. Cory used LinkedIn to raise money, gather the team for this project, and promote the product.

Navigating LinkedIn

While Facebook is effective for socialising with family and friends, for Cory, LinkedIn is the platform that can best cater to his needs. When people started doing videos there, he followed suit even when nobody was watching them. He kept going and tested algorithms: When is the best time to post? In which time zone was his content resonating? Which hashtags are working?

When he started applying his learnings on his LinkedIn content, that's when he started getting attention from people. Accolades, media exposure, and ultimately, customers and investors also came afterwards.

From Waiter to Entrepreneur

As a waiter, bartender, and restaurant manager, Cory has always been talking to strangers. The customers want to hear about his life, where he's from, and what his plans are. He is used to putting himself out there and talking. Nonetheless, he was selling without really selling – because his customers are those who are already hungry and know what kind of food they want.

When he transitioned into being a tech entrepreneur, he used the same approach in handling social media. He put himself out there, but he also used the so-called blue ocean strategy. It's a business and marketing strategy wherein you don't go to where everybody else is.

On LinkedIn, he started to post early in the morning and late at night. He also set himself apart from other entrepreneurs by not talking about entrepreneurship itself. He aimed to be different and have a unique selling proposition. And for his part, it was about working as shift workers. From there, he branched out so that more people could relate. He learned that what resonated on a bigger level are topics about job-seeking.

The Law of Reciprocity

Everybody thinks that what they put on LinkedIn is valuable. However, Cory begs to differ. In reality, nobody cares to learn which strategies worked for you or what are awards that you won. When using social media, especially LinkedIn, you have to apply the law of reciprocity: What you put out is what you get back.

Everyone on LinkedIn is trying to sell something and make money, in one way or another. People sell a product, their service, or their book. People emulate themselves as job-seekers who are fit for a certain job to make money. Therefore, if you want to resonate with people, you have to talk about how they can make money with what you are sharing. Talk *with* your audience – don't simply talk *to* them.

For instance, instead of simply telling that you've had an amazing career, gather people who have cracked the code and share it with people around the world who need the code – freely and with no expectation. When you put it out there, people will start to notice you, go to your profile, and see your work without talking about it yourself. This is what the law of reciprocity is about.

Understand that every platform has a specific purpose. On LinkedIn, people put out content to help people make money. Cory, whose friend is a co-founder of the said platform, shares that LinkedIn was created as an avenue where you can look people up, see what their careers are like, and who they are as a professional before you officially reach out to them. It wasn't intended to be a social media platform.

Only a few people truly get what LinkedIn is about. But once you learn about it, you can easily replicate it, play with the algorithm, and give your audience what it is that they want on LinkedIn.

How to Get Your Audience's Attention

Generally speaking, short videos and high-quality still images paired with an engaging question work well in capturing your audience's attention.

Apart from the visual aspect, you also have to know about the importance of a LinkedIn headline – or what can be found underneath your name. Instead of simply stating your position at a certain company, use a headline that starts a conversation. It can be whatever, as long as it resonates with your audience.

By having a strategic headline, you can attract more people every time you engage and comment on posts. In Cory's case, as he uses "Waiter-turned-Entrepreneur," he gets to receive enquiries from people looking for a restaurant tech figure. And these are people who are exactly his ideal client.

Through using an apt and catchy headline, he gets clients for his coaching service – and investors for his various initiatives. Now that he is set to launch his own cryptocurrency, he also plans to use his LinkedIn headline to tell something about that.

The law of reciprocity is also applicable if you want to reach more people and get more engagements for your posts. For instance, if you want to get 10 likes and a hundred views for your poster, you should scroll through a hundred posts on your newsfeed and like 10 of them. Once you intentionally engage more, people will start visiting your profile and look at your content. And when you engage more than the kind of engagement that you're expecting to receive, it will come back to you more quickly and on a bigger scale.

On Remaining Authentic

Cory is all for having an authentic, personal relationship with his followers. This is why he does not use and recommend any tools.

Algorithms and computer science can also pick up on patterned matching and automation, and penalise them eventually.

Cory emphasises that his personal brand is his asset and his currency – and that he has to be very guarded with that. Incorporating personal touch is also a far better way to grow your brand. While his service in Cory Connects involves sharing tips and tricks on how to use social media, it's still up to his clients how they can personalise them for their business needs.

When you use LinkedIn, let the law of reciprocity be your guiding light. Be willing to give, share, and serve because all of it will find its way back to you.

Chapter Six
Avoid Podcast Fade.

Interview with Miami-Fort Lauderdale-based Sebastian Rusk; a Podcast Launch Specialist. Digital Storyteller, Author, Speaker, Corporate Event Emcee, and Online Personality

By June 2023, 4,105,166 podcasts registered have been registered around the world. Podcast specialist Sebastian Rusk joined me in an episode of The UnNoticed podcast and talked about how people should start their own podcast – and more importantly – how to keep it going.

Know Your Why

For Sebastian, the number one thing you have to do is to know why you're starting a podcast. As with a lot of other things, like business and life decisions, you have to be clear with your *why*. When you find the authentic space of your why – which could be the story you want to tell, the value you want to bring to the world, or the message you want to communicate – it's going to impact your listeners for the better.

Next would be making sure that you're in line with your level of commitment: Are you willing to do the work that needs to be done to launch the show, continue to produce the show, and grow the show? These three components have to work simultaneously, or you're inevitably going to be headed to the podcast graveyard.

Having 5600 new podcasts on Buzzsprout is excellent. But you have to wait a month or two because statistics will tell that the average show doesn't make it past seven to nine episodes. In 2020, there were roughly a million podcasts on Apple Podcasts. By the end of the year, the figure was down to around 850000. So there were 150000 shows that went into the "pod fade."

Sebastian is in the business of helping people start a podcast and get to the finish line. The biggest challenge that he's encountered over the past five years is figuring out how to get somebody to continue and stay committed to what they originally did. Therefore, he and his team are very careful when identifying shows that they want to potentially launch. They make sure that their clients understand both the micro and macro work involved in podcasting.

Who Should Do a Podcast

You may ask: Is there a type of personality that's more suited to launch a podcast?

Sebastian has a background as a master of ceremonies (MC) and his father was a radio disc jockey (DJ) for 30 years. This gives him an edge in things involving audio and entertainment, like doing a podcast. But according to him, if podcasting is something that you want to try, you should definitely do it. You shouldn't let anybody stand in the way of you being able to do that.

While he did grow up in a radio station, Sebastian shares that he was never excited about it. He never had any desire to follow in his footsteps. His dad would only drag him there on weekends, helping him cut tracks for the ads that he'd go sell to local businesses in exchange for a McDonald's Happy Meal.

However, a friend (upon hearing the story) told him a few months back that genes are indeed powerful. Sometimes, what you don't realise is that a part of your upbringing or of what you're exposed to could end up being a component of what you'll end up pursuing.

Sebastian said that what he wanted was to find his place in the social media world. When he started his first company in 2010, he realised that he knew more about social media than the average people. That was the first advantage that he had, although he really had no idea how his company was going to make money.

After five years, he decided to pivot while staying in the digital marketing space – and that's when he ventured into podcasting. He successfully turned it into a business that bridges the gap between "I don't know" to "I know a guy who knows and he's taught me, and now I do know." It just happened that he grew up in a radio station.

Focusing on What's Possible

Through his business Podcast Launch Lab, he helps people get their podcast up and running.

However, not all people do podcasting full-time. It's something that only complements a part of their lives. There are also cases wherein people would give 100% to podcasting only to find that they're not getting listenership and revenue.

To help you not lose heart and even scale over time, Sebastian advises focusing on what's possible on the other side of getting your show launched and sticking with it. If you start today, you're going to be glad this time next year that you did.

Look at it as if you're becoming a media company or a brand starting a podcast or a YouTube channel: You are creating content on a platform that you can control. If it was 20 years ago and someone offered you a spot on a local radio station where you can talk about your business on Tuesday mornings for an hour, you wouldn't sleep about it – you would talk to a friend about it; you wouldn't procrastinate; you might even say yes, jump off the cliff, and figure out a parachute on the way down.

In truth, nothing has changed in 20 years, except the fact that it's easier to produce audio content. You don't have to go anywhere or get anybody's permission. You make up the rules, you create the content and you can talk about anything you want – including your business.

Whatever the case is, Sebastian notes that you can figure out a way to justify having this additional platform. And you can dissect podcasts into micro-content for your community. This is not just to create more content for them but to allow you to promote and advertise the show and the episodes.

There's never been an easier time to start a podcast and become a media company than today. It does sound crazy if you have an insurance office with a podcast studio. But it can serve as a platform to interview people doing really cool things. You can end up converting that business into something based on the content that's being created and the people who are actually consuming it. And to think that you can actually monetise your podcast, efforts can really pay for themselves. It's only 2021 and the whole podcasting landscape still has possibilities to offer.

Planning Podcast Content

One of the challenges of podcasting is planning out content. This is why Sebastian recommends not going out alone.

Sitting there and killing dead air by yourself because you think you're an expert is a bad strategy. You can sprinkle in micro episodes that are 5–10-minute long of something that you're passionate about or something that fits within the context of the content you're creating. However, the majority of your episodes should be interview-based. You should be connecting with people who are smarter and cooler than you – those who've done more things and are more successful than you. You can actually serve those people by putting them in the spotlight and benefit from the process because you're the one hosting the conversation and creating the content.

Never go, "What am I going to talk about in this podcast episode?" Because what you're going to talk about is whatever it is that your guest does, how cool they are, and how they got to where they're currently at. There is no lack of information on a complete stranger that you don't know, or on someone that you do know but want to know more about.

What Sebastian experienced in his YouTube channel was less than a pleasurable experience. However, the reward was worth it, knowing that YouTube is compensating you every time you put a new piece of content there. He worked at it for 16 months before he finally got into the Creator Program. Now that he's already built the channel, every content he puts up is being monetised. There are also now people calling him saying that they've watched his videos and asking for help on how to start a podcast. These components are information enough for Sebastian to consider that his YouTube channel was well worth the time he invested – even though it's less than a pleasurable thing for him.

How to Get Other People on Your Show

If you've got a show with almost no audience, how do you get someone on it?

For Sebastian, there's a little bit of luck and persistence involved in that process. If you're connected with somebody of notoriety and you've met in an event, you'll have some sort of rapport built without having a point of contact just to get the conversation initiated (which takes a significant amount of time). Just like how it went with Gary Vaynerchuck, whom he met through different interactions. The first time they met was in 2011, when he had a signing event for a book that he released. Sebastian got the chance to sit down with him for about an hour. The second time was in a green room of an event where Gary Vee served as the speaker and Sebastian was the MC. Another instance was when Gary Vee had his own event in Miami and Sebastian had the opportunity to spend the whole day with him and his team. That relationship grew, but behind that were a lot of tweets, emails, and connecting with his assistants.

Sebastian experienced the same thing with Marie Forleo, who's another rockstar in the marketing space. During an event, she was three hotel rooms down from him. She's an attendee while he was an MC. They met in the elevator and Sebastian took the opportunity to ask her to be on the podcast. Two months later, he was able to get her on the show.

These are just some examples of how some notable individuals in the digital space aren't easily accessible. However, you've got to work the angle as you get it. When you're reaching out to someone – whether it's an A-lister or a B-lister – you have to figure out what's in it for them to take the time to be on your show. Take note that they're getting requests upon requests, so forget about what's in it for you.

Remember that in podcasting, it's going to be a very one-sided situation and that there's going to be a lot of asking and falling on deaf ears before something actually happens. And as mentioned, Sebastian believes that it's a mix of luck and persistence that could get people of notoriety on your show. Apart from that, it's also being in places such as Clubhouse, Twitter, and LinkedIn.

How to Monetise Your Podcast

Sebastian doesn't depend on his audience to monetise his show. If you start right out of the gates, you can monetise your show right out of the gates.

Of course, it's great to have people download your show and continue to grow the community – that is a goal of the show. If you want to monetise the podcast, however, you should also aim to have an interesting conversation with interesting people who are doing cool stuff and creating content but don't have a podcast. Before or after the show, you can talk to these people and offer your services to help them start a podcast.

This strategy of interviewing people who can potentially be your clients is part of Sebastian's book (he wrote a whole chapter about it). It's about being able to identify your ideal client. In fact, a lot of the shows that they launch are for sales reps, insurance reps, and people who have a business that they're continuing to grow. And these are people who don't just want to be recognised in their existing community but also to be able to connect with new people.

If you're trying to sell employee benefits to a company, you're trying to get hold of the CEO and you're cold-calling this person every day. That CEO would have a gatekeeper that takes pride in making sure that you never reach the CEO. However, if you're telling that you want to interview the CEO, it becomes a whole different conversation. Now you're talking about ego, edification, publicity, and additional exposure. If you're smart about that and you understand the ability to be able to embrace social selling through content, that's a winner chicken dinner all day long.

You can also productively prospect. If you're going after these CEOs, you'd want to sell stuff too while you're going after them to get them on your show. Help them, interview them about the biggest struggles that they have, answer questions in real-time, and provide value to them. This way, you'd make them sound awesome while also helping them solve some issues. After that, you can expand the conversation and introduce solutions that you think will be fit for exactly what your guest has got going.

On Uploading Your Podcast on YouTube

Though he considers it a less favourable opinion, Sebastian doesn't suggest uploading podcast episodes on YouTube. By producing a podcast and throwing a video component, you are doubling the amount of work that you have.

If you think for a minute that you're going to take the archive video of your podcast on Zoom and publish it on YouTube and pray that it gets traction, you're being grossly negligent. The reality is that people come to YouTube to be entertained or to get their questions answered. If you can nail both, you're really doing a great job. But usually, it's one or the other. And these are the components that you have to look at.

If you simply post a podcast episode on YouTube with no strategy (e.g. you're uploading your whole 45-minute interview when YouTube videos are ideally between 5 and 20 minutes), it won't work. If you have a video team and the resources to produce videos, go for it by all means. Make sure that all hands are on deck to capture the video component of your podcast. Figure out a strategic, SEO-friendly title. Build other content around it. Have your team create a thumbnail that relates to the topic. Make sure that all components of YouTube production are being done with the actual video component of the podcast.

Not all people have Justin Bieber's luck (a video of him playing the guitar got uploaded on YouTube and the rest was history). A lot of people look up to Joe Rogan and other celebrities and people of notoriety who have podcasts. But take note that these people have a video company: They have a studio and an entire team to produce everything. Their job is to show up and be the talent of the show.

What the average person should focus on is getting really good at creating and recording podcast episodes, and interviewing people. And then if you want to introduce a video component, take the archive video and chop it up into small bits of content (i.e. micro-videos that are 30–60-seconds long with two or three keywords in the title that pique people's interest).

With this, you get to have a piece of content. You're also creating a call to action inviting your audience to listen to the actual episode. You can create two to five micro-content out of a 20- or 30-minute episode, and you can post it throughout the week before a new episode drops. You can check out YouTube Shorts, which allows you to upload one to two-minute videos that are short yet impactful.

Chapter Seven
Get Onto Digital Platforms.

Interview with Arvind Murali, Prosper, Texas; Chief Data Strategist of global digital consultancy Perficient

The Evolution of Platforms

Back in the 1980s, software and hardware companies dominated the world. Think about Intel, Apple, and Microsoft. Then a new family of businesses and small companies such as Netflix and Amazon started emerging in the 1990s. Basically, they are internet-based companies offering commodities and services via the internet. In the 2000s, social media companies started popping up: Facebook, LinkedIn, and Twitter among others. This social media revolution has allowed people to talk to families and friends over the internet.

Now, we are in the age of platforms. Uber, which is the largest taxi company in the world owns zero taxis. Airbnb, the largest real estate company in the world, doesn't have much real estate at all. These companies use the power of platforms – and it is today's digital economy that is driving these platforms to be extremely popular.

In 30–40 years, people will be talking all about blockchains. The value of non-fungible tokens and cryptocurrencies is slowly but surely getting their way into the mainstream. And because digital economy is going to be the future of any country in the world, it's important to talk about digital platforms.

What Can Small- and Mid-size Companies Do?

If you're a business that's only starting out, Arvind notes that you don't need to be *the* platform itself. You only need to be a part of a platform. And if you want to be on a platform, you have to think about the value proposition you're going to offer.

If you're a retail company starting out somewhere in the US, your goal should be to make yourself appear on Amazon because it's a platform where everybody around you shops online. If you're a restaurant, on the other hand, your objective should be to be part of Uber Eats. For example, if you're a Chinese restaurant owner, you should make your small business show up as the No. 1 Chinese restaurant on the said platform.

When participating in a platform, you got to have the technology to support your operation and make it seamless. Think about the application programming interface; think about how you can make it easy for your consumers to pay, interact, or choose a menu. But apart from making your company appealing, you have to make sure you're offering a good product. If you own a restaurant, make sure that your food is good.

Stepping Foot in the Platform Economy

The competition in the platform economy is rather tight. If you're a new business owner, Arvind says that the first thing you need to do is to think empathetically. Put yourself in the shoes of a platform like Amazon. And there are different ways you can approach this one.

First, look at it from an experience perspective: How is your customer's experience with you? You can get insights about this through a rating system. The more your rating grows, the more Amazon will consider you as a business that should appear at the top of their list. This is a standpoint that involves algorithms. No human beings are working behind the scenes – the platform is using machines to calculate these data.

Second, look into the number of transactions that take place in your business: How many transactions are happening in a day, a week, a month, and a year? The more transactions, the more the platform will favour you, whether you're on Amazon or Uber.

The third is keyword recommendations: Do you use keywords that your target consumers are using? If you own a Chinese restaurant and you're offering the best type of food in this class, you should use keywords that relate to what you offer. And your value propositions have to be there.

If you want to get noticed, you also have to put out lots of content. It can be a video about your company. It can be PDFs and brochures that you upload on social media. There are powerful tools such as LinkedIn and Facebook that can help your business get found. Think about the so-called network effect: If you show up on LinkedIn and a user presses the "like" button, that activity by the user will be sent to the networks of people that include that certain user. Through machine learning algorithms, you can appear in the feed of other people. This is why you shouldn't be discouraged if you have a low engagement for now. Keep uploading content and the network effect can help you reach more people.

The Role of Data

One of Perficient's clients is considered the largest online pet adoption company. When you visit their platform to look for pets, you'll be required to put your name, address, phone number, and other basic information. Their technology allows you to map all the pets around you, including those in shelters, retailers, or any other owner. They will also give pet recommendations based on certain qualifications, like vaccinations, behaviour, reviews, and their level of being allergenic.

Through machine learning, the company combines these pieces of data with a certain variety of parameters to match adopters with pets. Essentially, they are working as a technology platform. The same is true for Uber, which connects passengers with car drivers.

With the Uberisation of the industry, as how Arvind calls it, traditional marketers can also leverage it to promote their businesses. Worldwide industry analysts Gartner and Forrester recently named the customer data platform as one of the top technology trends in 2021. Using CDP, marketers can personalise their interaction and content based on the particular characteristics of their prospective consumers. Again, these are based on data and machine learning.

Marketing in the Digital Age

Arvind considers marketing to be in a sweet spot right now. And this can be attributed to traditional marketers' inherent need for data and analytics. To build and launch a campaign and to measure its success, they need to rely on financial data, customer data, transaction, data, and inventory data among others.

Now, the new breed of marketers is also getting trained in academic institutions on how to use analytics and make the most of information to create an effective campaign. They look into digital data – How many Facebook likes did they get? How many of those people who liked your post have moved into filling out a form or have been converted into a customer? How many have become loyal customers? Are they advocating the products to their friends and family?

Marketers also have *that* need to personalise messages. Because this way – if they offer something unique to their consumers based on their pattern of shopping – they can generate more sales. And all these data come from the platform that they are using.

For Arvind, Microsoft Excel is still the best tool in terms of managing data. However, there are other tools such as Alteryx, Tealium, Salesforce, and Adobe. No matter which tool you use, it will come down to how you will use your information about your customers effectively and ethically.

Today, regulations such as the California Consumer Privacy Act of 2018 (CCPA) and the European Union's General Data Protection Regulation (GDPR) exist to tackle data privacy. If you're a business, make sure that you're using your consumers' data properly, ethically, and legally. Violating these rules can get your business into trouble.

Chapter Eight
Data and Disruptive Content.

Interview with Colonel Aaron Perlut, St Louis Missouri; Partner Elasticity.

Everything is Data-Driven

For Elasticity, every problem begins with data. They try to infuse data with everything, from understanding the audience, developing creative solutions, to reaching the right people. Data can be used to implement the two primary elements of marketing communications: content creation and distribution.

Elasticity's mission is to create compelling and disruptive content and deliver it via a 360-degree marketing plan. They do this all-encompassing approach because getting people to pay attention to just one channel is rather challenging.

The idea of bringing data and communications together can be attributed to Aaron's background in media relations. He began his career as a producer in television and has always been passionate about creating interesting content.

Throughout his career, he witnessed how the changes in the media landscape have sapped revenues out of many media outlets. Today, it's important to think about what's the most effective channel that can be used to reach someone; which platform makes an impact. For instance, you were able to land a four-to-five-page story on *Fortune*. But if you think about it, who is reading *Fortune* magazine today when everyone has already moved online?

Aaron and his partners' vision is to use data to create content and a PR approach that integrates traditional media relations and social media.

If you're a media relations practitioner, you don't want to go to 300 different media outlets to pitch a story. What you'd want is to go to the most effective ones to save time, energy, and resources. At Elasticity, their media buyers are using data to determine where they'd place their client's money for advertising. This concept of data sharing makes their media relations practice far more effective.

The same goes for content creation. Today, data dictates that you're likely to get more attention if you upload a short, compelling video on Facebook rather than some static post, even if the latter also features compelling content.

The Rise of Data Targeting and Analytical Tools

Elasticity uses proprietary tools and paid subscriptions to do data targeting and analysis. These include Nielsen and Facebook (which is free for anyone who has an account on the platform).

Aaron notes how Facebook has been a game-changer. On Facebook, if you have a million followers and you are dropping content – only 3% of your followers are going to see it at most. However, if you boost your post even for a little amount, that number can dramatically broaden. You will not only be able to reach your current audience but new audiences as well. Facebook allows you to segment your data and reach new users. When Facebook did that, LinkedIn and Twitter among other platforms followed suit.

Now, these platforms have become tremendous tools that can be used to deliver the right message to the right people.

With the rise of these tools, the nature of what PR used to be – which is to release content with integrity chosen by an editor – has dramatically diminished.

Today, even the so-called bastions of earned media also use pay-to-play opportunities. For example, Aaron mentions that Forbes has public relations and advertising councils and you can pay $1200 per year to have your content published on Forbes. Several editorial contents on CNN or MSNBC are actually paid ones as well. From a thought leadership perspective, it might be a heady thing but it's still an advertising opportunity.

Though lines are being blurred now, it doesn't mean that there are no credible news opportunities anymore. But oftentimes, what media outlets are paying attention to are either industry Goliaths and game-changers or unfortunate events happening worldwide.

What's a Disruptive Content

For you to catch attention, Aaron shares that you have to have disruptive content.

When people hear the word "disruption," there's immediately a negative connotation to it. However, in this case, being disruptive means doing something different – not just different for you as a company but for your industry as a whole. An example of it would be what Elasticity did for H&R Block.

H&R Block is a tax-processing firm and they process more tax returns than anyone else in the US. But if you're a reporter, you'd prefer to broadcast something more interesting and disruptive, like what tax returns preparation software TurboTax is doing: To make sure that you can do it on video.

Elasticity, therefore, created a disruptive campaign for H&R Block called the Million Moustache March. For this campaign, they tapped a tax policy professor to write a white paper arguing that people with moustache should have a $250 tax deduction because they are improving good looks in America. Then, they also held a physical march from early February until 15 April, which is the deadline for filing tax returns. On Facebook, they encouraged people to show support by putting a branded moustache on their photos. Every time a consumer did it, H&R Block donated to a charity called Millions from One, which offers water access to third-world countries.

Though it may sound a ridiculous argument, it was indeed disruptive to connect H&R block, moustaches, and a charitable endeavour altogether. It ended up being covered not just in the US but globally as well. It also generated great interaction online because it was different. In general, the campaign had amazing coverage although it was only a drop in the bucket from an investment standpoint (because H&R Block was also running traditional advertisements on paper media at the same time).

Aaron remarks that being disruptive can also mean doing something that is purely movement-oriented; something that can drive change and help improve humanity. It all comes down to finding a way to step out of the norm.

Listening to Your Audience, Being Aware of What's In

With their work with GoDaddy, a brand that was previously linked to racy advertising, Elasticity helped soften their image. The client wanted to appeal to the doers and entrepreneurs who need web services. For that campaign, Aaron and company used different colours and scenarios to bring to life different stories, which mostly involved female entrepreneurs.

With the wide array of problems people are forwarding to Elasticity, Aaron points out a common denominator to what they do: Listening.

Often, companies have these preconceived notions wherein they think that they already know what a customer wants; that they already know the answer to something. Instead of doing this, Elasticity steps back, gets rid of preconceived notions, looks at data and research about customers, and derives insights from that. He further emphasises that it's not that difficult and expensive to research what people think of a certain brand.

Even if a particular strategy doesn't appeal to your own sensibilities, you need to focus on how you're serving your audience. If you're trying to serve a specific demographic, it begins with throwing out any preconceived notions, looking at true data, and understanding what your audience really wants.

Apart from listening, another important thing to do is paying attention to pop culture. Even if Aaron doesn't know who Camila Cabello is, if he would sell a product to 17-year-old girls, he'd need to know about figures like her.

Being keen on what's in can be seen on Elasticity's Million Moustache March campaign. At the time of the campaign, young people everywhere were really getting into moustaches. The culture has evolved and there are a lot more people now with facial hair than in the past.

Part of Elasticity's approach when working with a brand is to identify which are the trends that they can jump on. This comes on top of what they can already do to make a campaign work with their client. So, it's about looking at data and resources, throwing preconceptions out the door, being realistic and diagnostic about what customers want, and thinking about how that ties with a certain pop culture phenomenon or technology.

The Power of Search

Traditionally, PR practitioners do not pay attention to search, which is a rather important aspect of digital marketing.

Though search algorithms constantly change, search has become the ultimate arbiter of everything. It helps people find things, determine whether they want to work for you, whether they want to move somewhere, or whether they want to purchase a product.

Based on experience, Aaron notes that search has been the most under appreciated aspect of reputation management of brand marketing. Everyone relies on search, whether it's Google or YouTube. Even Facebook and Amazon (where you can find his disruptively titled book, *F!!ck Your Formula: Why Following Rules Is the Worst Marketing Decision You'll Ever Make*) has search technology. Search couldn't be more important.

Chapter Nine
B2B Content Marketing.

Interview with Serbia-based Ugi Djuric; Co-Founder and CEO of Podino, Founder of Contenthorse.

Content that Gives Real Customers

95% of B2B SaaS companies do content marketing the wrong way. One of the main problems that Ugi's clients have is not getting a clear return on investment (ROI) on their content marketing efforts. They don't know how to produce content that gives them real customers – not just vanity metrics like traffic or search volume. At the end of the day, what matters is how much money their content brings to their business.

To generate such content, Ugi shares that there are two things you need to keep in mind:

The first one is the maturity of your company. Depending on which stage your company is – whether you're an early stage company or an enterprise with 50+ employees – your approach in content strategy should be different.

The second thing is the maturity or saturation of your market. If you search the marketing and sales industry, you'd find that there are millions of articles out there. However, if you will narrow it down to a more specific niche, for instance, marketing for real estate or injury law firms, it will be less saturated. And it will be easier for you to penetrate that market.

When working with early stage companies, or companies that don't have big resources and millions of revenue yet, Ugi and his team first write content dedicated to the bottom of the funnel. The bottom of the funnel includes those people who are ready to make a purchase; they only need a little more information on which vendor to choose. To make effective content for them, they incorporate keywords that these people use when searching for a particular product.

For example, when they worked with GetResponse (which has over a hundred competitors, including Mailchimp) and did keyword research, they found that Mailchimp alternatives has a search volume of 2000–3000 a month. To target people who are using that keyword, they advised creating an in-depth article about the best Mailchimp alternatives. The article included their client's product as one of the alternatives.

If you're an enterprise company, the approach will be different. You should produce content that can position you as a thought leader. You should offer new innovations in the way that the market thinks about your industry.

Proper Positioning and Messaging

Many companies make the mistake of positioning themselves in the market by emphasising their product features and specifications. However, the truth is, thousands of other companies are completely offering the same thing. For instance, there are many tools that provide what Mailchimp does. And 99% of them have the same features.

For Ugi, this is where proper positioning and messaging come in. To differentiate yourself from the competitors that arise daily, weekly, and monthly, saying that you have a better product is not enough. You have to differentiate yourself through your messaging.

First of all, you need to know who exactly is your target audience, which needs to be a specific group of people. You need to know where they are hanging out on the internet, what types of content they consume, and what words can be used to engage with them. From there, you can craft better messaging for your landing page and inject lead magnets into your content.

Founders of companies also have an important role to play, according to Ugi. Today, many founders are considered to be the main driver of growth for their respective businesses. Take, for example, Russell Brunson of marketing and sales tool ClickFunnels. He has authored a number of books and many of ClickFunnels' customers are people who came because of him – not because of their product. While there are other products better than theirs, Russell has been successful in positioning his company through himself.

Nonetheless, this capacity of the founder will be futile if you don't know who your dream customer persona is. It is only upon knowing your customer that you can write about big things and ideas and create a buzz around your name, your product, and your industry. One good example is what Slack, a messaging app for businesses, did when they were launched. They rolled out a public relations (PR) campaign that positioned themselves as a company that killed the email.

On the Effectiveness of Podcasts

When you're on the road at 70 miles per hour, you hardly notice the billboards that you drive past. The same is true on the content that you scroll through Instagram or LinkedIn.

However, with podcasts, you will have access to an audience who dedicate 20–30 minutes of their time to listen to the host and the guest. These are consumers who attentively listen and remember the things that you have to say. This is why Ugi – co-founder of Podino, which helps businesses get on top podcasts in their niche – considers this medium as one of the best ways to reach your dream customers and engage with them. It allows you to build a relationship with your audience and, over time, position yourself as their go-to choice when they're looking for a certain product.

While understanding the metrics of podcasts can be challenging, there are tools that can help. Listen Notes, for example, works like Google for podcasts where each podcast has a global rank. If your podcast has a global rank of 10%, it means that you are in the top 10% of the podcasters that they're ranking.

However, at the end of the day, it's not about the quantity of the people that hear you – it's about the quality.

Repurposing Content

No matter what industry you're in, everything comes down to creating content. And there are different types of content that you can create.

To help you be more efficient, repurposing is recommended. For example, if you have an article, you can repurpose that to create 10 social media posts or three newsletters, or five podcast episodes. If you have a podcast, you can use that audio material to create 10 other social media posts. Creating as much content as you can is helpful in your pursuit of becoming a leader in your industry and in your market.

There are several tools that you can use for content repurposing. Choosing which tools to use depends on which type of repurposed content you're planning to create. If you want to create social media posts from a podcast episode, you can use Wave.Video. For creating visuals and infographics, there is Canva. Effectively repurposing content entails getting creative. With creativity, you can take, for instance, one article and create five different LinkedIn posts or a Twitter thread for that.

Chapter Ten
Using Gated Content for Leads.

Interview with Israel-based Omri Hurwitz; Founder Omri Hurwitz Media, Podcast Host, Blogger at Times of Israel.

Any company can build their brand by themselves and work with an agency like Omri's once they want to scale things up.

Omri notes that one of the first tactics that can be used is to set up podcasts. This avenue offers an amazing networking environment, allowing users to reach many people. The second one is to write blogs and post thought leadership videos on LinkedIn, Facebook, and YouTube. The last one is to pitch to journalists and create a network of these professionals with specific niches. These are things that virtually everyone can start off with right now.

As content creation is easier said than done, Omri advises companies to kick things off with key players in their organisation. Let these people write about the things that come very naturally to them – and not those complicated articles or blog posts. They can use emotions and their own experiences from their profession, and let things flow from there. For example, a chief technology officer or a sales development representative can talk about their experiences working in their respective positions. Once blog and media articles are treated more like personal posts, these can snowball naturally and allow companies to write the way they really want to.

Ensuring Consistency of Voice

With different personas contributing content, how, then, can companies ensure that there is a consistency of voice? With the internet breaking that norm – wherein a company would only have one author, one press release channel, or one person dealing with external affairs – how can businesses obtain that consistent look, feel, and narrative?

According to Omri, the key is strategically tapping only two to four extroverts in the company. In a company, people would find that not a lot of employees are actually comfortable expressing themselves on social media or news coverages. Therefore, you only have to select a few who like being publicised and play on the strengths. Every company has these natural communicators who, given the platform, can market and brand themselves out well.

For employees who cannot write but can communicate orally, Omri encourages creating audio-format content. In recent years, the use of audio has significantly increased. For instance, there's a social media app called Clubhouse. It's a platform wherein instead of posting writings, you can simply talk, record your audio, and post the clips.

Given audio's effectiveness and emerging popularity, companies can leverage this trend and allow their people to talk about valuable things on record, and make a podcast out of them.

It's All About Advertising

Building a media company around a certain brand is one thing. But getting people to know that it exists is another.

For this, Omri has one tried-and-tested solution: Advertising. When you promote thought leadership pieces, podcasts, or blogs – that's a form of advertising. However, when it comes to advertising, there is no shortcut. If you've got a great piece of content, you need to get past the saturated market and advertise it to a very targeted niche.

For Business-to-Business (B2B) companies with a budget, Omri recommends advertising on LinkedIn and remarketing on Facebook (which has a wide audience). Meanwhile, for Business-to-Consumer (B2C) companies, he advises sticking out to Facebook, Instagram, and YouTube (which has a very low cost-per-mille or CPM).

Each of these platforms demands different budget allocations. Omri shares that the people who advertise on LinkedIn usually have a budget of $3000 to $15000. He recommends using 30% of that to advertise on content that promotes demand generation (e.g. thought leadership pieces). On Youtube and Facebook, spending $1500 per platform is a good place to start things off. What's important is to test these allocations and see if it works for you?

Compared to other platforms, LinkedIn charges higher advertisement rates because users can target specific people in specific companies. This narrowed-down approach can't be found anywhere else.

B2C companies can also promote on LinkedIn organically. For instance, if you have podcasts, you can cut a few clips from your episodes, promote them on the platform, and allow them to organically grow.

But if your company is already doing advertising but it's all about lead generation, Omri can come into the picture and help add ungated, creative content.

Meanwhile, if you're already doing both demand and lead generation, what Omri and company can do is to help you get quality media coverage, which completes the whole picture.

The point is, the minute you start advertising and you're doing it correctly, your company will grow – you will get more leads, improve brand awareness, and eventually increase revenue.

Gated Versus Ungated Content

Contents of a company's brand-awareness plan can be gated or ungated.

Gated content, as its name implies, refers to content wherein you'll ask your potential customers to fill out a form before getting access to the information you are providing. The form may entail asking for the user's phone number or email address. It's considered a lead generation strategy.

On the other hand, ungated content includes content that demands no commitment from potential clients. An audience can click on your link and read your content without leaving any contact information.

Omri recommends for companies to produce 70% ungated content and 30% gated content. The gated ones will be the re-marketing stuff. This will allow you to capture audiences who have already been exposed to your previous content, such as podcasts and blogs.

When it comes to tracking how content traffic is generated, tactically speaking, Omri shares the benefits of using Google

Analytics. The platform offers a feature where you can see where the traffic to your website is coming from. For example, if a New York Times article included a link to your website, you can track how much of your traffic can be attributed to that link.

On the philosophical side, Omri, however, notes that companies that are doing PR correctly won't need to let the numbers tell them how they are faring.

Role Models to Look Upon

If you're looking for companies or individuals to draw inspiration from when it comes to effectively building a brand, Omri mentions New York–based real estate expert Ryan Serhant. Through amazing PR and marketing tactics (he's virtually everywhere, from LinkedIn to YouTube), he was able to build a billion-dollar real estate business.

Another is Gary Vaynerchuck, who, in a way, has invented digital, personal branding. He is the chairman of Vayner X, which is an innovative media and communications holding company.

For companies, Omri cites Gong, a company that uses Artificial Intelligence (AI) to help clients increase their sales. The company, which has already mastered B2B marketing, actually even had an advertisement shown on Super Bowl.

Red Bull, on the other hand, is doing a great job doing influencer marketing projects.

When building your brand, think about how you can do so with multiple sources of content. Building a brand for your business is as important as operating the business itself.

Chapter Eleven
Leverage Online Events.

Interview with Spring, Texas-based Toni Kaufman; Founder and CEO of Standout Universe.

The key to getting yourself known to the online world is to establish authority. Toni points out the significance of having the credentials to prove you can be the go-to expert in a certain topic. We're in a community, a huge expanse, wherein almost everyone wants to make a difference.

Tapping Technology

For someone like Toni who used to work as a Microsoft technical evangelist, setting up conference calls via Polycom dialling, the online conferencing system is a mind-blowing concept. She particularly commends Zoom, a video conferencing platform that was at the right place at the right time.

Today, several webinar platforms emerge and grow daily. And it's really impressive how servers are able to handle online events without a hiccup or a glitch. Before, it took about half a million dollars to setup two rooms in two places to have a video conference. Fast forward to today, this service can be availed for only 30 bucks a month.

Gamification of Online Events

Toni says that the online events landscape has undergone what is called "gamification." People are now like the third or fourth generation of video game players.

Through gamification and Artificial Intelligence (AI), people can now use avatars and enter a conference centre, enquire at the front desk about what kind of events are ongoing, and attend a variety of these meetings at the same time – similar to what Toni has witnessed at a recent conference that made over a million dollars.

Nowadays, people are making some serious sales through online conferences. Technology has allowed audiences to attend events of their choice from the comfort of their homes.

Replicating Traditional Trade Shows Online

Toni and the rest of Standout Universe do the exact same things as what salespeople can expect during traditional trade shows, except that things are done online.

They still host VIP dinner parties before the event proper, conduct breakout rooms for lunch with their sponsors, and have the happy hour at the end of the day. Hosted on Zoom, they play music and games as well. One of her business partners, Linda Kane, was able to bring in an escape room of sorts to the said platform.

The important thing that they keep in mind is to execute what their clients want and even go beyond what is expected. For instance, they recently ran a 12-hour summit that featured giveaways and 20-minute talks on a Saturday. Due to popular demand, the summit got extended until Sunday.

Another helpful thing about online events is that they are more economical. Before virtual shows, someone would need to spend a minimum of $2500 per event to cover travel, accommodation, and food expenses. This is on top of the programme or product that he or she is going to invest in. Because the $2500 is eliminated in online events, people can now better afford to buy your programme.

Creating an Environment That Doesn't Aim for Perfection

With virtual conferences now booming, there's also an increasing demand for high-resolution digital assets.

For Toni, it's not all about creating the perfect online setup or environment. It is the imperfections that attract people to work with you, not perfection. It's the ability to create a common character that people can resonate with. Because when you host a summit or a podcast, you become the authority figure and the go-to expert.

Maximising LinkedIn

Business-to-Business (B2B) companies can also take advantage of online events.

Toni recommends promoting an event on LinkedIn. When she created a B2B Thanksgiving event on the platform, her post earned responses from around 8000 people. Afterwards, she exported the list to create a mailing list and develop a campaign from that: Ask if they're interested in your service and tag your list according to the responses.

What B2B companies need to ensure is that they have a landing page or a community page to start with (may it be on Twitter, Instagram, or Clubhouse). You can start small and use free tools like Facebook Live, in order for you to be seen. Then build your audience and participate and join other communities to build your list faster.

Chapter Twelve
Virtual Events Online Forever.

Interview with Mia Masson, Paris; Content Director at Swapcard.

Mia Masson works for a company called Swapcard that was started in 2013 by three French men who were childhood friends, and Swapcard is slowly revolutionising the way that people hold events. Surprisingly, none of the founders had a background in technology or in events management, but one day, they decided to start a company together in that industry because they found that there's a demand on the market for swapping business cards. They thought, "Who's still going home from an event or a meeting with physical business cards and typing details into their computers?" They figured one could misspell an email address, lose the business card, it could get wet, and then you lost your contact, so they decided to create an app where you could scan a business card and all that info would be directly saved on your device.

After a few years and a few funding rounds, though their idea didn't work out, they had the resilience and the stamina to keep going, so they decided to completely change their product. For them, the execution was more important than the idea anyway. After a while, they decided that the market was in need of an online event platform. Originally, they were handling physical events. They managed huge conference centres where it would sometimes be difficult to find the right booth, so they made an interactive map and had an online agenda. Early on, the value of artificial intelligence (AI) came to light. They wanted to use AI to connect people with each other and with the right sessions to watch according to their data, their profiles, their interests.

That was going great, and then COVID happened. Mia says they've come to realise that there is a need to evolve and adapt their product once again. This time, it needed to all go online and to cater to virtual events, as there wasn't much of a choice. That's their strategic vision, and they hope to have events changed for the better. These long-lasting changes they're implementing are going to make all events hybrid models in the future. It is their belief that the value of technology in events, shows, conferences, and the like cannot be lost because it's making people more data-driven. It's helping them increase ROI, and it's connecting people globally especially in a time of need like now when people can't see each other. People are missing human contact from being in lockdown, and so being able to connect with a global audience and a global network of peers is very valuable.

There are two views to it: some people like the physical contact and really miss it, while others miss it but can find replacements online. Swapcard caters to that with features on their event platform that allows chatting with other attendees, taking part in live discussions during a session, polling, and content which can make the session more interactive. It's a great way to network with people, make new contacts, and approach people through messaging online. Swapcard caters to clients big and small, including SMEs. The virtual events platform works with associations like IAEE for an event called Expo! Expo! They work with NAMM which has a "Believe in Music" event. They also cater to smaller events, and those are just as interesting for them to take part in.

How to Create an Event Using Swapcard

To create an event with Swapcard, first decide whether to turn a current event into a virtual one or to create a new virtual event, then think about what's needed to make it happen. Key aspects of this would be a good platform, a place where everyone can come together and follow all the news, content, data, and the people in the events. Once there's an event platform that meets your needs, look at your content, because when going virtual, content is king. If you are at a physical show and you're watching all these different sessions and speakers, if it's not to your taste or you find it boring, you could simply leave or attend a different session. With virtual events, you could just exit that tab at any point if it's boring, so content has got to be extremely valuable and engaging that it makes viewers or listeners want to stay and pay attention.

Once you have great content, great speakers, a great platform, and all the other tools like registration, then think about engagement and how your audience can meet, what you can offer to both attendees and exhibitors. With Swapcard, organisers get online support that's available 24/7. They conduct trainings as well. After that, the next steps are just to ensure that the speakers are engaging and that the exhibitors are going out there and getting leads.

One of the challenges for speakers at virtual events Mia shared is that it's not necessarily possible to see who's currently watching, who's exiting, who's messaging whilst they're supposed to be paying undivided attention to the event. Luckily, Swapcard tracks the activity and behaviour of everyone on the platform, and this is all GDPR-friendly. Everyone that enters and uses the platform agrees to this. At the end, it's very helpful for organisers to become data-driven and know where to invest. Swapcard provides them with detailed data so they can analyse who watched which session and for how long, which systems were the best ranked, which speakers were ranked the best, how many messages were exchanged, how many calls were planned, etc. The speaker also has a unique view of seeing the live chats, the question and answer portion, and the polls. They can see people chatting in the live discussion and asking questions. They can see who's interacting which would be similar to seeing faces in the audience.

Virtual Events Are Here to Stay, Literally

Community building is one most important aspects of an event, and at Swapcard, they believe it can happen online, but there must be opportunities for it. The platform needs to be open for longer than just two or three days in a year. At a physical event, it's normally only two to three days. At the end, you say your goodbyes, and if you remember, you'll connect with each other on LinkedIn and maybe chat. But with an online event platform, it can be open a month prior to the event. People can already start looking at the attendee lists, the exhibitor list, stock networking, making meetings, and it can be open weeks or months after the event has finished, so the content that's in demand is free for people to rewatch, or if they missed it due to timezone issues. They can keep networking basically.

Mia says that eventually, platforms or online communities will have to be open 365 days a year, as this builds a much greater sense of community than people travelling from show to show and losing touch with one another. The beauty of Swapcard is that you can connect any platform to it. In terms of registration, they sync with all major registration tools in the market today. That means you can upload or download all the attendees, exhibitors, and speakers with one click. In terms of content, you can do live streaming, or you can do pre-recorded, existing content. As long as the video player and streaming tool has an iframe player built in, it can be embedded onto the platform. Native players like YouTube and Vimeo can be automatically put in easily. That creates a very efficient way of repurposing one's content.

Say you're an attendee that wants to network and meet new people. Thanks to Artificial Intelligence (AI), it will send you pop-up recommendations of people to meet, and you have the option to say yes or no, sort of like using a dating app. The more you say yes or no, the better the understanding of the AI becomes in terms of your tastes and interests, and then it will send more accurate contacts that can be downloaded at any time, even once the event has finished. It's possible to even rate contacts and add notes to contacts for contextualisation, which is important for exhibitors.

Lower Cost, but Greater Return

In the past, with physical events, even with the biggest booth, it still didn't guarantee leads. The cost of lead acquisition was high, but with not a lot of guarantees. Now with virtual events, the cost of lead acquisition is much lower. There are no travel expenses and no need to pay for a physical booth, so the overhead cost is much lower, but on average, you get three times more attendees than any physical event. On top of that, they're global attendees and they can connect at any time zone. You can talk to more than one person at the same time, which you can't do at a physical booth. So with virtual events, the cost of lead acquisition is lower, but the potential is much higher.

The chance encounters or random acts of business that are often pivotal with going to a show are one of the most challenging aspects of going virtual, and that sometimes translates to serendipity happening right in the chat box. The industry is still figuring out ways to make it as valuable as in-person chance meetings, and online, there are tools for it. Coffee breaks, happy hours after events, online roundtables, or speed meeting features are great ways to make this happen.

Online event management does require a whole new skill set, which is why event organisers should invest in training their teams on that immediately, because even with event managers, that's not going to be sustainable, according to Mia. They need to learn to do it on their own. If you choose not to have a dedicated project manager which is your go-to person for events and someone who is with you 24/7, there's a very thorough training process and support all the way through from way before the events, as they do understand that the platform can be difficult to grasp. That's why they have many tools available including webinars, demos, and calls to train clients.

Chapter Thirteen
Your Own TV Station.

Interview with Cleveland Ohio–based Audrey M. Wiggins; CEO of the Mason Wiggins Media Group.

Creating Her Network

Audrey hosts shows twice a week and simultaneously works as a full-time administrator and a branding and technology consultant.

One of her programs is "Make Something Happen," which aims to promote what people are doing. Similar to what The UnNoticed podcast is all about, it puts the spotlight on deserving figures such as local businesses and entrepreneurs, ministers, and politicians among others. It's a mix of a showcase and an infomercial, and by the end of each episode, guests can promote their website or any other offering. The second programme is "The Audrey Wiggins Show." It is more into public affairs wherein she features human interest stories.

MWMG.tv started when Audrey realised that her shows needed to have a platform. From there, things snowballed and grew into what would become a network: She started asking other people to get featured, and people came up to her as well. Though these individuals aren't well-known, her internet-hosted network gave her and these people the opportunity to be seen around the world.

Democratising Communication Through Technology

The UnNoticed podcast showcases how technology is able to democratise communication. Regardless of the size of your audience or your message, you can distribute your own content through technology.

For Audrey, building your own network and streaming from home is practically easy. All you really need is your computer. Even through a tablet or a mobile phone, you can upload and set up a stream.

As she also offers domain names and other related things through Altogether Marketing LLC dba Mason Wiggins Media Group, she could get her own server. With MWMG.tv, she could upload content and give people on-demand access to them by simply logging on to the website.

If you have your own WebTV, you don't have to compete with other content or have unwanted advertisements. It is also possible to make money through affiliate links and pre-roll ads among others.

Uploading content can also be automated through built-in software. So, for example, even if you have recorded your show on Wednesday, you can schedule it to air on Friday at 7 p.m. Eastern Time. After that, the uploaded content can be accessed on-demand. For MWMG.tv, Audrey uses WebTV Solutions. Everything is self-contained in there except for the fact that you have to put it on your own server (in which Audrey's service can be of help).

When it comes to licences, she pays for the $497 package so she can accommodate a number of channels. However, there are also lower-tier licences worth around $100 that allow you to run one channel. The choice of licencing depends on your goal. You can opt for a low-tier package and upgrade it anytime.

Growing the Organic Way

When it comes to content, the creation is relatively the easier part – especially for creatives who were simply born to do such things. The more difficult aspect is distributing it and reaching the right audience.

For Audrey, though, the best way to grow is through organic means. Nowadays, people can buy likes and subscribers. However, this does not guarantee engagement. There won't be follow-up comments, likes, or shares after that one time that you've bought them. While building traffic organically will take time – let's say, you'll have a starting audience of only 5–30 – you can be sure that these people are really listening to and sharing your content. They are genuinely engaged. And that is worth more than 300 or 3000 people who do not engage.

Over time, traffic will grow. What Audrey advises is for you to be consistent in creating content, to know who you're trying to attract, and to promote persistently. Promoting on the Internet today is not that expensive (You can spend $30 per week for a show). The key is identifying who your audience is and being specific when it comes to demographics.

Audrey advertises and directly promotes her station. At the same time, she uses other social channels such as Facebook and Twitter to share links directing people to her content on MWMG.tv.

Opportunities to Earn

WebTV offers a world of opportunity when it comes to earning revenue. One is the subscription revenue model wherein a user needs to pay, for example, $1.99 a month to access your content. Another is the pay-per-view, which is similar to what broadcasting networks do during major events.

For MWMG.tv, Audrey uses a built-in system to collect earnings. But others shouldn't be limited to that. If you want to use Patreon or any other network or gateway to receive payments, you can do so.

She also earns through affiliate links. For instance, she works with entrepreneurs and authors (which ended up to be a good affiliate to sign on to because there, she gets up to thousands of affiliates). She includes their affiliate links not just on her WebTV network but on her newsletters as well. She also uses Amazon affiliate links to further reach wider audiences.

Changing Trends

Over time, different sectors and industries experience different buoyancy because of technology.

Today, the real estate and insurance sectors are booming. On the other hand, the beauty and barbering industry seems to be hard-hit. In social media, the audio-driven Clubhouse app, which offers intimacy and newness to users, has exploded recently. As many organisations have started focusing on their internal operations, many opportunities for web design and marketing have also emerged.

However, even if you're new to your industry or you're already a veteran, Audrey points out that the important thing is to have that constant need to grow.

Chapter Fourteen
Case: Joking Apart, Amazon Ranking.

| *Interview with Morry Morgan, Melbourne; Group CEO at The Rubber Chicken.*

Morry Morgan is an entrepreneur and author who now brands himself on LinkedIn as "The Wisecracking entrepreneur." The development of Morry's personal skill set started when he took up microbiology in university. He was in the Australian Army as a member of the Medical Corps and as a microbiologist in that capacity, so there was no way he would have ever imagined that his skill sets would be in training, in China, in stand-up comedy, and in entrepreneurship. He'd use a microbiologist to describe what he's learned, and that is, "Chance favours the prepared mind." Louis Pasteur, the French microbiologist coined this, and Morry absolutely agrees. He says the more input you give yourself through life experiences, whether they're intentional or not, the more ready you are when an opportunity presents itself.

He calls himself "wisecracking," because he likes to consider himself relatively intelligent but with a sense of humour. He sees opportunities where others have not. Currently, Morry has a web series entitled "Is This Thing On?" The name was derived because anyone who grabs hold of a microphone, particularly in comedy, says that especially if they're a bit unsure of themselves. Only the first two episodes are on YouTube while the entire six episodes will go to Apple TV. Morry says this whole thing is actually a marketing and PR exercise. What is the purpose of this PR and marketing? It is for the stand-up comedy school he founded called the School of Hard Knock Knocks.

The School of Hard Knock Knocks

Morry came up with his stand-up comedy school through a motto that he developed in Shanghai. Go big or go home, he says. When you're in China, everything's difficult, and nothing's impossible. That's what he thought with the School of Hard Knock Knocks. They only have a few competitors, and in order to differentiate themselves from the market and create a barrier to entry for anyone else thinking about it, he created a TV show. In terms of setting it all up, Morry befriended a director who turned out to be an ex-stand-up comedian and was even on a TV show himself. So, when the idea came to Morry to make a show, that friend was the first person that came to mind. He happened to also live about 2 km from where Morry was living at the time, so he considers it quite serendipitous.

When it comes to his show, Morry says there are two ways of looking at it. If you're a small business and you're thinking, "Oh, this is beyond me," Morry's here to give you some numbers. $50 000 AUD was spread out over two years, so it wasn't a huge chunk of change in one go. The show went through a couple different ideas, but eventually, they settled on a factual show versus one that was scripted. That meant that they were a fly on the wall. They had 10 wannabe stand-up comedians from different backgrounds. They had a couple of people in their 50s, some in their 20s, and then people in their 30s and 40s. They had an equal amount of men and women. Some were from Sydney, some from Adelaide, and some from Melbourne. It was basically a good mix of personality types and backgrounds, and they put them in a room for five days. The activity was to learn stand-up comedy, and they occasionally had a relatively famous guest comedian.

Regarding PR and marketing, Morry has always been a big fan of Key Opinion Leaders (KOLs), so they embedded names like Greg Fleet and Glynn Nicholas, a great Welsh-born Aussie comedian and performer, and they took a day for each of the five nights. Morry's team filmed them, and what they filmed them doing was quite unusual. For example, on one of the nights, Mayumi Nobetsu, a Japanese-born Australian comedian, took them to do life drawing. That's nude painting to the layman, but then she told them that everyone had to get naked as well. She forced a group of 10 strangers to strip off except for an apron (so you wouldn't get paint on you), and that was the second episode. You get to see them learn stand-up comedy, but you also get to see them go through these emotional challenges and rollercoasters. They have a behavioural analyst as well who does hypnosis on one of the people, Steve Mackey, and makes him forget his name. Generally, it's a bit more organised than just walking into the factory floor and pressing the record button.

What Made Morry Pick Apple TV

Morry says they actually chose Apple TV by accident. Initially, he thought they would be able to get onto the ABC or the Australian Broadcasting Corporation (or the BBC of Australia). But unfortunately, the timing was wrong. They were going through turmoil, a new CEO, and no one wanted to take a chance on an Australian unknown. So, they looked at alternatives, and Morry reached out to Netflix, Apple TV, YouTube Premium, and he found out through Apple TV that almost anyone can get their own show on Apple TV. You just have to go through a company that augments and brings everything together. They ensure that the quality of the video is great, that any captions are included, and that the format itself is the right format for Apple to stream.

In Australia, there are five such companies, so Morry spoke to them. They said, "Look, this is what we can do for you. There's a cost." Morry believed that at the end of the day, in terms of PR, if they had given it to the ABC, they'd pay them a chunk of change, stick it in a warehouse forever, and then Morry will have lost that PR opportunity, so they decided they'd rather put it on YouTube, at least for the first two episodes plus a teaser and run that continuously. Now, they've got over 5000 views on both. In fact, the trailer on Facebook has got over 13 000 views, and then they built up that subscription for people watching them on Youtube, and then they'll put all episodes onto Apple TV.

The big advantage of using Apple TV is that it allows them to get ranked and pulled onto IMDb which is the Internet Movie Database. This creates an IMDb account or listing for them, of which Amazon owns and has one of the highest authorities in SEO alongside IMDb, so by adding "Is This Thing On?" to IMDb produced by the School of Hard Knock Knocks and the fact that this show is a comedy, they're immediately attaching the brand of the School of Hard Knock Knocks to the word comedy at a massive level in terms of SEO, which is the goal of PR. That then gives Morry the chance to put it on YouTube and gain views, and they can link that to Facebook ads. Currently, Morry says they're paying $0.08 per view at the moment on Facebook which is unheard of, because one typically has to pay anywhere between $0.40–1.60 minimum to get a view. Remember, it's essentially an ad. It's a show about his stand-up comedy school, but the great thing about Facebook is that they can do geo-targeting and send those $0.08 to people in Melbourne, Sydney, or Adelaide.

On the School of Hard Knock Knocks website, they use a tool called Proof Factor, which Morry heard about on a podcast, and that led him to start investigating. Proof Factor is a free tool that can be attached to WordPress sites, and it's a tool Morry recommends. Morry also has Google My Business for three venues around Australia, and he's got five-star ratings. To get his customers to write reviews, he simply asked them. The School of Hard Knock Knocks is a community, and so for each review, he thanks the customer who wrote it, and that reminds them. Anything to note about his business is they don't actually have a location. They use the services of venues. They play with the algorithm to be listed within an existing venue, because they're a service. To get around the technicalities that Google My Business requires, such as a postcard address, every time Morry does a show in a venue, he just gives them a call and says, "Do you mind if we list in your venue?" and they say they're perfectly fine with it. This is why they have venues listed in Adelaide, Melbourne, and Sydney. Their competitors started doing it as well, but they don't ever have as many reviews as social proof.

The idea of making your own TV series, which then becomes an infomercial, is very powerful, and Morry is one of the few people who have been able to do that, but by sharing how he has done it, may be an option for your business too.

Chapter Fifteen
Case: Punk Rock Live.

▌ *Interview with Drew Stone, New York; Filmmaker and musician.*

A filmmaker and a musician, Drew Stone grew up in the American hardcore punk scene as a teenager. And the ethos of that scene is do-it-yourself: You get up, go out, and make it happen. If you're into music, don't wait for a record company. Put a record out yourself, make flyers, and push through with your own shows.

Filming Music Videos

Though he came from a family of filmmakers, Drew's career focused on filming music videos.

It began when he was the vocalist of Antidote, one of the early hardcore bands in New York. During his stint on the band, he got to play and meet a lot of other musical acts. Soon, people started asking him to do their music videos.

One of his films is called the "New York Hardcore Chronicles" and is currently available on Amazon Prime. He has also done music documentaries, one of which was on Netflix for a couple of years.

Over the years, his film catalogue has helped him earn a fanbase.

The Birth of "New York Hardcore Chronicles Live"

Somebody once invited Drew to guest on a show. Upon guesting, that person also invited him to subscribe to his YouTube channel and follow him on Facebook.

This instance made Drew realise that he has also his own following on YouTube (which is Stone Films NYC, with around 11 000 subscribers as of writing) and on Facebook (which is New York Hardcore Chronicles, with 90 000 followers). And with the pandemic prompting him to be locked down for a while, he started his own show titled "New York Hardcore Chronicles Live."

Drew put his show on a platform called StreamYard. It's similar to Zoom but you need to pay to avail of a certain tier. In his case, he's paying $24.95 a month to broadcast his show on three platforms: his YouTube channel, the "New York Hardcore Chronicles" Facebook page, and his personal Facebook account. If you want to have your show broadcast on five or six platforms, you can pay for a higher tier.

"New York Hardcore Chronicles Live" is a live video streaming show (episodes can be viewed on-demand on his YouTube channel afterwards). It airs at 3 p.m. New York Time, equivalent to 8 p.m. in Europe, which is a prime time.

When he broadcasts live, there's also a live chat room wherein people from European countries like Italy and Germany are interacting. By a stroke of luck, as Drew calls it, he was able to garner a worldwide audience; a global community of hardcore punk aficionados.

Using Hashtags, Ensuring Brand Continuity

Drew doesn't regard himself as a casual music lover, but a music historian; a music archaeologist. What began as a passion became an obsession of sorts.

When he delved into filmmaking and started putting out clips on YouTube, he carried the same spirit and would always include tags and hashtags to make his content more visible.

Apart from tagging, another important part of promotion is brand continuity.

For instance, his brand is Stone Films NYC, which is in line with his name, Drew Stone. It's also the name of his YouTube channel and film production company. Meanwhile, his Facebook page is called "New York Hardcore Chronicles." One of his films, which bears the same name, is essentially about the hardcore scene that he talks about on his Facebook page. For his live streaming show, he used the name "New York Hardcore Chronicles Live."

More Than the Sum of All Parts

Drew shares that there are different things that enable him to be financially stable. And it's more than the sum of all parts.

One is his Patreon page. Patreon is a platform that allows people to support an artist through a multi-tier system. In Drew's case, he offers a $2, $5, $10, $25, and $100-dollar tier; each tier offers different incentives and products to his supporters.

He calls his Patreon followers, which is now close to 200, a community within the community. In this community, he invites people to support and watch his show and offers unique content – he uploads never-before-seen photos and video clips, and even does short, private shows.

Another thing is sponsorship. Drew's sponsors are still in keeping with the ethos and brand of what he does. For example, two of his sponsors are a record store in Denver, Colorado, and a comic book store in New York. When a sponsor approached him for an exclusive sponsorship deal – which is something he's not ready for yet – he turned it down.

Apart from Patreon and sponsorship, he also has YouTube monetisation.

Moreover, Drew has a merchandise line available through the platform called Teespring. Teespring has a fulfilment house in China and they can put your logo on all kinds of products and ship them anywhere in the world.

His products include t-shirts, sweatshirts, and mugs, and some more unique items such as girls' leggings and shower curtains. He incorporates links to his merchandise on his show to promote them.

Building His Network

Luckily for Drew, talent and talent management runs in the family. Sister Kelly Stone-Binday runs Integrated Marketing Management and drives Drew's media engagement including placing him on podcasts like The UnNoticed Show. She was the one who encouraged him to go on as many podcasts as possible because it helps in cross-promoting things. Sometimes sibling support can be really instrumental in building a business.

PART FIVE
Know

Chapter One
Introduction.

"Through great input, you get great output."
— RZA

The ultimate measurement of my success in China has been the commercial results and that some of the events and brands have continued their momentum after I have left, which means that we built brands to last. I've always kept simple measures of performance across the business from the obvious ones like cash flow, sales leads, media coverage and now social media metrics. We have to engage in measurement as the best guide to our future decisions.

It seems an obvious point to say that we should know more about the performance of our public relations activities. The good news is that digital technology now allows for much greater analysis with Artificial Intelligence (AI) tools which can track sentiment, stance, and relativity. The "second golden age" of marketing technology offers over 8000 tools to us, which is a bit overwhelming really, and so I've invited some experts to share their insights here. The key point that I'd like to share is that these significant results only come because of implementing a solid and structured content creation and amplification plan.

Guests on The UnNoticed Show discussed many fascinating forms of measurement, which now extend beyond statistics into analysis to form decision making. In reviewing the podcasts in the Know category I came to see it is an area of marketing which has become so much more robust since the days of Advertising Value Equivalent (AVE) and the Barcelona principles laid down by the industry. This is because of big data, AI and also our control of our own channels for amplification. As you'll read, the impact of technology is that we no longer need to just look at historical data, the tools available provide predictive and contextual analysis which help in the entire life cycle of the content creation strategy, but there is still a place for simple email surveys.

Chapter Two
Second Golden Martech Age.

Interview with Scott Brinker, Cambridge Massachusetts; VP of Platform Ecosystem HubSpot, Editor of Martech.com.

Agility and Low-Cost Development

When it comes to what he thinks technology can do for the small business owner, Scott says he's biased on this, but he believes that the marketing technology revolution has served small businesses far greater than it has served large businesses. Large businesses have always had large technology budgets, and while they sometimes have the challenge on how quickly they can change and adapt, which is perhaps one of the downsides of a larger organisation, they could certainly spend money on it. When it comes to the large marketing and e-commerce platforms, for years, they were very expensive propositions. But what's happened over the past couple decades, he says, is the cost of developing software has dropped so dramatically, thanks to all these cloud platforms like AWS or Microsoft, Azure, and all these open source projects.

Creative software developers now confer a fraction of cost, create a great product, sell that at a very different price point, and help you build a great business. As a result, entrepreneurs have started building tools that marketers and salespeople at smaller companies can take advantage of, and they can now afford the technology. But because they're also small companies and they're entrepreneurial, they tend to be a bit more agile in how they actually adapt and experiment with that technology than some of their larger competitors.

Scott believes the adoption of these platforms has accelerated in recent years, mostly because small businesses are adopting marketing technology sometimes without even really thinking about it. Most of them start with wanting to build a website, so they might do something with Squarespace or Wix. All of a sudden, they realise they could use a CRM. That's why one of HubSpot's strategies has been to offer a free CRM that a lot of small businesses can use. And so without really thinking about needing a technology strategy, SMEs are creating their own websites, utilising a CRM application, and developing their own email system to stay in touch with people. It's become a part of daily life.

The "Second Golden Age of Martech"

In one of his articles, Scott mentioned "the second golden age of martech." He says it began with around 100–200 companies offering marketing technology, which at the time seemed like a lot.

But over the past 10 years, because of those absence of barriers to entry and software, the landscape of marketing technology solutions has grown to thousands, and they were able to map out 8000 companies, which was still by no means comprehensive, because he heard from all the people they've somehow missed. Evidently, there is an explosion of technology. The challenge, however, was that most of those technologies grew independently.

If a non-technical business owner wanted to bring several of them together, it was often on their shoulders to figure out how to, for instance, integrate a CRM or email marketing platform to a website, and that hindered adoption for a lot of folks. One of the things he talked about in that trend for the second golden age is that the platforming of marketing technology is being highlighted. He likens it to a phone with this universe of apps that can be downloaded onto it, and they work because iOS and Android are designed as a platform. In the marketing technology space, many of the large marketing companies like HubSpot, Salesforce, Adobe, are starting to shift their product strategy to more platforms. They're working with more specialised martech apps and making it easier to plug in. Ultimately, this is about getting business owners to a place where they can harness these different technologies without having to be a systems integrator himself or herself.

Five Things Every Business Should Have When Going Online

For every business owner that's starting out on their journey to digitalising their marketing, Scott believes there are four or five core capabilities that pretty much every business needs. The first thing is a website. There needs to be a way that people can find the business online, where the company can share content and get discovered through search engines. The second is a CRM, which doesn't have to be super sophisticated. It could simply serve as a common database to keep track of all customers and prospective customers and how those relationships evolve. The next thing that's needed is an email marketing solution. These are also what they call marketing automation platforms, because it's not just about sending out emails to everyone at the same time. This is for when the business owner starts to get a little bit more clever and discovers that there are trigger moments for individual customers or prospects when they're sent a specific email.

Next, every business will want some way of managing their social media, and Scott's not just talking about being on Facebook or Twitter. That might be part of it, but Scott is referring to simply paying attention to reviews that customers are saying about your company in different communities and forums and sites. This is so that when people are talking about you, or they're looking to engage with you, you're able to hear them and represent yourself. The fifth ingredient depends on the nature of the business, but there's usually some sort of e-commerce layer to it. For a consumer business, the ability to transact and deliver certain goods or products to customers would be very useful. In B2B, that's still a little less common, but nowadays, things continue to change rapidly. More and more B2B-oriented businesses are doing transactions with customers online. If a business has these five, that's a pretty complete set of digital capabilities.

Another key aspect is a strategy to manage the workflow and the content within that universe. When it comes to managing this, which was a job companies didn't really have before, the most important consideration is how to engage with the audience effectively. Setting aside the technical details of operation and execution, why would people want to visit your website? What value are you trying to provide for them? Why should people talk about your products positively on social media? Who is your tribe? Who is your target audience?

In the digital world, competition is, as they say, just a click away. So, on one hand, it's an advantage for companies in that you can compete in almost any market if you want. On the other hand, you have to be really clear on your strategy of why customers should pick you and not the other options in that field. A lot of small businesses are getting started in implementation, and this is seen when they work with small digital agencies that are serving SMEs and getting them up to speed on what needs to be done and for a modest price point.

In terms of case studies on how companies have gone from offline to online and how that's impacted them, what challenges they faced, and how they overcame those with or without an agency or maybe through guidance from HubSpot itself, Scott suggests checking out HubSpot as they have lots of case studies on there, and picking one that you feel is best aligned to your particular industry. For an existing business that is looking to add this new digital layer, Scott says the first step is understanding how the existing customers want to interact with the brand and what they are looking for.

AI and Budget for the Small Business Owner

An advantage of being a small business is the more intimate relationship with the customers. One can start by simply speaking with them and asking, "How can we serve you better? What would you like?" It really emphasises understanding the rationale behind all the actions of the company. Once there's that clarity, then the ability to hire someone or engage one of these agencies to help becomes easier. There are even some agencies now that will do some of this work on a contingency basis. They will put their money where their mouth is.

One of the areas that's getting traction nowadays is AI, and Scott's opinion on the impact of AI on Martech is it's a really fascinating topic to begin with. When people talk about AI and marketing, they're actually usually talking about a form of machine learning that essentially looks at a whole collection of data. It determines what the signals are that indicate a certain set of customers who have a higher propensity to purchase, and it helps predict which customers will have the greatest lifetime value. Now that computing and data storage are so cheap, with the help of these machine-learning algorithms, all this digital data can be analysed and predictions can be made that will identify where to prioritise time. Many companies now use these predictive algorithms without even really thinking about it as deploying AI. It almost just becomes a feature in the software they're using. These more generative AI models that have now reached a level of sophistication where they may not be writing Shakespeare, however they're able to generate a lot of viable creative output from modelling on whatever you point them to. And so, Scott's not sure if we're quite at the point where we're going to just turn the whole thing over to those machines, but the idea of marketers using these tools in partnership with the algorithms to generate new ideas and then choose, craft, and iterate will accelerate quickly in the next couple of years.

In terms of the budget required to get started and move up the martech chain, Scott says there are now a lot of solutions for small businesses, and these are often presented in a freemium model, which is perfect for those who are just getting started and want to try it out but don't have much data or content running through it. Once the businesses start to get traction, a lot of them then offer packages at affordable starter prices. It's not unusual for these starter prices to be under $100 a month for some of these tools. And then as the business grows, and more and more is done through these digital platforms, then you will get to a place where you will pay more as well. The great thing about these freemium models in the way so many Martech companies have structured them is you really only end up starting to pay a meaningful amount at the point in time that you've actually now started to see it work for your business and you've decided to scale it, and that's a great relationship to have.

Chapter Three
Choosing the Right Martech.

> *Interview with Frans Riemersma, Amsterdam, North Holland, Netherlands; Founder of the MartechTribe.*

As a son of a radiologist, growing up in Holland, Frans Riemersma was taught to value functionality over features. Now an established marketing technologist, the Top 10 Martech influencer in Europe and founder of MartechTribe shares valuable insights on how you can leverage Martech solutions to augment your business' marketing efforts.

The 30-Minute Rule

People often make the mistake of looking for marketing technology solutions right away. However, Frans points out that it's important to understand first what you're trying to solve. If you know what your goal or aim is, formulate it in one sentence. For example, "I want to set up a LinkedIn campaign," "I want to set up a calendar," or "I want to get a better view of who's visiting my website."

Afterwards, go online, search up for a tool that will help you meet your goal, and check out the free trial. If, within 30 minutes, you haven't achieved your goal yet then it means that the tool is not intuitive or not doing the job for you.

Trends Your Business Might Not Want to Miss Out

Frans mentions four Martech trends that businesses can adapt.

First is to gather your clients in one place with a Customer Relation Management (CRM) platform. This is how you can cross and upsell and make money more efficiently. Today, there are free tools that you can use, such as Agile CRM, Close.io, and HubSpot. These can provide a lot of services even to entrepreneurs and small businesses.

The next one is to automate your lead generation (one tool you can use is LinkedIn automation). Leads refer to people who aren't your client yet but have the potential to be one. After generating them, the next step is to have your leads in one place. HubSpot and Agile CRM also offer lead management tools.

The third trend is to understand what your clients are doing across different channels. This is where Customer Data Platforms (CDPs) help. Big corporations, for example, use CDPs and customer journey tools to understand their customers' behaviours across the entire spectrum of their channels – how they flow from another. This way, you can give your customers the right message (e.g. offer the shorter messages on mobile and the bigger ones on the web). Some of the customer journey tools that Frans mentions are Heap.io, Woopra, and Mixpanel.

While these three trends are already being done by corporations and can be applicable for small-scale businesses as well, Frans shares a fourth trend that has not been widely used yet: to personalise content. With AI tools such as MonkeyLearn, you can put all reviews, comments, and emails sent by customers into one document and analyse which are positive, negative, or neutral. You can also identify five or 10 topics that your customers talk about the most.

From there, you can make sure that your content reflects the needs of your customers. If you want to create a copy that's gender-specific or neutral, there are also tools like Textmetrics that can do just that.

What About the Data?

Given the different tools that you can use, data can oftentimes be overwhelming.

Frans advises starting looking into your clients: Who are your clients? What about their firmographics – are they Business-to-Business (B2B) or Business-to-Consumer (B2C) companies? Afterwards, identify the clickbait across these channels then examine the words that they commonly use. After pulling out the keywords, incorporate them in your Google AdWord campaign. These words would be effective as they are basically generated by the public – your audience and your clients.

The Democratisation of Marketing Technology

Scott Brinker, a leading figure in the Martech space, has previously mentioned that technology today is now being commoditised.

Before, Frans shares that you would need to hire and brief a developer to help you manage your data. With this process becoming more taxing, professionals (including Frans) started doing things themselves. And with the democratisation of marketing technology, you can now use online no-code and low-code tools such as Zapier and Blender.io in lieu of a third-party developer.

These platforms also allow you to create workflows and your customer data flow. For instance, if you get a new website visitor from a specific country, with a specific background, these tools can help you enrich such lead information (e.g. identity which company does your visitor belong to based on IP address). These can also help you automatically send data from your site's form submissions to your Agile CRM account, populate it there and put them into specific buckets. With this technology, you can send out personal emails and even address them on the chat function of your website.

Why Engage with Your Audience

Websites are designed to help businesses with their search engine optimisation and marketing endeavours. They help people be found.

When asked about the content heaviness of a website, Frans notes that it has nothing to do with informing your audience but with attracting them. Based on the AIDA model (AIDA stands for Attention, Interest, Desire, and Action), informing and attracting audiences are separate things.

But if you really want people to come to your website, the key is to chat and engage with them. Drift, which is a brilliant chat programme, uses AI that allows you to create a chat flow. Similar to an email flow, you can initiate a conversation, automate your response (e.g. if they don't respond, you can remind them of what they can do to reach you out; if they respond, you can provide a particular corresponding answer). If you're into Martech auditions, an example of a chat flow that you can use is to ask your website visitor how many people do they have in their marketing team. If it's above 10, you can offer them your service.

With these tools, you don't have to be awake 24/7. You can simply automate answers.

These chatbots also have different variations. Intercom, for instance, offers a chat functionality wherein you can automate conversations and break in or overwrite the bot when you're at your desk.

Chat flow cuts down response time into just a couple of seconds or minutes – and allows you to catch your target client right then and there. It's advantageous because people have a short attention span in today's consumerist society. By getting an immediate response, they can easily make up their mind if they will avail of your service or product or not.

The Impact of Video

When talking about marketing, the impact of video is not one to be ignored. Videos convert really well and they're also recognised by Google. They help improve your SEO performance.

Today, there are tools like Bonjoro that can help you personalise videos and send them directly to your customers. Video-based platforms such as Zoom and TikTok are also on the rise because they help give your audience an idea that you're a real person. They also correspond with the so-called global village idea, which tells that you can find somebody across the globe who shares the same thoughts with you. All these are possible without you having to go big on money.

Taking Geography Into Account

With services and products now becoming more accessible, he notes that there's a need to have multiple strategies. This is because the type of technology a country like the US has is different from what's available in Europe. In Europe, businesses are very much involved with content creation. European tools are also at the forefront when it comes to scaling content and creating them in bulk.

Having multiple strategies is also essential because one brand can be considered top-of-the-bill somewhere and low-end in another. Each country has a different language, currency, and metric system. And if you don't speak the same language, you won't sell.

Chapter Four
Bias-Free Views on Behaviour.

Interview with Dr. John Ricketts, Tokyo; CEO and Joint Founder of the Earth.ai Significance Systems.

Everybody Is Living in Media Bubbles

Significance Systems gives people the ability to identify emotions around a narrative and how the narrative changes and evolves over time. They're able to find the strongest stories or brands in a particular sector or category, and then apply that in lots of different fields. John says everybody is living in media bubbles these days, and these are pretty much by design. Google, Facebook, the newspaper, or TV channels, they're all media bubbles, so it's hard to distinguish what reality looks like. Anybody who's a business owner, a CEO, or in a managerial position knows how difficult it is to know what's actually going on, because of the reporting mechanism. People tell you what they want you to hear, and this is happening around everything, because what you hear is what you're going to click on. That's the business model, and because people are disconnected from reality, they start to make poorer quality decisions, whether it's around elections, investment strategy for growth, dealing with a crisis, etc. The onset of digital myopia is everywhere. To expand horizons Earth.ai looks past the media bubbles, finding out what emotions look like around that narrative and discovering the emotions that describe future behaviour.

On their website, one can easily input a company brand, and then they will see the conversations, the language, and the terminology used around that brand and it will be displayed graphically. It could be a brand, a positioning opportunity, an issue, an asset, or a need, whether met or unmet.

The Importance of Narratives

Narratives describe the world. Anybody who's been involved in communications knows full well that narratives are a very important part of what makes the world go round. They generate tremendous value. They steer the directions and the decisions that people make as societies. This is intuitively understood but poorly measured. If you think about a world where things are really well-measured, say capital markets, there's a huge amount of detail in terms of assets, balance sheets, and technical measures, but the idea that narratives could impact value is one that is novel and isn't fully believed. It would be nonsense to say that narratives don't impact markets, as people are seeing with the likes of Trump and Elon Musk. Nobel Prize-winner and economist Robert Shiller's book called "Narrative

Economics" is pretty much the longhand version of what John and his team are doing at the machine level. They both look at the stories around things like subprime or particular assets, etc.

At Significance Systems, their work revolves primarily around the narrative. Marketers want to grab hold of or become a valued part of a narrative that already exists, because nobody's got the time or the money to go and create a whole new narrative anymore. There is nothing new under the sun, and so it's best to find a narrative that is close to the positioning you want and become a valued part of that. Looking at the brands that have become successful, they're the brands that have understood that they have to be a relevant part of culture. Failing to do so in today's world means a failure to be relevant, other than at a purely transactional level.

Together with the University of Tokyo, Significance Systems has established a virtual living lab. They look at aspects of culture in Japan and in the UK and at the way values have changed in these two cultures. One value they're looking at is the notion of resiliency. Prior to COVID, in Japan, resiliency was all about one's work and career. That was the absolute centre of gravity. If one wanted to become better at being resilient, that would mean investing more time and energy around one's career by taking additional courses, spending more time working, and doing other activities that would build resiliency. As soon as COVID hit, there was a shift from focusing on work to being family oriented. Now, people believe they become more resilient by investing time and effort in their families. There's been a return to family values, so for businesses trying to connect their brand to an attribute like resiliency, the executions have completely changed.

Their platform enables them to look across all the major languages and provides clients with multiple country-multiple market studies the following day, making it a really useful and time-efficient tool. Historically, global positioning has been a very complex, time-consuming, and expensive exercise, but working with different companies, they've shown that to be far more straightforward, thanks to machine learning or AI. They find as much topical content around a particular query as they possibly can, then they study the data, and then they will boil it down to what really matters. That involves seeing through that media bubble, and then they'll look at the core pieces of content, the core locations on the web, the core emotions that are driving that narrative forward, and this all happens without human intervention. It's all up to the machines, so it's very scalable, it's very fast, and it's very cost-effective.

One example John gave was about vaccines and how there are anti-vaxxers or those who do not believe in the effectiveness of vaccines. The topic then came to the idea of what if it was a Chinese-developed vaccine and how the world would react to that. They were able to look at that in real time, and they found that there's been a significant hardening of Western attitudes towards China, that vaccine hesitancy is a very real thing in the world, and it's characterised by the depth of feeling, so don't expect to have a rational conversation with somebody who's anti-vax. This will be fight or flight for them. However, people haven't put China and the vaccine together yet. The China vaccine already has equity in the world, but there is no polarisation around it, and it hasn't gone tribal. John says that's a pretty simple exercise, where people can engage with their business partners, they can get engaged directly with the site and sign up, and for a few hundred dollars, they'll have a view on it.

Global Information Made Accessible

Significance Systems services many industries. Not only can they handle large amounts of data, but they can dig deep into a particular country or market sector as well. They can go that granular and study small brands or niche issues. While those who've tried social listening might find nothing or brief engagement there, with Significance Systems, they will go deep on B2B issues. Even if people aren't talking about it on Facebook, there's still proper engagement with it, but it'll be a very technical conversation that will require more technical forums. In terms of compliance, they only look at open data. That's part of their policy stance even from the prior days, and they make that very clear.

Aside from the amazing services that they offer, as part of their journalism without borders initiative, they also provide an opportunity for journalists to use the platform for free. This is not simply just for data journalism, but it's about media. It's about thinking in terms of "we" instead of just "me," and this goes back to the media bubbles. It's about understanding a culture's feelings around certain issues, because having a view that isn't tainted by particular media bubbles is increasingly important to have. The goal is to create a common framework where the emotion is removed to be able to look at issues more clearly.

The platform, which is called Earth.ai, represents this vision of global information made accessible, one where people can look across the walls from their own walled gardens, which is kind of what everyone is experiencing now. Their tool sets are great for helping clients define the positioning of their brand and looking at key topics taking place that clients want to take part in. It's powerful for aligning the messaging and the future messaging with the global and prevailing trends not just on social media but in deeper channels as well.

Chapter Five
Social Listening as Protection.

❚ *Interview with CHATGPT about social listening.*

Forewarned Is Forearmed.

AI tools are helping companies and brands understand what's being said about them across all channels, not just in text but also in photographs and videos.

Social listening is a term which addresses the task of tracking and breaking down conversations that are happening online. These days, there are so many different conversations happening online and at such speed that it's essential to use these new AI-powered social listening platforms.

Social listening involves monitoring discussions and references about a particular subject on social media platforms and examining them for valuable information to enhance the experience. For businesses, it entails comprehending the online dialogue concerning their brand and offerings.

These conversations and mentions may be directly aimed at the brand (talking about or replying to your brand) or broader, where the brand still needs to be mentioned (talking about your brand). According to the State of Social Listening 2022 by Social Media Today, almost 61% of businesses now have a social media listening system and monitor for keyword mentions. More than 82% of enterprises consider social listening to be a critical planning element.[1]

The practice of social listening has been in use for many years. Traditionally, people would gather feedback through surveys and other methods. However, with the development of technology, it has become possible to extract this information from social media without asking for it. This practice of gathering information means it is now easier to collect large amounts of valuable data effortlessly.

Social listening is crucial to any brand strategy as it provides valuable insights into what people say about your business. By analysing data from social media platforms, you can better understand customer feedback, employee opinions, and brand perception. An entrepreneur can then use this information to enhance the overall experience for their stakeholders.

Listening platforms like Ipsos Synthesio, Talkwalker, and other social listening tools can be invaluable for companies, as they provide a great way to track and analyse conversations around a particular brand or industry. While Talkwalker is a well-established social listening platform, several other platforms offer similar functionalities.

---

[1] URL: https://brand24.com/blog/what-is-social-listening/

One such platform is Brandwatch, which goes beyond social listening and is a consumer intelligence platform. Brandwatch's AI analyst, Iris, automates bringing insights to the surface, saving users' time. The platform also offers image analysis, allowing users to analyse visual content related to their brand.

Another notable social listening tool is NetBase Quid, which provides historical and real-time social media analysis. Their AI-driven platform offers insights into various topics and brands, making it useful for brand management and market research.

Additionally, there are other social listening tools available in the market. Hootsuite, a well-known social media management platform, also offers social listening capabilities. Their social listening tools allow businesses to monitor social media channels for brand mentions, competitor brands, and related keywords. It provides valuable insights into customer sentiment, pain points, and preferences, which can inform marketing strategies and customer service efforts.

With social listening, businesses can track how customers and prospects perceive their brand, product quality, and overall sentiment. By actively listening to conversations and monitoring mentions, businesses can efficiently identify potential issues and promptly take action to resolve them.[2]

Social listening enables businesses to:

1. Assess Brand Health: Companies gain insights into how customers and prospects feel about their brand through social listening. It helps identify positive sentiments, excitement about new product announcements, or areas where improvements may be needed. By monitoring social media mentions and comments,

---

[2] https://www.agorapulse.com/blog/social-listening-case-studies/.

businesses can proactively address concerns and ensure customer satisfaction.

2. Manage Customer Complaints: Social listening allows businesses to identify and respond to customer complaints, even when they don't directly mention the brand. By monitoring conversations with relevant keywords, companies can quickly address issues, resolve customer problems, and retain customer loyalty. This proactive approach helps prevent negative sentiment from spreading and turning into a full-blown crisis.

3. Address Potential Crises: Social listening helps businesses detect and address problems before they escalate into major crises. By tracking conversations and monitoring sentiment, companies can identify emerging issues, assess their impact, and respond efficiently. This proactive crisis management approach helps protect the brand's reputation and maintain customer trust.

Let's look at some cases when social listening impacted a business.

Hong Kong Airlines faced a pricing crisis that turned into a PR win through effective social listening and swift action. In this case study, the airline detected and reacted to the issue within hours, leveraging social media monitoring tools to track conversations and sentiments surrounding the crisis.[3]

The incident occurred on 22 January 2019, when Hong Kong Airlines accidentally sold business class tickets at a significantly reduced price. The airline's social listening platform, Talkwalker, noticed a sudden increase in conversations about exceptional pricing.

---

[3] https://www.talkwalker.com/case-studies/hong-kong-airlines-how-to-turn-a-crisis-into-a-soaring-success.

Recognising the significance of the spike in discussions, the airline dug deeper to investigate the situation.[4]

By promptly identifying the pricing error, Hong Kong Airlines swiftly addressed the issue. They could compare their response to a similar incident involving British Airways, which could have handled the situation more effectively. Hong Kong Airlines used social media to communicate transparently, acknowledging the error and offering solutions to affected customers. This approach helped them turn a potential crisis into a positive customer engagement opportunity.[5]

Through its proactive social listening strategy, Hong Kong Airlines achieved a remarkable 4900% increase in engagement. By monitoring conversations, sentiments, and customer feedback in real-time, the airline not only mitigated the negative impact of the pricing crisis but also strengthened customer relationships and improved brand perception.[6]

Many businesses have embraced sustainability to meet the growing demand for environmental protection. A global CPG manufacturer and retailer aimed to investigate the factors driving the trend towards sustainability among consumers. Synthesio identified ways to contribute to positive change and improve customer satisfaction using its social listening dashboard capabilities. For example, a global meat processing company aimed to understand the trend of meat replacement products and predict their future trajectory. Synthesio's

---

[4] https://www.talkwalker.com/case-studies/hong-kong-airlines-how-to-turn-a-crisis-into-a-soaring-success.

[5] https://www.talkwalker.com/case-studies/hong-kong-airlines-how-to-turn-a-crisis-into-a-soaring-success.

[6] https://www.talkwalker.com/case-studies/hong-kong-airlines-how-to-turn-a-crisis-into-a-soaring-success.

Signals software provided insights into the industry's major players' messaging and strategies, resulting in a claimed 15% increase in profits and an 18% increase in organic online conversations for the brand.

These examples show how social listening can guide companies to detect and respond to critical situations and accurately forecast consumer trends. That's because the social universe is already alive with chatter about what is essential to people, and social listening tunes into that conversation and then processes that data into insights.

When choosing a social listening tool, it's essential to consider various factors, including:

1. Determine the type of data you require and whether the platforms you're considering can provide it, such as brand mentions, impressions, and engagement.

2. Assess the tools' ability to analyse different types of content, including text, audio, and still and moving images. Visual analysis is fundamental in today's social media landscape, where much content is graphic.

3. Consider the customer experience and support provided by the platform.

These tools enable proactive monitoring and provide insights into sentiment analysis, competitor analysis, and brand perception. The ability to analyse conversations in real-time and receive alerts about brand mentions empowers the entrepreneur to capitalise on what's happening now and what's likely to happen. It's like a crystal ball into the future, which uses the data from the present to create a forward view. Social listening using AI platforms is the solution to knowing what to talk about, when, where, and how so that the message lands where it will be most impactful.

Author's Note

This article illustrates the power and potential of AI. The original article was written from an interview with someone which was featured on the podcast, but who is no longer employed by the company they represented at the time. I wanted to include an article about social listening, but our publishing deadline would not allow for another interview and edit. The management of the company, and the former employee, both declined to contribute, citing scheduling issues. Instead, I turned to ChatGPT and Grammarly, giving them both prompts for content and corrections for any plagiarism or non-sensical terms. Within two hours, I had an article with explanations, citations, and case studies ready for the publisher.

This is an example of the potential for this AI technology to replace those who can't keep up with the pace of content creation. It seems that time waits for no man, nor does AI.

Chapter Six
STOP! Don't Post Too Much.

Interview with Bant Breen, New York; Founder and
Chairman of Qnary.

No Longer Window Dressing

Bant Breen is an entrepreneur himself, has a PhD, and is the Founder and Chairman of Qnary in New York City. He founded a business which helps executives leverage their social media presence. He's done a survey with the Center for Global Communications between Emerson College and the Blanquerna School of Communications, and he said that the findings included the conclusion that we should not see digital reputations of key executives as mere "window dressing."

When he started the business eight years ago, he would simply tell people, "Your online presence matters," because it operates essentially as an instant background check. Without it, you're not aware of all of the digital and scaled opportunities that could come from anywhere. Post- COVID, remote working has become standard for organisations of all sizes around the world. Bant says your online presence is not only important; it's everything. It is the way people know you. It is your calling card.

Bant publishes a white paper annually, and over the years, they've discovered interesting things, one of which is that when an executive or a professional shares content via LinkedIn or all the other channels, it's eight times more likely to be engaged with than if it was shared on a brand channel. It's connected to a very obvious but very important insight, which is people like to connect with people.

The second statistic of interest which came out of Asia was that individuals that follow an executive and a brand are twice as likely to purchase from that company. Even with an excellent LinkedIn score, at Qnary, they focus not only on LinkedIn, but on your entire online presence, what you look like in search, what you look like across the multitude of social platforms, business platforms, etc. They don't want to overweight one over another, but he says it certainly matters today. And if this COVID pandemic continues, it potentially could become quite a game-changing moment for everyone, as this could be the new way people do business.

The Problem Qnary Solves

Coming from the world of agencies, his last roles before starting his businesses were running agencies in the IPG family. He had worked at WPP and Publicis before that, so he's very aware of agencies, marketing, and all that. The great things about agencies, he says, is that they're filled with problem solvers and creative thinkers, and they're service-oriented. But, as Bant looked forward eight years ago, he realised that the challenge with agencies is that they didn't scale as businesses. They didn't utilise technology as effectively as they needed to be using them. And so, he set out to build a solution that didn't exist in the agency world, and then he came up with Qnary, a technology platform and a solution that works for executives and professionals to optimise their online presence in search as well as in social platforms. It creates thought leadership content, whether that be short-form or long-form content, and then it grows their audience and engages with other key influencers in topics that they care about.

What sets Qnary apart from an agency is that their whole solution begins with their technology platform and ends with their technology platform. They have a product mindset. It's very different from what happens in an agency which is focused on the number of FTEs that you put on a problem. You might have some brilliant thinkers, but it's very hard to scale agencies. Their whole process over at Qnary is very much made around the technology, and one of the main things they do is produce content. In fact, according to him, they actually generate more digital content for their clients than *The New York Times*. They are generating content across 36 different business verticals, and they have a team of creators that are vetted and are experts in specific topics, and they utilise Qnary's tools to generate content. Some of that content is pre-structured or pre-formed using some machine learning tools that they apply. It is then formed into final pieces of content through the creator network that they have, and then sent to an internal team of editors to be reviewed. Once the editors give it the green light, it goes to a Customer Success Manager (CSM), which is assigned to the executive, and it is then reviewed one last time before it goes out.

The technology also monitors whether the client makes any changes in it. If you receive the content and you change a sentence, word, or structure, the technology learns that and says, "Oh, Jim doesn't like the word 'like,' so we'll avoid using that." It learns your tone of voice and your structure, and that gets fed back into rules that are seen by the creators going forward. It's basically a combination of technology and human intervention.

With a PhD in Artificial Intelligence and Marketing, Bant's take on AI is that there are incredibly useful ways to utilise it, so that it can support us in the jobs that we do. That's what they believe in at Qnary. There's never going to be just a tech solution that works or just a person solution. The best way is to bring the two together. On the one hand, it's exciting how AI can generate articles and other forms of content from a sentence or phrase, but on the other hand, it could possibly go very wrong too. Bant says they do consider all of those.

Qnary has a mobile application that operates as a place where a client will receive notifications on various optimisations. They'll receive their content there, and they'll also receive notifications saying, "Here's a post by an influencer in your space. You should engage. Here are some potential ways you could engage with that." It operates like a media hub or media agent, and there are some basic metrics too along with a dashboard. On a monthly basis, the Qnary CSM sends over a measurement report and walks through that with the client. That will cover a lot of things that Qnary believes are important, which is, are you findable? Are you connected with the topics that matter to you as a business executive? Are you connecting with the influencers in your particular field? Are you growing your audience? Are people engaging with you? Qnary tracks all of those metrics and shares that with their clients on a monthly basis.

As Qnary is growing and engaging on people's behalf, they are applying a variety of tactics to do that. The ongoing interaction when the client receives a report offers that opportunity to discuss additional moves that would be recommended by the team. They have a growth and engagement technology platform baked into their technology and a team of experts who support that process of providing information like, "We would like to consider X, Y, or Z for you. Are you interested?"

The Best Way to Understand Your Customers Is to Be One Yourself

Interestingly enough, not only is Bant the founder of the company, but he himself is also a user of Qnary. He has his own client services manager who recently advised him during his monthly review to post less. As a hyper-social person who wants to post all the time, he said they took him through the math of the diminishing marginal returns. This is not about trying to post a million times a day on every channel, he says. Everybody has their own optimal number.

Chapter Seven
Tracking Content Context.

❚ *Interview with Ant Cousins, London; CEO of Factmata.*

From Fact-Checking to Media-Monitoring

Factmata started off in the fact-checking space back in 2014 when Founder Dhruv Ghulati, who then acted as their CEO of sorts, started working on this problem academically and scientifically. However, fact-checking was useful, but it doesn't touch on the commercially sustainable, scalable, and exciting part of the story. There's a lot of harmful content out there. It's not just mistruths, disinformation, and fake news – there's racism, sexism, toxicity, and hate speech.

So it become imperative to not just measure quantity but sentiment and stance i.e. how people are representing opinions and ideas about topics or companies.

There are a lot of other things that are harming people, brands, and organisations. And this prompted Factmata to broaden their scope and refine their vision and approach, taking them to where they are now, which is the media-monitoring, brand-protection space.

Ant sees their company as something that can be compared to bigger players such as Brandwatch and smaller ones, including Social Mention. These companies work like how public relations have been previously run: It's about getting the volume and sentiments as high as possible. Businesses want people in their target market to talk about them as much and as positively as possible. While accomplishing this is a great job, what they've found out is that there's a need for more nuances – because negative narratives and sentiments being shared online can have a massive impact on one's brand reputation and, ultimately, their bottom line.

Competitors that follow how PR can tell you how much you're being spoken about and what the audience's sentiment is, but they don't tell you why that conversation is taking place. They don't analyse the reason why these volumes and numbers are the way they are. Ant says that this was indeed hard to do until recently, when Factmata was able to develop a technology that allows this kind of analysis.

In comparison to the other players in the media-monitoring space who only provide numbers, Factmata can go behind those numbers: Why is the volume the way it is? Why is the sentiment trending this way? Factmata automates the analysis – and this has been possible because of the recent advances in Artificial Intelligence.

Understanding Sentiments

To understand these numbers and sentiments, Factmata uses a topic clustering technology.

In terms of gathering data, they do the exact same thing what other players do. They go out and find out all those mentions about you – including tweets, Facebook posts, articles. Then, it will produce a word cloud. However, as this doesn't really state reasoning, they then run it through their topic clustering technology and get narratives out of it. They're able to find common threads and narratives across different mentions and platforms. They use automation to identify these and provide you with data that you can look at and interact with.

Currently, most of their clients get mentions from the broader, easy-to-access platforms. Factmata focuses on content coming from such avenues, including social media. But as they also have arrangements with data aggregators, it's possible for you to obtain a more specific set of data.

How Their Technology Can Be Used

Ant says that in general, their technology is being used to identify threat opportunities.

They can conduct a narrative analysis and give you the Top 10 by any metric – by the most positive, the most negative, the most racist, the most toxic, the most popular. With this, they're able to provide you with the ability to understand those narratives in terms of whatever's important to you. You can find the most negative and even identify the most negative influences or sources of these negative narratives. Who is promoting this? Are those significant people that you can engage with? Can you educate them to switch their views? Or are there people who disagree with their particular stance and counter those narratives?

Factmata can tell you both the narratives and the people that influenced these narratives. However, it all comes down to what really matters to you. If you're interested in avoiding risks and crises, you can use their narrative identification service and look for the riskiest, most threatening, and most toxic content out there and base your strategies on that.

It's important to note, however, that they can help with longer-term kind of planning. The data that they provide is not real-time. One reason is that running a huge amount of content through AI entails hardcore computing. What they can provide is historical data, which can then be updated on 24-hour cycles going forward. With this, you can gain insight into whether a narrative is bubbling away or has the potential to trend.

During the podcast episode, Ant also shared that Factmata can currently work with English-language content. However, they're now in the process of tackling other languages such as Spanish (which has a high volume of content). In fact, they've won an award from Innovate UK for developing multilingual models that deal with media monitoring.

On Choosing a Topic to Track

With Factmata's technology, it's absolutely possible for you to keep track of both absolute and relative narratives. You can track a topic that directly involves your business or a topic that's about your competitors. For instance, if you want to track Pfizer or Moderna, you can use their technology to look into the conversations that go around these topics – the misinformation, the people's sentiments, and others.

One thing that they do differently from other players is that they don't just track sentiments objectively (i.e. is this sentiment positive, negative, or neutral?). They are also about stance. They go for the layer on top of the sentiments. For example, there could be a tweet about a politician which has a negative sentiment. However, if you look at the bigger picture, that tweet can be treated as positive and in favour of the topic of that politician as a whole. With Factmata, you'd have two different lenses that can help you analyse so much more, especially when you're doing influencer analysis.

Another example of how their AI technology helps, in this case, is when they did an analysis about a company that makes protein powder. Their client wanted to know what people are saying about their products. When they tracked, there's one specific comment that has the phrase "sickly sweet." They identified it as a negative though it has a positive word ("sweet"). Because when that positive word was paired with "sickly," it becomes a negative sentiment towards the product.

Understanding the sophistication of the English language (e.g. when an adjective is attached to a noun, the whole meaning can be modified significantly) is something that Factmata has been working on over the last three or more years. And their models have been trained to take on that level of complexity. Because of it, they're also able to track and pick up ironies and other modifiers in context. Though it is not 100% perfect, their technology is reliable enough to give sound data and statistics.

What's Next?

The first step in their process is identifying a narrative. You've got to know what's being said about you and understand who is behind it – their motivations and intentions. With Factmata, you can find all this information. They can also arm you with keywords and associated phrases that go along with those. This is vital especially if you're trying to track hashtags or finding where else those conversations are happening.

The next on their roadmap is to help you with the creation of content based on their analysis. After knowing the narrative that you want to beat, you can then look into a narrative that can counter that. What is the volume and sentiment of that narrative? Who are its influences? By knowing these, the least that you can do next is to support and help facilitate the counter narrative's exponential growth.

The next phase in their intelligence roadmap is to automatically identify such narratives and influences on your behalf.

On Countering Bots

Today, companies are also vulnerable to foreign agents and bots that post negative narratives about them.

For Ant, however, it really doesn't matter where the negative narratives are coming from. Once these have already been picked up, then there are already going to be humans involved. In the first place, this is the aim of bot farms: To get humans to see what they post and immediately share it. By the time you are seeing those negatives, it's already too late because the bots have already done their job.

What Factmata can help you with is to identify those narratives much earlier in the cycle – when it could still be largely bot-driven. What they try to do is give early warnings so that you can already start measures to take them down, or identify their potential trajectory then head it off afterwards.

Here, contextualisation is also being used. Factmata's technology works to get that context as early as possible before humans can spot the trend. They will spot a narrative – which can be potentially toxic, racist, or harmful – and flag it to you.

The opposite also applies. Think of their technology as a tool in which you can find positive opportunities for your brand as well.

Chapter Eight
Only Qualified Leads Matter.

| Interview with Stapho Thienpont, Belgium; B2B Lead Consultant.

Marketing Qualified Leads

Unlike Sales Qualified Leads (SQLs) – or people who are also already interested to buy from you right now – MQLs are those who are in the earlier phase. They fit your requirements as people to whom you want to sell your product or service.

For you to identify your MQLs, it's important that you understand who your target audience is. Instead of simply launching a podcast or posting content on LinkedIn or Instagram, you have to ask yourself first: Who is it that I want to sell to?

If you already have some clients, you have to look into your Customer Relationship Management (CRM) tool and determine which companies or clients are making you the most money. Then, assess what is it that they have in common. You can interview, for instance, your top 10 customers and identify their common denominator. After doing that, you can start finding more people that fit the bill.

However, if you don't have customers yet, you should start by making a list of companies that you'd love to work with. Stapho notes that you should only list down companies that are as similar to each other as possible. This way, it will be much easier and efficient to make a piece of content that will be valuable for your intended audience.

After you've made a list of 100 prospects, interview at least 10 of them, if not all 100. Your interviewee should be the people who are likely to be interested in this kind of conversation – marketing research interviews and surveys. For example, if you have a PR firm, you would want to interview the marketing manager of a company because he or she will be the one to determine that their company indeed needs some PR. These people are called the champions. Champions are easy to have a sales conversation with. In the first place, they're the ones who will appreciate talking to someone who will actually listen to them.

How Do You Reach Out and Get People to Talk to You?

Coming up with a list of MQLs can be made mostly by googling. If you want to target startups specifically and you want to know about their funding, you can use platforms such as Crunchbase.

For the next phase – which is reaching out – you can start a genuine conversation by sending out direct messages (DMs) on

LinkedIn or Instagram. You can also roll out a cold email campaign using tools like lemlist, which is a software that allows you to customise outbound solutions (e.g. attaching personalised images in your emails).

In terms of incentivising companies to be interviewed or surveyed, Stapho shares that many people consider the mere participation in marketing research already adequate. However, you can also offer something such as Amazon gift cards.

The key is being genuine in your conversation. Before you converse with them, you should do some research. You can look at their website and prepare a short video pointing out what can they improve – and how you can help them improve it. If you're a graphic designer, you can review some of their designs or even make a free design for them. Leverage your expertise to do something beneficial for them. This way, you'll make them feel that you've done something for them, incentivising them to do something for you as well.

For Stapho, one of the most effective techniques is starting a podcast targeting your MQLs and inviting them to get featured on your show. Apart from giving them media exposure, you're also showcasing their expertise in a particular topic. In the process, you'll be able to sustain a podcast that your prospective clients would really want to listen to and be featured in the future. For instance, if you're doing PR works for manufacturing companies, you could make a podcast that talks about manufacturing.

Whether you're reaching out through DMs or a podcast, what's important is to know why you want to interview them. Though having a conversation that can lead to a sale is one thing, understanding these companies' problems is significant as well, because it will be helpful in your marketing campaigns. For instance, when you're making a landing page or creating a cold email, you can use this information to entice your prospects to buy from you.

However, such vital information isn't something that you can simply guess – you can only know it by reaching out and asking them. And as you get to know your customers better, you will start seeing common traits. This will help you create content that will be useful for all of them.

Podcasting and the Edge It Offers

As stated earlier, a podcast is an effective means of reaching out to MQLs. Stapho points out that launching one shouldn't be considered overwhelming.

Come up with a list of guests, record, add descriptions and show notes, and attach a cover image. There are tools like Fiverr wherein you can get everything done by paying $15. You can also pay an additional fee if you want to incorporate a piece of engaging intro music. If you want to take it to the next level, you can also upload and distribute your podcast on platforms such as Podcast.co.

There's an article by Sweet Fish Media that rounds up 26 steps on how you can start a podcast. It goes to show how launching a podcast is much easier than you think.

However, it doesn't end with just recording podcasts. Stapho points out that it's also important to help your podcast guests – your MQLs – share the content on social media as well. Promotion is vital because it's one way of tapping into other companies that are similar to them. You can propagate your reach to other people who fit your Ideal Customer Profile (ICP).

Apart from reaching other potential customers, you're also allowing the very people within their company to see your content. For instance, if your interviewee is a marketing manager and he shares your podcast episode on LinkedIn, there's a chance that his supervisor will get to see it, too. This way, you can get people who need to know about you, know about you.

The content that can be shared on social media isn't limited to the whole podcast episode only. With Podcast.co, you can splice your content, get an interesting clip, and have it automatically captioned. There's also an app called Headliner that can help you promote your podcasts through social videos.

When it comes to boosting content engagement, Stapho recommends lempod (it comes from the same people behind the aforementioned lemlist). Through this tool, you can make a group of people who agree to automatically engage in your content. For example, if you post something on LinkedIn, you can make a setting wherein the members of your lempod group can automatically like it. Boosting engagement on LinkedIn can help you expand your reach from first connections to second connections.

You can also utilise podcasts as an avenue where you can strike up a sales conversation. As an expert in high-ticket B2B, Stapho recommends asking qualifying questions during the podcast. From there, you can figure out during the show if the person is indeed a qualified lead. After the recording proper, you can transition into discussing business matters: What is it that you do? Will your interviewee be interested in availing of your product or service?

After the podcast recording is done, you can send an email thanking your interviewee for agreeing to be featured. In your email, you can incorporate a discovery call, or the conversation you make with someone who has initially shown interest in your product or service. Once the episode is live, you can also make a follow-up email and tag them on your social media promotions.

Podcasting gives you an extra edge because it lets you show that you appreciate your prospects – and that you regard them as experts in their field. It's also a way to establish good rapport and kick off discussions that can naturally flow into a sales conversation.

Chapter Nine
Case: Pew Research Center.

Interview with Washington, DC–based Dan Morrison; Senior Advisor, Acumen Public Affairs, Former Vice President of Communications, Pew Research Center.

The Pew Research Center is a nonpartisan American think tank that shares information on relevant issues around the world.

"The Single Biggest Problem with Communication."

One thing Dan has been working towards is harnessing cognitive diversity in the workplace. He has had the privilege, as a communicator, of working with people very much unlike himself at IBM when working with technologists, at the OECD working with economists, and now at the Pew Research Center working with researchers. He likes to live by the saying from George Bernard Shaw, *the single biggest problem in communication is the illusion that it has taken place.*

This talks about cadence, messaging, and the moments where you think you have communicated, but you realise you haven't, in some way. Everyone needs prompts in communication, especially since the coronavirus and the inability sometimes to see a face on the other end. Even when you do see a face, you don't get those facial prompts, making it hard to communicate.

When it comes to communication, Dan emphasises taking into account the other person, whether it's someone sitting across the table, someone on the other end of the phone, or someone on the other end of the website, as deeply understanding that audience will dictate the manner of communication. One can't say they've really done their homework unless they know the audience they're trying to appeal to. Another tip from Dan is to imagine yourself in their shoes. What's going on in their lives? What are the hindrances they see in the message you're trying to deliver to them? Why is that not going through for some reason?

Scale is about audience and growing it. That's true across any discipline, be it the private sector, the public sector, or nonprofit. Aside from understanding the target market, another element of that is writing down in the strategic plan who that audience is and who that audience isn't. For the Pew Research Center, their audience tends to be decision makers, journalists, and the informed public. Internally, determining the audience is just as important, because it will save time and avoid problems of people speaking in a way that isn't relevant to the people listening. If the audience or current strategy of the company are in sync, a diplomatic and productive way to have that conversation is to suggest postponing an activity or plan until the vision and the target audience are aligned.

How Pew Research Center Gathers Information

To better understand their audience, the Pew Research Center does a lot of data essays. They find it to be a compelling way to share data across a set of audiences, and when assessing different technologies, they discipline themselves when there are new products or when new technological developments are on the horizon. They assess first whether those technologies are good for the organisation, because what may work for one organisation may not work for another. They also don't diminish or cast aside existing technology, because it can still be used in a different way.

One thing they've experimented with at the Pew Research Center is something called an email mini course, where they quiz people on their knowledge of a particular subject with information coming from their existing resources. So far, topics they've covered include immigration in the US, how much people actually know about the US census and what it's trying to achieve, and facts and figures about Muslims and Islam. They've taken an old technology, email, and added a different capability to it, and they find it rewarding as they've received positive feedback on it, one of the reasons being that it gives the respondents the freedom to do it in their own time. Through this, they're able to share their brand and share knowledge, which is the goal in their business of providing data about what citizens are thinking and feeling around top issues of the day.

Face-to-face used to be one of the main methods for gathering data and information, but since the coronavirus, one of the challenges faced by Dan and his team was having to find other ways to collect data from citizens. They've had to pivot along the way, not to mention the fact that they're on a global scale in terms of communication. In the long run, it comes down to knowing the audience and being conscious that what is said in one part of the world needs to be consistent with what is said in another part of the world yet specific to each locale. Back then, the assumption was you say different things in different places when communicating, but it doesn't work that way anymore in a globalised world. Cultural sensibility plays a major role in the way questions are asked, and the message needs to be global but explained in the local context, which can be quite challenging.

Storytelling has two sides to it: the actual narrating and then the listening, and people often forget the significance of the latter. For organisations aiming to tell a story, they must take into account global as well as local headlines and how those two may overlap. In the way that people are getting their information from the news, there's sometimes a heightened expectation on the part of the reader or listener to understand where those messages are coming from and to understand how it is relevant to their own lives. It actually serves as homework for them as consumers of information, which is new, as it didn't use to be that way. Not so long ago, major networks produced news that people would consume, and it was delivered in a way that was nationalised. But now with the emergence of the internet, people are getting their news in many different ways, and the onus is on the reader to understand and filter through that where the information is coming from, what it means for them, and then tie those strings together.

In other news, Dan and his teenage son have written a book entitled "Backpacks and Baguettes: Colouring the World through Young Eyes", the premise of which is understanding the world through a child's eyes. Dan explains that the formula for each chapter begins with his son's impressions of a place, their food, and then the children in these different places. Dan believes his son's youth makes him hypersensitive to what's going on in the lives of the children in the cities they've been to, and his son was very attuned to that possibly in a way that adults aren't. One realisation that came out of writing this book together was that children, or people in general, are the same and yet different. People are essentially the same everywhere around the world. They speak different languages and approach their lives in different ways, but there's a lot of commonality there, and understanding that is one of the main points of this book, making it a worthwhile read.

Dan sharing about international communications and his experience on the need to really listen and be sensitive to the people on the other side can hopefully help more business owners communicate more efficiently and get their message across to the appropriate audience.

Keeping the audience in mind is paramount, because for them to understand a business, the business needs to understand them first.

Conclusion:
It's Your Thymōs Time

Thank you for taking your valuable time to review these conversations with entrepreneurs, experts, and technology developers. I apologise for the inconsistencies in tone and style which I hope were not a distraction; I wanted to faithfully capture the sense from the transcripts as if you were part of the conversation. One of the learnings is of course that none of us speak in sentences and paragraphs with the same grammatical discipline in which we write. It is often up to the audience to interpret what it is that is being shared, and it is no wonder then that Wiio's law of miscommunication so often prevails when we are ill-prepared for presentations and conversations. The Finnish Professor Osmo Antero Wiio in 1978 sardonically wrote, "Communication usually fails, except by accident".

My hope is that you will have interpreted useful information from these 50 articles. It was hard to decide on the first 50 episodes, but I intend to curate another 50 as there is a lot of other good information which I believe will help you. I really hope that you have found at least one piece of information or one person who will help you in your journey to get your venture noticed. I would like to invite you to reach out to each and any of the people listed here as within 20 minutes and these pages I could only hope to introduce a small slice of their brilliance. You could tell them you read about them in *The UnNoticed* book. There are over 300 episodes of The UnNoticed Show available on iTunes, Spotify, and all other players, and so if you've found this selection useful I do invite you to come and listen to more episodes; some of which are interviews, and some are my own theories and explanations of public relations for fellow entrepreneurs.

It's a brilliant time to be a business owner because we have at our disposal all the tools to create, amplify, and measure communications with the people who matter most to our business. The bad news is that everyone else has these opportunities too, so we have to be quick to adapt and effective in our implementation. However, because audiences engage with authenticity and creativity delivered in person, and not spurious and dull generic campaigns, the entrepreneur has a massive advantage because we simply know our customers better and have the autonomy to have fun and get personal.

As a foreign entrepreneur in China without language skills nor a budget, launching the Morgan Motor brand demonstrated to me the commercial potential of public relations. I have tried to demonstrate in these pages that public relations isn't a narrow discipline but all the ways that a company communicates with people who matter to the business. It's the best form of marketing because it is essentially free. Of central importance is that we are active consistently over time, and that we give Thymōs to the people who matter to our business, and in doing so we will #getnoticed for all the right reasons. In truth, everything that we do communicates something about ourselves and our company, even if we are saying nothing we are making a statement. As an entrepreneur you know that you can deliver value to others, how you communicate that will impact how many people will let you help them, and in turn how well your company will grow.

Keep on communicating.

Acknowledgements

Recording, producing, compiling, and publishing this book has been possible due to the support and encouragement of many others. I give thanks to my family: Erika, my wife, who has cared for our wonderful daughters, Amity and Halo, whilst I have been in Shed Studio each night over the past 12 months during lockdown, and to my amazing daughters who have brought me tea and home baked biscuits to keep me going. I thank my sister Dr. Shelley James, internationally renown Lumenologist, for being my inspiration as I thought about what knowledge would help her on her journey. To my father Professor Louis James and my step mother Louis McConnell (both acclaimed authors in their own right), for their review of my early ideas and manuscript, although all the errors and inconsistencies are entirely mine. To my mother Jill and sisters Nikki and Hilary, who are examples of the unnoticed good people who constantly strive to serve their communities, to learn and grow whilst being amazing parents. To my great Auntie Mimi who has constantly sent messages of support not knowing just how welcome those communications have been to receive. To Binkie our beagle, who deserves a special mention as he's been the most loyal studio companion a producer could ask for (and tested my editing skills when he barked mid session).

To my fellow entrepreneurs and good friends and who have encouraged, guided and inspired me. Richard Robinson whom I first met in Hong Kong in 1998 and continues to be a trusted friend, mentor, and cheerleader. To the EO Beijing chapter entrepreneurs who shared openly and courageously their own plans, which taught me so much about building a business better than I could have ever known, and whose determination to succeed regardless of circumstances never fails to amaze me. To the Class of 1990, the Manchester University friends who welcomed me back into the fold with open arms (virtually due to COVID) upon my return to the UK after 25 years, and to Danny Goldman specifically who both appeared in one of the podcasts and kindly gave his insights to make this a better publication.

To the people who have worked with me on the podcasts and this book as part of my extended and virtual team I owe thanks. To Grace Eio of EASTWEST Public Relations in Singapore who has always encouraged me and carried my weight on client work when needed. To Kelly Stone-Binday in New York who had faith enough to entrust her clients to me to be interviewed. To Alecs Magtoto my VA in the Philippines for working through the logistics of this production. These projects are never a solo effort and I am grateful to the people who have all made it possible.

Everybody deserves thymōs for their contributions, and I apologise to those I have inadvertently omitted. Finally, I thank you for taking time from your business to read this; my hope is that you find the time is well spent.

About the Author

Jim has built businesses from a suitcase on three continents over 25 years, all using public relations. His first brush with #gettingnoticed was at 18 when he jumped out of a plane in return for sponsorship and received expedition equipment in return for media publicity. He hasn't stopped this model of brand+business building ever since.

Having grown up in Europe, Africa and America, it was perhaps inevitable that Jim would move to Singapore at the age of 28 to start his first company, EASTWEST Public Relations. Since 1995 the B2B agency opened offices in Singapore, China, India, and the UK serving over 500 clients. In China between 2006–2019, Jim built the business importing and distributing Morgan Motor Company cars, was interim CEO of Lotus, Vice Chair of the Chamber of Commerce, founded the bi-annual British Business Awards managed by the British Chamber of Commerce, and was the President and co-founder of the Beijing Chapter of the Entrepreneur's Organization.

Jim returned with his young family to the UK in June 2019 to provide his daughters with a British education, and works with entrepreneurs to ensure that they are able to get noticed so that they can eventually sell their company, He hosts "The UnNoticed Show," and provides consulting from his base in Wiltshire.

He can be contacted at: https://www.linktr.ee/jimajames

Guest Directory

Listed in alphabetical order, the people who kindly shared their knowledge with me on The UnNoticed Show.

Aaron Perlut, Co-founder, Elasticity (p. 227)
> LinkedIn: https://www.linkedin.com/in/aaronperlut/,
> email: aperlut@gmail.com

Alex Greenwood, Public Relations Consultant | Founder | Podcast Host & Producer, AlexanderG PR (p. 143)
> LinkedIn: https://www.linkedin.com/in/agreenwood/,
> email: alex@alexgpr.com

Ant Bohun, International Sound Specialist, Owner of Sound Please (p. 126)
> LinkedIn: https://www.linkedin.com/in/ant-bohun-aaa354a/,
> email: ant@soundplease.com.au

Ant Cousins, Executive Director for AI, Cision, formerly Managing Director of Factmata. This company was acquired by Cision
> LinkedIn: https://www.linkedin.com/in/antony-cousins-6004b264/,
> email: antcousins@live.co.uk

Anthony Hayes, Founder and President, The Hayes Initiative (p. 148)

> LinkedIn: https://www.linkedin.com/in/anthonyjhayesnyc/,
> email: anthony@hayesinitiative.com

Arvind Murali, Chief Data Strategist, Perficient (p. 222)

> LinkedIn: https://www.linkedin.com/in/iamsmarchitect/,
> email: nmarvind007@gmail.com

Audrey Wiggins, Founder and Executive Producer, Mason Wiggins Media Group (p. 253)

> LinkedIn: https://www.linkedin.com/in/audreywiggins/,
> email: audrey@altogether.biz

Bant Breen, Founder and Chairman, Qnary (p. 293)

> LinkedIn: https://www.linkedin.com/in/bantbreen/,
> email: bantbreen@gmail.com

Brandon Watts, Founder and Principal, Wattsware (p. 137)

> LinkedIn: https://www.linkedin.com/in/brandonwatts/,
> email: brandon@wattsware.com

Catherine Griffin, Managing Director, ImpactableX Analytics (p. 160)

> LinkedIn: https://www.linkedin.com/in/catherine-griffin-0a07976/,
> email: cgrifc@gmail.com

CHATGPT

Chris Martin, Owner and President, Atlas Marketing (p. 46)

> LinkedIn: https://www.linkedin.com/in/atlasstories/,
> email: chris@atlasstories.com

Chris Robinson, Founder, Boost Marketing Ltd (p. 153).

> LinkedIn: https://www.linkedin.com/in/chris-robinson-0381aa1/,
> email: chris.robinson@boost-awards.co.uk

Cory Warfield, LinkedIn micro influencer & Chief Communications Officer, CoryConnects (p. 208)

LinkedIn: https://www.linkedin.com/in/corywarfield/, email: cory@shedwool.com

Dan Morrison, Senior Advisor, Acumen Public Affairs, Former Vice President of Communications, Pew Research Center Vice President of Communications, Pew Research Center (p. 310)

LinkedIn: https://www.linkedin.com/in/dan-morrison-40842b40/, email: danangus_2000@yahoo.com

Drew Stone, Owner, Stone Films NYC (p. 263)

LinkedIn: https://www.linkedin.com/in/drew-stone-8817794/, email: stone4124@aol.com

Eric Mitchell, Co-Founder, LifeFlip media

LinkedIn: https://www.linkedin.com/in/ericlmitchell/, email: info@lifeflipmedia.com

Frans Riemersma, Founder, MartechTribe

LinkedIn: https://www.linkedin.com/in/fransriemersma/, email: FransRiemersma@MartechTribe.com

Gerry Foster, Brand Strategist, Owner of Big Brand Zone

LinkedIn: https://www.linkedin.com/in/gerryfoster/, email: mktgman@aol.com

Guillaume Portalier, Co-founder & COO, Waalaxy, the company formerly know as Prospectin

LinkedIn: https://www.linkedin.com/in/guillaume-portalier-66996b1b2/, email: guillaume.portalier@gmail.com

Helga Zabalkanskaya, CMO, Newoldstamp

LinkedIn: https://www.linkedin.com/in/zabalkanskaya/, email: helga@newoldstamp.com

Howard Kaufman, Co-Founder, ORL
LinkedIn: https://www.linkedin.com/in/hojo5/,
email: hkaufmanusa@gmail.com

Jimmy Cannon, Voice and Performance Anxiety Coach
LinkedIn: https://www.linkedin.com/in/jimmycannon/,
email: jimmycannonsinger@gmail.com

Joanna Drabent, CEO and Founder, Prowly
LinkedIn: https://www.linkedin.com/in/jdrabent/,
email: joanna@prowly.com

John Lee Dumas, Founder, Entrepreneurs on Fire
No LinkedIn, website: https://www.eofire.com,
email: team@entrepreneuronfire.com

Dr. John Ricketts, CEO and Joint Founder, Earth.ai Significance
Systems
LinkedIn: https://www.linkedin.com/in/john-ricketts-a4b706a8/,
email: john.ricketts@significancesystems.com

Justin Goldstein, President and Founder, Press Record Communications
LinkedIn: https://www.linkedin.com/in/goldsteinjustin/,
email: justin@pressrecord.com

Laura L. Bernhard, Inbound Marketing Expert, Host of Marketing
Bound podcast
https://linkedin.com/in/lauralbernhard
laura@marketingbound.com,
email: hourihanepaul@gmail.com

Martin Barnes, Pitch coach and Founder, 8Seconds2Connect
LinkedIn: https://www.linkedin.com/in/martinbarnespresentations/,
email: martin@mountainsofimagination.com

Matthew Law, Co-Founder & CMO of Telum Media.
LinkedIn: https://www.linkedin.com/in/matthew-law-76800510/,
website: https://www.telummedia.com

Mauricio Duarte, Justice Entrepreneur and
Chief Operating Officer at Access2Justice Tech
LinkedIn: https://www.linkedin.com/in/mauriciodrt/,
email: Info@GoA2JTech.com
website: https://www.goa2jtech.com

Mia Masson, Content Director, SwapCard
LinkedIn: https://www.linkedin.com/in/mia-masson/,
email: mia@swapcard.com

Michelle Griffin, Personal Branding and Marketing Consultant, BRANDthority
LinkedIn: https://www.linkedin.com/in/michellebgriffin/,
email: michelle@michellegriffinmedia.com

Morry Morgan, Group CEO, The Rubber Chicken
LinkedIn: https://www.linkedin.com/in/morrymorgan/,
email: morry.morgan@icloud.com

Nigel Sarbutts, Founder, PR Cavalry
LinkedIn: https://www.linkedin.com/in/nigelsarbutts/,
email: nigel@prcavalry.com

Nitin Pandey, Founder, Parentune
LinkedIn: https://www.linkedin.com/in/nitinparentune/,
email: nitin@parentune.com

Omri Hurwitz, Founder, Omri Hurwitz Media
LinkedIn: https://www.linkedin.com/in/omrihurwitz/,
email: omrihurwitzmedia@gmail.com

Park Howell, Founder and President, Park & Co
LinkedIn: https://www.linkedin.com/in/parkhowell/,
email: park@businessofstory.com

Paul Hourihane, Founder, ReMark Asia Pacific
LinkedIn: http://www.linkedin.com/in/paul-hourihane-2824a4,
email: hourihanepaul@gmail.com

Peter Dorrington, Founder and Chief Strategy Officer, Anthrolytics
LinkedIn: https://www.linkedin.com/in/peterdorrington/,
email: Peter@XMplify.co.uk

Sabrina Scholkowski, host, Pretty Sure Podcast
LinkedIn: https://www.linkedin.com/in/thatgirlsabrina/,
email: sabrina.ssch@gmail.com

Sander Nagtegaal, CEO, Unless
LinkedIn: https://www.linkedin.com/in/centrical/,
email: sander@silicane.com

Scott Brinker, VP of Platform Ecosystem, HubSpot
LinkedIn: http://www.linkedin.com/in/sjbrinker,
email: sjbrinker@gmail.com

Sebastian Rusk, Founder, Podcast Launch Lab
LinkedIn: https://www.linkedin.com/in/sebastianrusk/,
email: srusk@socialbuzztv.com

Dr. Shelley James, Lumenologist, Owner and CEO of Age of Light
Innovations
LinkedIn: https://www.linkedin.com/in/dr-shelley-james-53592229/,
email: shelley@ageoflightinnovations.com

Stapho Thienpont, B2B LeadGen expert
LinkedIn: https://www.linkedin.com/in/stapho/,
email: staphothienpont@gmail.com

Dr. Stylianos Kampakis, CEO, The Tessaract Academy
LinkedIn: https://www.linkedin.com/in/dr-stylianos-kampakis/,
email: stylianos.kampakis@gmail.com

Toni Kaufman, Founder and CEO, Standout Universe
LinkedIn: https://www.linkedin.com/in/tonikaufman/,
email: toni@kddminc.com

Ugi Djuric, Founder and CEO, Contenthorse & Co-founder, Podino
LinkedIn: https://www.linkedin.com/in/ugljesadj/,
email: ugi@contenthorse.com
Zachary Nadler, CEO, VaynerSpeakers
LinkedIn: https://www.linkedin.com/in/zach-nadler/,
email: zach@vaynerspeakers.com

Bibliography

Podcasts I listen to about PR and business:

7 Figure Small with Brian Clark

https://podcasts.apple.com/gb/podcast/7-figure-small-with-brian-clark/id1017418913

Business of Story with Park Howell

https://podcasts.apple.com/gb/podcast/business-of-story/id1012379862

Buzzcast with Buzzsprout team

https://podcasts.apple.com/gb/podcast/buzzcast/id1446336657

Beyond the Story with Sebastian Rusk

https://podcasts.apple.com/gb/podcast/beyond-the-story-with-sebastian-rusk/id510904010

Content Inc with Joe Pullizi

https://podcasts.apple.com/gb/podcast/content-inc-with-joe-pulizzi/id948387773

Entrepreneurs on Fire with John Lee Dumas

https://podcasts.apple.com/gb/podcast/entrepreneurs-on-fire/id564001633

Genius Network with Joe Polish

https://podcasts.apple.com/gb/podcast/genius-network/id1161195772

Marketing Bound with Laura L Bernhard

https://podcasts.apple.com/gb/podcast/marketing-bound-podcast/id1495717454

Marketing Secrets with Russell Brunson

https://podcasts.apple.com/gb/podcast/the-marketing-secrets-show/id1315130618

PR After Hours with Alex Greenwood

https://podcasts.apple.com/gb/podcast/pr-after-hours/id1496015627

PR Resolution with Stella Bayles

https://podcasts.apple.com/gb/podcast/pr-resolution-podcast/id1423627061

Small Business Radio Show with Barry Moltz

https://podcasts.apple.com/gb/podcast/the-small-business-radio-show/id288125609

Systemize your Success with Dr. Steve Day

https://podcasts.apple.com/gb/podcast/systemize-your-success-podcast/id1560955240

The Agency accelerator with Rob Da Costa

https://podcasts.apple.com/gb/podcast/the-agency-accelerator/id1491143609

UnLeashed

https://podcasts.apple.com/gb/podcast/unleashed-how-to-thrive-as-an-independent-professional/id1227297532

Youpreneur with Chris Ducker

https://podcasts.apple.com/gb/podcast/youpreneur-the-profitable-personal-brand-expert-business/id590043753

Books: [in alphabetical order]

A Simple Model of Global Cascades on Random Networks by Duncan J. Watts

Backpacks and Baguettes: Coloring the World through Young Eyes by Dan and Sam Morrison [sold out and no longer in print]

Brand Bewitchery: How to Wield the Story Cycle System to Craft Spellbinding Stories for Your Brand by Park Howell

Business Storytelling from Hype to Hack: How Do Stories Work? Unlock the Software of the Mind by Jyoti Guptara

Habits of a Happy Brain: Retrain Your Brain to Boost Your Serotonin, Dopamine, Oxytocin, & Endorphin Levels Kindle Edition by Loretta Graziano Breuning

Lead with a Story: A Guide to Crafting Business Narratives That Captivate, Convince, and Inspire by Paul Smith

Narrative Economics by Robert Shiller

The Common Path to Uncommon Success by John Lee Dumas

The One Thing: The Surprisingly Simple Truth Behind Extraordinary Results by Gary Keller and Jay Papasan

The Decision Maker's Handbook to Data Science by Dr. Stylianos Kampakis

The Structure and Dynamics of Networks (Princeton Studies in Complexity Book 12) 1st Edition, Kindle Edition by Mark Newman, Duncan J. Watts, and Albert-László Barabási

The AMEC Framework can be seen here: https://amecorg.com/amecframework/

Index

W

Website 9, 14, 30, 37, 43, 45, 71,
    85–91, 98–99, 109, 127, 138,
    164, 186, 242, 253, 254, 261,
    271–273, 278, 280–281, 309,
    313

Z

Zachary Nadler 202
Zoom 39, 44, 123, 150, 155, 204,
    220, 243–244, 264, 282